CHICAGO QUARTERLY REVIEW

Volume 37
Spring 2023

The Chicago Quarterly Review is published by The Chicago Quarterly Review 501(c)3 in Evanston, Illinois. Unsolicited submissions are welcome through our submissions manager at Submittable. To find out more about us, please visit www.chicagoquarterlyreview.com.

Proud Member

[clmp]
COMMUNITY OF LITERARY MAGAZINES & PRESSES
W W W . C L M P . O R G

TABLE OF CONTENTS

NONFICTION

POETRY

ART

EDITORS' NOTE

For us, the best part of the AWP Conference is when our past, present and future contributors drop by our booth to say hello and let us know what they're up to. This year in Seattle, we caught up with (from left to right) Rich Simon, Alta Ifland, April Nauman, Barbara Tannenbaum, Ben Masaoka, Catherine Segurson, Charles Johnson, Gemini Wahhaj, George Choundas, Janice Nakao, Jessie Ren Marshall, Micah Perks, Karen Yamashita, Moazzam Sheikh, Richard Huffman, Sean Towey, Sharyn Skeeter, Faisal Mohyuddin, Thomas Dodson, Zack Rogow, Christine Sneed, and Steve Woodhams. Great to see everyone! ■

THE SOONER STATE
Eireene Nealand

1.

Trains hadn't even reached Oklahoma before the Civil War, but he knew nothing about Native Americans or the hammering in of the first railroad spike, nothing except for what he'd seen in Westerns, where they seldom distinguished between the arroyos of New Spain and the Oklahoma Reserve. Fyodor was interested only in freedom, that vast unregulated space where you could stretch your will and learn to drive.

Most often found in a ten-gallon cowboy hat and pink sweatshirt imprinted with the words Escaped from Alcatraz, he'd head to the train tracks after bodybuilding in his tiny apartment with its bed on the floor. His first car was a sleek gray Ford Taurus, low-to-the-ground and reminiscent of outer space— completely unlike the red pickup truck he'd later find himself needing, along with the loud motorboat he repeatedly crashed into sandbars.

Doctors blamed Fyodor's thyroid for every usual action they saw, but his mother claimed the water pooling under his skin and around his heart was due to the pressure of his enormous drive pulling against the Soviet bureaucracy's slow, bumbling drag.

Back when Communism's bulwark still retained its umph, Fyodor had been a "sprout of the revolution" and "struggler for peace" who collected recyclables door to door. Beside a thousand stalwart comrades he'd roughened his hands digging potatoes in mandatory summer service and joined the military when it was his turn.

Then perestroika schmaltzed in, all the nineties. Long before the Soviet Union split into a series of ethnic states based on feudal boundaries, Fyodor understood the military was little more than an accessory to graft. By the age of sixteen, he'd begun to strain against the weight of a vast historical dialectic, betraying a long line of communal principles by sneaking away from the army barracks in Poland to test the concept of "buying low and selling high," transporting t-shirts bought in Krakow across the border to Moscow.

Immigration wasn't a given back then. Despite generations of relatives turned down from university seats and party jobs, Jewish being marked on their identity cards, Fyodor's family's paperwork lingered in the refugee lottery for years, the prospect of immigration little more than a dream Fyodor watched his mother blow the candles out on just about every year since he turned five. It was luck, really, and a series of unrelated political maneuvers related to aluminum sales that expanded the refugee pool enough for the family lottery number to be pulled.

Though Fyodor's elder sister was better at math, Mama Dezhda chose Fyodor's 'y' chromosome to stake out the family claim because "boys marry quicker...if my son took to drink..." No matter that the doctor continued to warn about Fyodor's thyroid. America's bustle was bound to steam off any water that pooled in his chest.

And so it went. While the Soviet Union sagged under the weight of its inner conflicts, Fyodor boarded a plane with only a slim duffle bag, the hopes of his whole family rattling along behind.

2.

In Oklahoma, the cowboy hat didn't make him an equal. Fyodor felt lonely in the gray cubicle he'd been assigned to by a red-nosed rancher who knew enough to mine his Soviet education, but never said where sausages could be smoked. Tulsa's Sooners squinted fiercely under the hot sun and spat in the red dust with an individualistic ferocity Fyodor could never quite match.

In long hours spent before the white screen's bright glare, his face swelled. His voice became hoarse. The underactive thyroid bloated his jowls. The doctor's theories would have been proven right had it not been for the cheerful whistle supposedly announcing the progress of man.

Trains on the Missouri-Kansas-Texas "Katy" line could be heard as far as the suburbs, which is where Fyodor lived that first year with graying sheets and a pillow that sagged beneath his prematurely balding head. In the evenings, he'd grab his cowboy hat from the coat rack and drive out to that all important finger of commerce whose freight-carrying function refused to be dwarfed by the dot.com boom. Watching the Tulsa-Wybark run rush toward the open plain, Fyodor's whole self swelled in his throat. History was on his side. The engine's massive will-less disinterestedness seemed ready to barrel him into the future, caring nothing for his accent, or the country he'd left behind.

That, at least, is what Fyodor thought before he was dragged.

3.

A train at full speed involves a violent mechanical hurtling, useful to some, deadly to others. It has little in common with the slow shudder of cars that jerk forward at the station and later grind to a halt, shedding sparks with a hopeless squeal. Precisely at 5:55, Fyodor revved up the Taurus's V6 and raced out onto the frontage road, where he zig-zagged around potholes in his attempt to race the great beast of enormous beauty that drew so many tons of history behind. When he came close to matching the KTY's speed, his pectorals swelled and his thyroid gave a little skip, every pore of his hairless chest open to whatever ran on ahead.

It was winter, already, when he finally caught up. A thin layer of snow had settled on the frontage road. Driving advisories warned of tiny spikes of ice. Fyodor, however, was from a cold country. Dale Carnegie's Win Friends and Influence People played on the Taurus's tape deck. Clank-a-clank the weight of the self, Fyodor thought as he peered through the frosty windshield, gripping the steering wheel he'd waited so long to hold. When the descent from a particularly bad dip in the frontage road caused the Taurus to swivel and skid, the increase in speed felt like a triumph.

A lonely immigrant—from Portugal—sitting by the window of her crummy cottage 200 feet from the track was the only witness when the hood "crumpled like a daisy." She'd been studying for her citizenship test, but jumped up, girding her bathrobe around her, when the Taurus's displaced engine thudded across the snow-covered red dirt. When describing the scene for the *Tulsa Herald*, she compared the wall of orange sparks to the spectacle of Daniel Boone's last stand when the Alamo burned.

"John Wayne couldn't have played it better," she said, smiling seductively into the camera. She'd painted her nails and waved her hair before calling 911.

Was this any way to become American?

Fyodor thought that it was.

4.

When we met that spring in the Rocky Mountains for the mile-high hike we'd planned at the age of sixteen, I wanted to kiss him, like we had in Red Square, and comfort him, folding him into my arms, but all Fyodor could speak of was the airbag and its amazing speed.

"A thump hit my chest," he said. "Powdery flecks flew out like stars. The Taurus's airbag deployed faster than any race to the moon."

He seemed to have forgotten our youth exchange to thaw the Cold War, and how, during our first kiss outside Lenin's tomb, our chapped lips melted Red Square's thick snow. That spring we tramped through long grass near the Dezhda family dacha, and drank frothy milk warm from the udder of a cud-chewing cow. In love with Fyodor dark curly hair, I accepted her slow, serious eyes as akin to my own. Yet Fyodor had no memory of helping me mount the Dezhda family's one rusty bike or his valiant pledge to run alongside. It had seemed romantic when his thyroid had pumped out a river of sweat. Maybe I liked that he couldn't keep up.

When, however, he charged up at the Rocky Mountain, leapt up onto a boulder and took firm charge of our packs, he stayed two steps ahead, pushing on so quickly he barely had time to shout about the speed of the train or how its noise was so great the engineer failed to hear the sirens of Tulsa's five dispatched fire trucks. Cradled as he was by the airbag's big hand, Fyodor had emerged without even a shard of glass in his cheek.

"It's how I knew I'd become American," he said, smug eyes avoiding my own.

We hiked, ignoring the steam that rose from his chest. Halfway up the mountain, Fyodor spotted a fraying rope tied to a big-branched pine near a giant placid lake. When we climbed the tree and balanced side-by-side in the crotch of a branch, I realized Fyodor was several feet taller than I was. Taking courage from his bulk, I swung out, letting the rope burn my hands, then plunged deep enough to scoop up a handful of the lake bottom's rich sediment. Once Fyodor and I were married, I decided, the mud could consecrate our future organic farm. I thought he'd take an interest in the mineral-rich sludge, but by the time I'd cleared the wet from my eyes, Fyodor was already scrambling up onto the furthest shore.

That was how speedily he'd remade himself. Ignoring the rivulets of murky lake water that ran from our underpants, he pushed on toward the 2.7 mile-high mountain's peak. Just as we reached the thinned-out tree line, he keeled over and projectile-vomited against a scrubby bush, then looked proudly at the mess.

"Consider the rate at which that spewed from my gut," he said, looking down at me as I rushed up the trail. "Even the airbag never deployed at such a great speed."

I stood awkwardly, catching my breath. Realizing he wanted no comfort, I stared at the stalk of a mushroom he'd inadvertently nudged aside with his toe.

That night while we roasted the mushroom over our fire made of sticks, Fyodor confessed to having eaten eight eggs that morning to boost his libidinal drive. And listen, my Russian had plans. The crash had convinced him to quit his programming job in Tulsa to apply for an MBA in the City of Big Shoulders where — history having run off its rails — he planned to immerse himself in discussions of market collapse and sheer. "I'll slam so quickly into the new economy, it'll be like immigrating for a second time," he said, watching our fire's smoke rise and rise.

It was then that I realized the mushroom I'd picked was filled with tiny wriggling worms. "In the capitalist world, you defeat a superior force by giving way," Fyodor said, stepping into the dark to jointly zip our sleeping bags. Who cared about mushrooms or Soviet heroes, when there were such great safety features in the new American cars? Soon, he promised, the pistons of sex would produce a fountain that would soften my vagina, causing a malleable airbag-like yield.

"It's what makes you better than me," he said.

5.

"When they say jump, you jump," screamed a small blonde girl in a sateen shirt, when I visited Fyodor in Chicago the very next year. The blonde was pretty and slim, and might have contended for Fyodor's heart had not they both been more attracted to the numbers scrolling across the ticker tape just above the whiteboard. Sitting outside on the college's close-mown lawn, I listened through the window, while they discussed perpetual motion trains in Beijing that never needed to stop because passengers loaded themselves into cargo-pods. These pods stood still at the station until a crane lifted them up, and dropped the passengers down onto the chassis of the always-speeding trains.

Fyodor's chest had softened in the City of Big Shoulders. His lips were cold when we kissed and he seemed not to recognize himself when I reminisced about his struggles for peace and how I, myself, had briefly worn a pioneer's red scarf. From Tulsa the only remaining trace was a single barrel shotgun that reminded him— pow!—of the airbag's rapid trajectory across a distance.

"You've got to work your competitive advantage," he said, unbricking the artillery he'd stashed in the wall of a sleek new house bought with proceeds from illicit AK-47 sales. His most American moment, he said, was arranging the delivery of a Soviet nuclear submarine to a Saudi Arabian oligarch through the dark web.

Watching a powdery balloon of happiness billow out from Fyodor's newly remodeled open kitchen plan, I wondered what had become of the Dezhda family's rusty old bike. Even Brezhnev, that petty materialist, could not have predicted that the stout, kerchiefed pioneer, named Fyodor, would trade his little red wagon of recycled cans for civil disputes about the length one's lawn could be grown.

"He kept a Beretta under the pillow," I said, explaining our breakup to ecologists later that month in my new home on a cooperative farm. "The sex was too rough." Maybe that wasn't the full reason I canceled our wedding plans, but the long and short of it, the clank-a-clank, the whoosh-and-pop is that I wasn't there when the doctor removed Fyodor's thyroid.

I was browsing about on Facebook when I saw, as if through the wrong end of a Hubble telescope, pictures of Fyodor vacationing in Australia with a parrot on his shoulder, sunburned chest exposing a four-inch surgery scar. The big bird had raised its wings to increase its seeming size, and the scar curved upwards along Fyodor's neck like a bright crescent scythe.

Six months later I saw he'd married a Ukrainian girl with the same wide hips and cow eyes as I had. Their first child — Ezra — had my preferred baby name. When they sent the child to my preferred Jewish day school, it was as if Fyodor and his wife had stepped through my skin and drilled even more deeply into the simple life I'd always planned.

Was there some clue there about the Soviet Union's aborted progress? Realizing that history had recoiled like a bouncing spring, I left my cucumbers and squash to visit the new Dezhda family in Illinois, where they'd settled in a house with a rather large barn.

By then Little Ezra was nearly six. Fyodor had quit his programming job to open a warehouse restoring old industrial machines. Listening to him talk about welding torches and forklifts, I wanted to place my ear to his hairless chest to learn whether water still welled about his dear heart. Fyodor's wife, however, must have seen my look. She suggested that I go out with Little Ezra to search for fresh eggs in the little clumps of dirt that graced their lawn.

Crouching beside a clump of ancient grass, I froze, iPhone in hand, when I came upon the cold dark eye of a hen. Painfully, it pecked my hand, until Little Ezra came up beside me, sporting the dark curly hair of a guy who'd herd goats.

"Her name is Rex," he explained in his wise child's voice. "The dinosaurs had feathers, long poofy ones. And Tyrannosaurus ruled over everything. Then the comet hit, and chickens grew up from dinosaurs."

I looked at the chicken and it looked at me, and some big internet-informed truth pinged its ping. That's when I understood it: progress is a strange thing. Fly too fast and you'll smack right back into yourself. ■

THEY MUST COME FROM SOMEWHERE
Marcus Ong Kah Ho

EXCERPT A.

My father and I adore fruits.

We do not suffer from constipation—we eat an apple or an orange, seedless grapes or slices of guava dipped in plum powder while the evening news on TV comes to a close.

My father avoids dragon fruits because of superstition: a feng shui master once told him that dragon fruits are bad for the family's fortune.

I dislike honeydew because it reminds me of cough syrup.

B.

My father likes kway teow drenched in brown gravy.

He tells me why:

His older brother (my third uncle) and that brother's girlfriend (now my aunt) once took him out to Sentosa on a day trip, and they were on a tight budget and could only afford a plate of hor fun to share among three.

There is another story.

He ate hor fun at a coffee shop near Thomson Medical Centre while my mother was in the maternity ward giving birth to me. When he returned, the nurse said to him: "It's done."

I like hor fun because of that story.

C.

My father and I take coffee, but Fanta's orange soda has always been his sky, his first love. They used to come in glass bottles, he tells me. Before Chinese New Year, Grandma would purchase a dozen bottles from the grocer and line them up on the table for her guests to pick. And for two weeks, he and his brothers would be squatting in the living room, scrutinizing every guest who came, gripping each other's hands and praying for whomever it was that day not to touch those bottles. On the final day, just before midnight, Grandma would clap her hands, and the six siblings would dash out of their room and begin to share the remaining bottles on the table.

D.

My father is thrifty; he rarely spends money on clothes. He knows what is best for himself: he likes Dri-Fit polo tees because he doesn't sweat too much in them, and my mother doesn't have to spend time and precious energy ironing.

I, too, hate to spend money on outfits. I go for basic cotton tees and jeans and match them with black track shoes so that I spend less time in the morning agonizing over what top goes with what bottom, what bottom goes with what shoes, what shoes go with what socks. I alternate between white and black for my tees, and I have multiple identical ones in my cupboard. But my father pesters me to dress better so that I make a better impression on others. He feels I'm making a big mistake—"You're only young once!"

E.

My father removes his polo tee the moment he steps into the house. He says he feels warm and sticky. He walks about the house half-naked, eats dinner half-naked.

I turn on the air-conditioning whenever I feel warm and sticky.

F.

My father and I are sports fans.

He tells me that he admires the way a boxer can endure battering during a match, and sometimes the battered boxer can knock out the crowd favorite with a single blow—he says it teaches him something about life. At night, he watches boxing alone with the TV set to mute so that the noise doesn't disturb my mother sleeping. I grew up with friends who liked football, and we spent our teenage years playing and watching the game—it has taught me about friendship and devotion.

G.

My father washes his ass with water. I wipe mine with toilet paper.

He saves money by choosing to clean himself with water. And I feel I should pick up this habit, too, so that we can save twice the amount of money for the household. But it is easy to forget since he is the one who pays for the toilet paper.

H.

My father has a good sense of humor; we find the same things funny. Like, how my mother shuffles items around in the kitchen once every two weeks, and so the family can never find what we need. He laughs when he sees me hunting around for my vitamin C pills; I laugh when he can't find the fruit basket.

However, there are things that my father does not find funny. Say, if I borrow money from friends.

"Not even ten dollars?"

"Are you deaf?"

He sees this as an ill habit.

I.

My father was terrified of bumping into our Canadian neighbors in the lift. He jokes that thankfully, we live on the third floor, and so there's only time for short exchanges like:

Hello, how are you?

Good.

Going to work?

Nod of the head.

He is more comfortable in Mandarin.

He is proud that I teach the English language for a living. He doesn't understand why I would be terrified of bumping into the Canadians in the lift, and why I would find interacting with Caucasians so daunting.

Before the Canadians moved out last year, my father had a better excuse than I had for taking the stairs.

J.

My father knows how to change a light bulb, fix the plumbing, work with tools that repair the appliances in our house, but often has my mother do these things instead. I do not know how to change a light bulb, fix the plumbing, work with various tools from the toolbox, and I, too, have my mother do these things instead.

Both of us depend on my mother a lot.

K.

My father uses a razor and shaving foam; I use an electric shaver.

Yesterday, my mother surprised him with an electric shaver, and he loved it.

L .

My father and I love my mother very much. He met her when she was sixteen (he was twenty-one). He describes to me how she used to look like with shoulder-length hair. My earliest memory of my mother was when she was thirty-four. I have never seen her with long hair.

M .

My father and I have our own driver's licenses. He worked and scrimped and saved to pay for his, whereas mine was sponsored by him. He drives his car to work in the morning; I take his car out in the night to meet up with friends. He is a cautious and steady driver. Two years ago, he received demerit points for beating a red light, and so his thirty-nine-years-clean record now has a blemish. I, on the other hand, drive a little too fast and sometimes take risks making illegal U-turns, but I have never had points deducted.

N .

When, at age twenty-four, I told my father I had only five hundred dollars in my bank account, he told me not to worry for he, too, had roughly the same amount when he was that age. However, he had tripled that amount within a year. At twenty-five, my account statement reads a hundred and sixty-six dollars. To make matters worse, a bowl of fish ball noodles cost fifty cents back in the day; today, it cost three dollars. My father and I have dreams, and I often tell him that mine is to become an accomplished writer. It makes him happy. He tells me to work hard, and he will support me for as long as he can. And not to worry, he says. He believes I can still enjoy a measly bowl of fish ball noodles. He tells me that he has dreams, too, but he hasn't told anyone what they are. I ask him what they are. Maybe someday, he says.

* * *

Dear Reader,

My son is full of shit.

He writes all this yucky sentimental stuff about us, father and son—which, by the way, is LIES!—and makes me look gloopy and weak.

Now my friends at work are going to ask what's wrong at home. My brothers and sisters are going to ask what's wrong at home. *Is somebody dying? Is it cancer?* Phone calls that'll come late in the night when I'm supposed to be reading the newspapers, enjoying myself. Already, my daughter has questioned why she wasn't featured, her feelings hurt. And my wife (good luck to her!) has friends who'll be dying for answers; they'll spam her texts. And she—so selfless and tenderhearted—will feel the need to satisfy them. Will she be shamed? I fully expect an interrogation to be coming my way.

So I ask myself, is there something wrong? I start to consider certain past actions and work out how they led me to today. It becomes a pastime. My mind drifts and drifts like that plastic bag in *American Beauty*. Say I'm on the toilet waiting for my bowel to move, or slumped on the sofa staring at the TV while the children are out on a Saturday night. I feel clumsy and misunderstood; I feel I should have a say. And so the question becomes for me—will my son appreciate the taste of his own medicine?

Since he was young, I've always reminded him about limits and boundaries. Self-preservation. Respect. Honor. Hygiene. Many, many other things. I find a man without his values no better than a spineless oxygen thief. Now, whenever I look at him, I picture this self-righteous, pen-wielding, narcissistic monster who can't stop grinning at his own belly button. I clench my fist. Where's his imagination? He acts like he has done me a huge favor and doesn't realize that I've stopped visiting bookstores: I see people checking out his book, and I can't breathe.

Look, I studied history in JC. I understand what a powerful thing a book is. That's why dictators burn and ban books. I just can't understand why anyone would care to read about a humble old fogey with one foot already in the coffin. The proudest thing I've ever done? Sending my children to university, giving them opportunities I never had for myself. When I look at their graduation portrait, this 60″x 40″ hanging in our living room under the IKEA clock, I see everything that is good. My wife often asks me what it is I see when I sit and stare at the portrait. I could be somewhere else, she says, watching a movie, attending Zumba or yoga classes with her. "I'm just sipping coffee," I say. "Let me nibble my Khong Guan biscuits in peace!"

Not that I wish to attract any attention. But I get it. I get why this can seem a little unusual. Why would someone who rarely looks at himself in the mirror spend his Sunday afternoons on his recliner staring at his family portrait like he's admiring a sunset? One time, my son took one of my biscuits and pointed to the picture and joked that his mother looked like the empress dowager.

I said, "How do I look?"

"I know the portrait means a lot to you," he said moodily. "But isn't publication a loftier achievement compared to finishing some stupid degree? I'd appreciate it if you could show more pride in my book."

How my heart sank.

I've slogged to send him to university; I don't tell him how often I've eaten oily sloppy cai fan or how many times his mother has nagged at me because she thinks I'm stingy.

This is the fruit of *my* labor. His book is *his* fruit, of *his* labor. Difference.

If I'd known he'd be publishing nonsense crap, I would never have supported him. Working odd jobs at this age doesn't look good on his résumé. I said to him, "Okay, you live with us, you use my water and electricity. Your mother will buy your favorite shampoo. But why do you need hair conditioner?" And he started twirling his fringe to spite me. He said he wants to grow out his hair like his sister's. I had to sit down. I thought, *Okay maybe he doesn't know that our government used to ban hippies from the cinemas.* Then he laughed when I asked him, "What's wrong with a clean buzz cut?" He said he doesn't mind the Singapore heat. And I looked down at all the hair on our tiles and recalled how I used to pray to the heavens to bless me with a boy. Now my boy wants to look like a girl. "Who's going to clean that up?" I asked him. "People are going to think our family is sick."

My wife tells me: times are different now. She uses the word *metrosexual.* I shiver. Our son is allowed do whatever he wants, she says. It's his life. I'm not supposed to *order* him to tuck his shirt into his underwear to keep it down and straight like working men used to do. He shall comply only if he finds it comfortable. Back in the day, my father would have given me a good wallop, disowned me if I'd done what my son did. My apologies would not have interested him. Papa was hard; he was head of some secret society. Which one, I'm not sure. We children did not ask. We didn't speak unless spoken to. We didn't ask, "Papa, why do you have three wives?" We'd be made to eat plain rice with soya sauce for three nights. It's funny: for a gangster who didn't gamble or drink, my father was surprisingly poor. Us siblings used to debate where his money went. To that smoking pipe that he never let anybody touch? Made of ivory? Gold? What was that special white liquid he poured into the pipe bowl every night, which, once dried, blended with the tobacco flakes to produce milky sweetness?

Eldest brother figured out it was condensed milk. He also found out that our father couldn't read, and we wept when we were told we weren't allowed to further our studies. *Shut up! Go scrub the kitchen floor!* Eldest brother had to kneel on beer bottle caps because he refused; he drives a taxi today. Our father was the most respected gangster number one in the kampung because he gave his money away—he couldn't afford to send us to university. How he moved everyone to tears! Our mother would always nag at him whenever he announced himself through the door. And when he had enough, he would escape to wife number one and wife number three. He did, however, love my mother the most. He gave her six children. Mother number one had two. Mother number three, only one. These days which woman would tolerate something like this?

I'm well aware that times have changed. Even if I still feel that a woman's place should be at home. I mean, have you tasted my wife's chicken rice chili? Her chicken macaroni soup? My god. Sedap. The fact that these things exist—and they do because my wife has stayed at home and perfected them over the years—makes the world a better place to live in. But I know these are things one can no longer say.

Never in a million years I'd have thought my son would become an artist. After all, it's impossible to predict what children eventually become. Maybe Lee Kuan Yew knew. But even our founding father couldn't foresee certain things that ultimately happened in his household. Did he, too, sit on his toilet in his later years, waiting, and drift just a bit? Perhaps. I'm not talking about the stuff in his memoirs, but the stuff he was too embarrassed to say. He must have brought it to his grave. I mean, he's still my hero. And no doubt I'll support his son, our prime minister, till the very end. Sadly, things have ceased to be as straightforward for my children. I see them roll their eyes at everything: when a public service announcement comes on, at national campaign posters in the MRT, at the news. "What's there to be so antiestablishment about?" I ask them. They assume the tall skyscrapers, our impeccable public transport system have always existed. They loll in their chairs, and they call for their mother. They ask her, "Was Pa this talky when he was young?" And my wife's eyes shine. "I couldn't stand him yapping away in the maternity ward," she says. She thinks she's a comedian.

It's true: I ate hor fun when my son was born. I'm not proud of it. I should've been there, waiting. But I was hungry; I didn't want to faint and drop the baby. My son doesn't know that he was a C-section baby. He doesn't know his mother had to go under the knife because he didn't want to turn the other way around and come out headfirst. Left a scar. A big, hideous one.

I should've listened to what the old folks say: open all the drawers, cupboards, cabinets before you leave the house to ensure the smoothest of deliveries. I can tell my wife's a little embarrassed that she didn't have a "normal" delivery. She thinks she didn't suffer the same (she was under anesthetics the whole time and was a little high after) like other mothers who had to *push* their baby out. But no, no, no. I don't think that way. I'm glad there's even something called C-section in our time. The position my son was in inside—my wife would've died if it'd been the old days.

So we clothed him and fed him and made him chuckle as much as we could. A year later, my daughter arrived. My wife hugged me. "We're now a well-balanced family," she cried. But then the economy crashed when it was time to send them both to primary school. I suffered a humiliating pay cut, and I remember those days walking up to the ATM to withdraw money was pure agony. Feared, too, when both of them refused to study hard or read books. When their teachers wrote on the report cards that they were working below potential, I asked myself, What *is* their potential? And so, who would've guessed that eight years down the road my elder one would tell me that he wanted to be a writer?

Is that a good thing?

I asked my daughter what she wanted to do; she couldn't say. Instead, she accused me of showing favoritism toward her brother and asked if I would support her as I did her brother if she pursued an unconventional dream. I laughed it off, told her to be grateful for what she has, and congratulated her when she took the first job offer that came. She draws a fresh grad salary now. Has started dating recently. Pretty normal. And I'm happy, at ease. Am I pleased that the other one wants to, as they say, "make art"? How do you go from tasting your first Happy Meal and catching your first cold to setting out to create something that will last perhaps even longer than me, him, his children, and his children's children? It's an exciting thought, yes?

Takes my breath away.

Also, will they still have Happy Meals then?

Come to think of it, I've never had a Happy Meal. I know the food is pretty much the same, only that they're fun size. And I'm glad my children still remember. They smile over memories of my wife and I taking them to Macs on Sundays; my son, in particular, remembers coming home with his belly full, holding a cute little toy in his cute little hands. I asked them if they recalled the open field at the end of the park connector where I'd taught them how to fly a kite. My son had a ruby-eyed bat kite, I remember, which he'd insisted was Batman's favorite bat. My daughter had this simple, rhombus-shaped one, white. And she could regurgitate that opposite angles of her kite had equal measure and the two diagonals were perpendicular with a consistency that was admirable. The children would scream when I started to run over the grassy strip, lifting the kite. I would do it over and over while my wife camped under a tree and fanned herself with a magazine. She would hiss at me whenever I paid more attention to our son. Her own mother, she told me, used to reprimand her for crying after her brother had punched her in the teeth.

Growing up, my two children hardly got along, and I could never understand why. The only time I ever saw them work together was when they came to my study to ask for a dog. They begged and threw tantrums. But I knew my wife was probably going to end up being in charge of not letting it die, so we lied to them that Mama was allergic to dogs' fur and bought them a robot dog from Metro instead. Boom. A hundred-plus dollars gone. And in the 1990s, a hundred-plus dollars was, well, equivalent to fewer oily sloppy cai fan. But robot dog sucked. Took the children a week to realize that it was lame as shit. But why, I asked them, when the Metro promoter had petted the dog's head (with touch sensor) and the dog "barked," had it felt so real to them?

It got worse: a Nintendo Game Boy (we refused), a swing set (we didn't have space), Pokémon cards and VCDs (we obliged because they were comparing us to friends' parents by then and guilt-tripping us), PlayStation 1, 2, and 3 (we obliged); PlayStation 4 he bought with his savings. Girl wanted Barbies, Polly Pocket, Magic Trinket Maker (okay, remember to study hard). Boy wanted football, football boots, football jerseys, football clinics (okay, don't forget to study). Both again: a computer desktop, then, laptops (okay, for schoolwork only).

Not once they'd asked for books.

Zero.

Got us so worried when they scraped through examinations each year. Sent them for tuition classes. Tried this center and that center. Continued to eat more sloppy, oily cai fan. More worries when my son sprained his ankles and knees playing football, and then having to send him to expensive chiropractors while his grades continued to plunge. Piling and piling worries because he always seemed in a hurry and never explained anything. He ate and slept at irregular hours, carried secrets, daydreamed, wasn't interested in studying. Was rude to my siblings and my wife's sibling at Chinese New Year gatherings. Dropped F-bombs here, there, everywhere when conversing with us on the day-to-day as if we were his enemies. When he was eighteen, he brought home a motorcycle helmet, and I remember wincing, feeling so upset that I recounted how a friend of mine had lost his child to an accident; I said they had to have a closed casket because the face was smashed in.

And he replied: "But death isn't such a big deal."

How could he say that when his mother and I loved him?

Once we got a call in the middle of the night, and the voice on the other side informed us that my son was in lockup at Ang Mo Kio Police Headquarters for shoplifting. So prideful he was, he didn't even apologize to us. So smug throughout the car ride home. Tried to trick us with words, calling it a "lapse of concentration," "fiasco," "tempest in a teacup," "once-in-a-lifetime experience," "not worth the trouble." Did he think we were fools? My wife and I were on the verge of tears. Then he said he wanted hot food, so we made a detour and took him for supper. His hands were steady throughout. His voice was loud and clear, and his appetite was great. He stuffed himself with rice and curry, swallowed three cups of iced lemon tea, and described to us the inside of a cell, the conversations he had had with the characters in there. My wife grabbed my hand; my ears rang.

We upped his allowance so that he wouldn't steal, but he never seemed to have enough to spend. He got his heart broken many times, oscillated between being a gentleman and an asshole; he was so confused. It seemed that all he was interested in was gaining muscles and impressing girls. I said to him, "Having a girlfriend isn't everything, there's more to life. You got to think about your future, slouch less, work harder!" He started coming home late, and one time with a cheap tattoo of a lion's head on his shoulder blade. In mere months his face had coarsened like mine, and his voice had turned husky and disturbing from all that cigarette smoking. Our neighbors would give him looks. And this reaction only seemed to reinforce his new identity. I suspected that an army buddy of his had hooked him up with a bet collection job for bookies. The signs were there: he was always nervous, miserable on match days; he had sudden cash; he talked big and talked loud about buying himself a sports car. I suffered nightmares as a result, about him lost among drug smugglers who saw their lives as cheap. Night after night I'd dream of him incarcerated, then hanged by our government; his name would appear in our national newspaper. I'd get up from bed, stumble into the bathroom to empty my bladder, and my eyes would burn once I snapped on the fluorescent light.

Meanwhile my daughter went through puberty, became sensitive to beauty, and started worshipping celebrities. She needed dresses, shoes, makeup, and these, my wife and I agreed, were simple enough to satisfy. Sometimes she'd come home from school with origami hearts and stars and roses cased in a clear jar, other times a handful of shiny but cheap-looking trinkets, and I'd look down or away when she showed them to me. Thankfully, there were no condoms in her bags and drawers when I checked. Clever of her to study with all those A-star boys in school who fancied her. Those boys, she explained, would help her with homework and revision. So tears of joy, really, when she completed her education with the National University of Singapore. Alas, more worries for my son; he could only manage a place in a private, god-knows-what overseas franchise university. Expensive. Demoralizing. Frustrating also because a risky bank loan was involved. The day I signed my name the dotted line, I shook his hand, and what followed were warning letters for skipped classes, months and months without us speaking to each other.

But today, if you walk into his room—

Books.

Books everywhere. Almost touching the ceiling.

What sorcery?

His room is so clean, even more so than mine. Twice a week he climbs the ladder to dust the ceiling, and he smiles to himself when he folds his clothes. He brushes his teeth, flosses his teeth. He hasn't missed a single night; I've been counting. He washes his hands at least ten times a day because he says he doesn't want to fall sick. He has important things to fill his hours with, and so he needs to work at optimal condition. No more junk food. Time set aside for exercise. He drinks only plain (warm) water and coffee (less sweet). He even called skipping breakfast a crime against the body when he took us out for breakfast once, and then he paid for our coffee! He hardly goes out anymore. Each night he curls himself in bed and reads. He doesn't lock his door; he keeps it open. But always I see the light in his room is a little too dim. "Take care of your eyes. You only have a pair of those things," I say to him, watching his silhouette against the books piled against the window.

"I'll buy you a new lamp," I say when he doesn't answer.

Slowly he looks up, and then, after a few seconds, he shakes his head and says no, thank you. He reads some more.

More books arrive in the mail.

"Where do you buy them?" I ask him, not because I'm interested, but rather I'm hoping to have a conversation.

"Well," he says, clearing his throat. "The consensus is that Book Depository sells books cheaper than Kinokuniya. That's only half true. Kino Members get ten percent off. Twenty during Christmas season. Waiting time nil, bar the occasional long queue. Then again, it boils down to what book you are looking for. Say, Sing lit. Do you think you're paying less to buy a book written and designed and printed in Singapore, shipped over to some Amazon warehouse in the UK or India or Malaysia only to ship them back here, in Singapore?"

I try to smile.

I suppose he's merely excited.

As I back away from his door, I feel a tiny sting. I tell him I'm going to bed. There's work early the next morning, you see.

Later I'm lying next to my wife in bed, paralyzed, puzzled at this metamorphosis he's undergone. He'd been this adorable child turned miserable adolescent gone astray, and now he's this artist, living, it seems, in a romanticized world of words and ideas, anchored by dreams that, surely, must have come from somewhere. But where? I cannot visualize this place. I cannot see the ground on which he now builds his life even though I tell myself that I've always been there.

As if she has heard me, my wife turns away from me, pulling the duvet.

Is this healthy?

I wouldn't mind some advice at this point.

Love,

A Parent. ∎

ELEGY FOR LORETTA LYNN
Dante Di Stefano

"The more you hurt, the better the song is,"
she said, and I can tell you the one time
I saw her in concert she'd cracked two ribs
falling down on her way off the tour bus,
but that night, onstage in her baby blue
sequined ball gown, her voice soared burgundy
as she belted out coal dust in the cornfield
and stars sprung from the theater's red rafters.
You could hear the resonant bruise in her,
the reedy, tart, bittersweet twang of pain
distilled like moonshine into a belief,
distinctly American and dandled
in the wind of a great granite refrain,
that want might could matter you into grace.

HOUSE OF CARDS
Paul Skenazy

Dad was an installment dealer. He sold clothes, bedding, watches, lamps, radios, televisions, drapes, towels and pretty much anything except food to customers who could not afford to pay all at once. Instead he drove to their houses and apartments all over Chicago and picked up weekly or biweekly installments on the bill—a dollar, two, five, ten. He started working for my uncle, Dad's sister's husband, when he finished high school in 1934. My uncle bought him a Model T and in the late 1930s sold Dad a portion of his business, which he then took back and tended for my father during World War II. For fifty years, six days a week, Dad would leave the house at seven or eight in the morning and drive around the city, moving from neighborhood to neighborhood, doorway to doorway. These were poor people for the most part who lived in cramped spaces in rundown buildings. Dad climbed the two, three, four stories through dark hallways. Or sometimes through alleys or tunnels that led to basement doors or wooden stairways and back porches crammed with refrigerators, bicycles and clothes hanging on lines stretched across from one apartment to the next. He drove more than 30,000 miles a year without ever leaving the city limits. I don't know how many miles he walked and climbed.

I never could figure out how to describe what Dad did to friends. "A salesman," I'd say. "What does he sell—condoms? Cars?" "Towels, clothes, radios, TVs." "Like appliances? Washers and driers?" "Household things: blenders, waffle irons, electric fry pans. Sheets, drapes." I would explain how my dad couldn't tell reds from grays, how even traffic lights baffled him except for the relative position of the red, yellow, and green. How they wouldn't take him in the Army or Air Force when he tried to enlist because he failed the color blindness test, so he wound up in the signal corps instead. Yet he chose clothes for hundreds of men and women every year, not to mention me until I had some say in what I wore.

Installment dealers kept records of their customers on account cards. The cards were a beige that darkened with the years. His sat alongside him on the front seat of his car. They said "Roosevelt Budget Co" across the top, though there was no "Co," since Dad was the business. There was a line for the customer's name, and alongside that the names of a husband or wife and kids; the address; the phone number—the numbers often crossed out and replaced by a second or third if the customer moved or was one of his oldest. The cards were three or four inches across, ten inches lengthwise, four columns: space for a descriptive entry, a date, a payment amount, a running tab. My father would note a purchase across the width of the left column. He would also add notes to himself about what he needed to buy for someone, say to someone. The notes went on torn scraps of white paper clipped to the top of a card so he had them when he got to the customer's house. Some of the older customers had two, three, four, even six cards; one active, the others archived in a rusty metal storage unit that lived in our basement. Newer customers had just a few entries on theirs, the beige card pale, clean, the edges sharp and not crumbling from years in and out of his hands.

Usually questions about Dad's work ended with me saying he was an old-fashioned credit card and catalogue: you told him what you wanted, he picked it out, brought it to you, you paid him in installments. He offered installments more than merchandise. His work was clear to me, growing up watching him each night, working for him from the time he let me when I hit my senior year of high school. Everyone I grew up with sold something: Dad's buddy Dave owned a dry cleaner's; my Uncle Max sold furniture; Uncle Abe sold cameras; Dad's three sisters were married to three other installment dealers. My friend Mike's dad was a butcher, my friend Dave's mom ran the knitting store where my aunts went every Saturday to buy their skeins and sit and knit with her for a morning. But it didn't translate, this kind of work, once I got to college, where my friends came from houses in the suburbs, parents who were doctors and lawyers, worked downtown in Chicago offices, had college degrees. So I stopped talking about it.

At five or six in the evening when my father got home, he would sort his cards. His card file was an old cardboard shoebox that he kept in the cabinet below his desk along with his adding machine, his account books and printed stationary that read "Roosevelt Budget Co. / 555 West Roosevelt Road / Chicago, Illinois 60607" at the top of each sheet. Before we moved to our house in 1953, we lived in a four-room apartment and Dad's desk was the Formica kitchen table, a bean-shaped thing with an aqua paisley design on the top, a metallic border and metal cylindrical legs. When we moved to our house, Dad worked at the dining room table, polished walnut though always covered with a thick protective pad. Eventually we added a den and he finally had his own desk: a small thing, about a third the width and half the depth of where I type this. Closed, it looked like a drawer; it folded down, then slid outward slightly, revealing a white working surface and six cubbyholes. He sat on a metal card chair with a vinyl seat that he kept folded in the den closet.

The "Roosevelt" in "Roosevelt Budget" came from Roosevelt Road, running east to west at 1200 South in Chicago. The area has been rebuilt. The University of Illinois Chicago Circle campus covers a neighborhood that once housed huge outdoor markets of stalls that went up early each morning, came down each night. This was the famous Hull House area, populated from the early twentieth century by immigrant communities: Italians, Poles, Greeks, Germans, Jews from all over the Mediterranean. It was where my father grew up. At home we called Roosevelt "the Street," as in, "Dad's working late tonight on the Street." "Tell him Dad's meeting a customer on the Street at 3:30 if he wants to find him."

After the open market days came buildings. Dad's first office on the Street that I remember was in a converted bank. The downstairs was filled with stalls, like an indoor flea market, each stall a separate business—people selling women's or men's clothes, canned goods, fresh fish and meat, salamis, bread. Upstairs a balcony ran around the perimeter, with cubbyholes created by thin plywood where the installment dealers worked. Dad's office had a large metal desk, a thin door with a lock, and a metal file cabinet. Settled at his desk at home, my father would turn over one card after another. Most of the customers paid in cash, a few by check. How much depended on how often they missed a payment, the time he knew them, how much they owed. He'd write the day's take in a neat column on a scratch pad, then check his figures with an old hand calculator that he cranked each time he added a notation. He'd compare that figure with the cash in his pocket. He carried around $200–$250 to start a day, most of it in small bills for change. He'd deduct the amount he started with from his new total—on a Saturday, often well over two thousand dollars—then reconcile that with his list of figures; if they didn't jive, he'd return to the cards, checking them again. This was as close as he ever came to his high school dream of being a CPA. When his cash flow and figures balanced, the cards for the day were divided, those on a weekly route into one pile, the biweekly customers in another. He wrapped the groups of cards in thick rubber bands, then dropped them into the shoebox, which had dividers cut from file folders labeled Monday through Saturday. The cash went into another thick rubber band for deposit at the bank.

* * *

When my father died, I lost forty pounds in a month. I had nightmares. I wanted to go to a movie, a baseball game. My father reached in his pocket for money but didn't have any. My father, who always carried a folded hundred-dollar bill in his wallet among the family photos; who bought gold Krugerrands he kept in a safe deposit box. I couldn't sleep. I listened to NPR news broadcasts. I spent hours in bed tuned to talk radio, absorbing insufferable right-wing arguments. A friend told me she lived through pain with the help of Bach's *Goldberg Variations*, so I tried Glenn Gould at 3:00, 4:00, 5:00 a.m. I woke at 7:00 a.m. to prepare lunch bags for my three children, draw funny faces on the bags, get my kids to school; I roused myself later each day to pick them up and drive to soccer games and karate lessons. One night I asked my ex to come hold me in her arms for twenty minutes while I cried. Another night I took the kids downtown to a film, parked the car in the city lot. When I came out, the front window was full of shit. There was a diaper plastered to the passenger side. I stood there and cried. For three or four minutes I think, long enough for the kids to come out, stand next to me, and rub up and down my arms. I stopped, got the kids back into the car, turned on the wipers and window spray, used the diaper to sop up what shit didn't come off with the water.

* * *

Eventually, the bank building was demolished. The people who owned the stalls found an empty lot on Roosevelt Road and built a tiny mall, with a guard post at the entry so you had to be cleared to come in and park. The stores were supposed to be strictly wholesale, only selling to the installment dealers and their customers, but that didn't last long. Most of the business still came through the dealers, though, who had a separate building with offices that were only slightly larger than the plywood cubicles in the old bank building. Independent Clothing Co., Associated Clothing, United Appliance: anonymous names. Dad reserved a couple hours each day to work on the Street picking up merchandise, meeting friends over lunch, schmoozing, playing cards when he had the time, calling customers. Dad hated selling but he loved to talk to people. People he knew, he felt comfortable with; when I started bringing college friends over, he was nervous, seemed to feel out of his depth, though he hid his uncertainties with affability. He hated going places he didn't know, stuck to the same restaurants and bowling alleys, golf courses and stores all his life. If it hadn't been for Mom and the chance to spend vacations with couples he loved, I doubt he would ever have traveled.

* * *

When I realized I wanted to kill myself, I started on antidepressants—one in the morning and one at night. I started seeing a healer. She led me through visions of past lives—Egyptian, Victorian. I was a peasant, a worker. I saw myself walking slowly down an endless highway in a flat, dry plain, weighed down by suitcases of parental grief and accusation. "Let them go," she told me. "Leave them along the roadside." I didn't believe a word and hung on to every one. I tried tai chi with a corporate guru and life coach, who traded me lessons in movement for my help with a book he wanted to write on mastery and power. I remember the jasmine tea we'd drink. He told me tales of wandering through multiple healing systems to discover what worked for him.

* * *

Because his desk did not slide out very far and Dad was six foot two, there was not enough room for his knees to fit straight under. So he was always turned a bit one way or the other, usually towards the TV in the corner, which was more or less always on. Walter Cronkite with national news just before dinner. Sports if he could find it: The Cubs played no night games then, White Sox night games weren't broadcast, no national games either until World Series time each year, and those too were during the day. Saturdays had college football and Sundays the pros. No ESPN.

I started working for my dad on Saturdays in high school. When I went off to college I lived at the other end of Chicago: 5500 South, versus our house at 5700 North. That meant fourteen miles across the width of the city, and about four miles east to west. I had a job on campus renting out televisions in the university hospital. I'd call in each day at three to get a list of the new rentals. I'd go to the storeroom, find the 19-inch black-and-white portables on their metal stands, plug them in to be sure they worked, ride the elevators, have the patients sign for the sets, do my best to get a decent picture with the rabbit ears, and then wander the halls getting renewals from other patients or picking up sets from empty rooms. Sometimes someone would die—"expire," the nurses called it, as if it were a magazine subscription. I'd find the bed empty, the mattress rolled up on the metal box springs, the TV waiting for me. I would walk home with a few hundred dollars in my pockets late at night, often in the middle of the quiet streets to avoid rubbing shoulders with anyone else out at that hour. I'd come home for weekends once a month; he'd hand me my pile of installment cards arranged in a route to travel from one stop to the next. I'd borrow his car at night to see friends, then head back to the university the next morning on the El so I could finish my schoolwork. I got to know my way around the streets, apartment buildings, the smells of the neighborhoods. I learned to be comfortable with some of the customers, though I never liked trying to sell them something. I also was embarrassed by what he did, or how what he did supported me, while I picketed against the war in Vietnam, claimed allegiance with the Black protests all over the North and South, discovered James Baldwin's essays about Jewish merchants in Black neighborhoods. And I cried each time he let me off at the El to head back to my dorm room, hugged me to him, rubbed his abrasive cheek against mine.

When his customers were not at home, or did not pay, my father phoned them. While my sister and I set the table and Mom cooked, or just after we ate while we started the dishes, he was on the phone complaining about a missed payment, working to nail down a promise about when he could come by for the cash. Or he would raise his voice and threaten to turn the account over to a collection agency. Frequently he would say he had to check with his boss before he could agree to the proposed terms—a boss who didn't exist but made it easier for him to pretend sympathy, one worker to another. After dinner, he would return to his desk to plan his next day's route through the city in front of sitcoms and quiz shows and sleuths: *Father Knows Best, The $64,000 Question, The Rockford Files*. My mother usually sat with him, darning clothes, riffling through magazines, folding socks. Dad would pull out his cards from his shoebox, unloop the rubber band from the accounts and imagine his next day—when he might find people home, who he needed to meet when. He'd calculate the one-way streets, the traffic flows that altered with predictable regularity. He spent his days in more and more comfortable GM cars: Chevies, then Buicks, finally Cadillacs. When he started making more money, he bought a new one every two years.

There are no more installment dealers. They have been replaced by credit cards and no-money-down offers from furniture and appliance stores. The business lasted from the end of urban street markets to the fall of Vietnam. It kept me and all my uncles and aunts, cousins and their children, in food. It taught me how to navigate Chicago streets and what work was. I keep a few of my father's cards in a shoebox along with his letter opener and fountain pen. ■

NONCHALANCE

Amy Marques

A WORLD OF HER OWN
Amy Marques

HUGHENDEN
Jack Norman

I t is a pallid drive west from Townsville on the way to Hughenden. Grey paddocks at the wings of the highway are fenced the length by barbed wire, lousy with rock and cattle and clusters of dry grass that burn with the stinging smell of sap in those rare periods after the rain. Bloated roadkill boils in the heat, melts to the bitumen, and wafts through the air-conditioner systems of trucks and family cars—they are kangaroos, mostly, but travellers spot the occasional deer bounding across the gravel, and a carcass begins to lose its form after a few days.

For the children asked to sit quietly in the back seat, there is something of the bushland and dirt, high rocks, and plains of brittle weed across the afternoon landscape that evokes the feeling of a Californian myth... but the spirit is all wrong: there is a white glare where an orange sun should be, cafés are made of linoleum and bargain plastics, rendered cinder blocks construct post offices, grocery stores, and general practitioners (each painted the same shade of aqua that is malleable and sticky when peeled), and people in their empty car parks fear for the death of their local newspaper that nobody reads, chalkboard signs request funding from donors in order to preserve this last symbol of themselves as a town.

Drought and ramshackle seem to have come at the same time, and now the earth begs repair as well as the highway. Termites take hold because they have stopped refusing to. Major leaks in the school plumbing linger as permanent puddles in the unlevel concrete beneath the rotunda. The drive across country takes longer now that it is being pulled apart by the earth as it drifts in opposite directions. Once it starts, it goes as fast as the standard years do. The suburbs cling to the center of town and the glass windows of heritage buildings reflect less and less of the same cars that have lived here and the highway signage as the distance between each is increased by the year... more space for the towns that are emptied like the old butcher's that has been closed for a long time now along the main strip, except for the front counter and its display case and the stray kitchen metals left hanging in the back room.

* * *

Against all tradition for cross-country drives, they stopped in Pentland so everyone could use the bathroom. It was an emergency, his mother had stressed from the back seat.

"You know I wouldn't bother you if it wasn't serious," she said, as he pulled off the road.

"Don't worry, Mum."

The children had enough sense not to complain. They told her it was okay, they needed to go as well. The girls filed across their grandmother's lap and helped to bring her down from her seat.

"You kids put your shoes on, please."

The dust from the side of the road had settled on the door of the car, and he could feel it very lightly on his molars when he ground his teeth. The children ran across the front yard of the roadside motel and urged their grandmother after them, around the side of the building where the signs pointed towards the unisex bathrooms and urged travellers to clean up after themselves. Men from inside glanced out the front windows at them, their eyes naturally attracted to motion. He had come to expect them: wiry, old, often with beards. Lazily, they turned their heads and went on as before as locals and regular customers with lives difficult for him to imagine.

"Where should we move to next?" Jill would sometimes ask, in bed or out for breakfast.

Certainly not Pentland, he knew. Charters Towers. Torrens Creek. Prairie. How many times did they have to come this way? They hardly felt like towns anymore, the way they encountered them. Checkpoints: numbers on the five-hour clock that recorded their journey to Hughenden; signage along the highway that spoiled the immersion of his daydreams or hopes they were almost there.

The road began to dip slightly as you got closer, up and down, and gravity rested heavily in your stomach and crotch. Tall, thin trees began spotty along the side of the highway and grew more plentiful the nearer you got to town, as if they were on their way as well.

"No," his mother had said, "it's not the sort of place for a young family, anyway."

He often wondered how it must have felt for her, coming back the same way, having done it as many times as him and as many times more. Familiar catalogue of rock formations, billboards, rusted homes, different colors of grass as weed and buffalo tides overlapped the nearer she came to home. Now that *her* mother was dead, it didn't seem likely they would ever be back here at all. There were no more funerals left to attend.

"Oh well. It'll just be me that's left now," she kept saying. "But I won't be buried out there. Dad and Noel can keep her company."

The children helped their grandmother climb back into her seat. They climbed through the other side of the car and grabbed her by the hands and pulled her into the cab. When she got in, she couldn't manage to bring her weight back up to a sitting position, and she laid over their laps, laughing at how helpless she was. They stayed tangled up like that as he started the car and put them back on the road. Everyone was pleased at how well they'd been getting along since they had left that morning. They continued along the Flinders Highway as it straightened out through empty paddocks and the car began to dip in the last hour of the drive, causing the children to squeal at how strange it felt.

By the time they arrived, it was still only late in the morning. They were ahead of most the family, but the back gate to his old nan's house was already wide open, and the head of the stairs was now empty of her as they pulled into the yard. The cold dirt beneath the heavy fig tree they parked under was the same on the soles of his feet, but she did not come out to meet him on the grass while he unloaded the bags from the back of the car.

Instead, it was a strange woman he recognized. Nan's cousin from somewhere in the Tablelands. He had seen her before when he was much younger. He remembered the short woman with orange hair and the pink collared shirt whom he'd woken from a nap when he was poking around downstairs, the same bottom story she had just emerged from.

"It's so good to see you, Ron!" she said, embracing his mother.

"Hello, Elsie. How has it been here?"

"Oh, it's all fine. There's not been much to do, really. I'm just waiting on the last call I think from the people up at the funeral home. They were pushing for an open casket yesterday, but I told them it wasn't the sort of thing she would have wanted."

His mother laughed almost hysterically. Jill and the children went by with smiles and good mornings, carrying their things inside.

"God love it! Elsie, she would have hated something like that."

"Yes, I said we all felt that way."

"I'm sorry, Else. Do you remember my son, Dougy?"

"I do! Hello, Dougy. It's good to see you."

"Was it you that roused on me when I was little? Do you remember? You were sleeping downstairs and I knocked all the porcelain pigs off the table."

"That was you! I do remember that now!"

"I thought so. I'm glad I remember it right. It's always a bit strange visiting Hughenden, I have a hundred memories that I can't tell if they're real or not."

"Oh god, don't we all. Well, you won't stay too long then, will you?"

"No, I've told him already," his mother said. "It's not a place for a young family anymore."

"It's really not, is it? It's such a shame in some ways. When I was a girl, we used to love coming down here. Do you remember the river used to be full half the time then? You could spend hours jumping off the bridge and swimming along the bank."

"There was all sorts of things wasn't there?"

"There really was. But, I suppose, it all moves on, doesn't it?"

"I've been trying to tell Mum for years. It's a dying town."

There was an unusual amount of empty space in the breeze and between the leaves as they rustled against something thin. The sky was overcast, so that it felt like the evening, and it seemed very far away. He had a petulant sort of feeling, now they were here, that there was nothing for him to do. The old Queenslander home presided over the yard with a tranquil understanding of the events it hosted, enduring each of them up and down its stairs (many trips that could have been avoided, if certain tasks at hand had been paid close enough attention). He had an idea that he would find his way into the living room and sit for a while. He might urge Jill into the fold with his mother and Elsie and get her to prove her woman's savvy even though she was only young. There was ham off the bone to look forward to for lunch, if Elsie kept the fridge the way his nan had.

In a way, he looked forward to funerals like this that doubled as reunions, because there was always something interesting to take back with you. You only had to sit through the chatter to get to there.

The children ran around the side of the house and kicked up the pebbles in the walkway and scattered them through the garden bed and over the stone stepping tiles.

"You girls be careful!" he yelled, and listened as they ignored him.

* * *

The small veranda at the top of the stairs sat outside the kitchen, and though it was situated at the back of the home, it was thought of as the main entrance by all her friends and relatives who used to visit, so that any knock at the front of the door was a certain sign it was a stranger come to call. They passed the rest of the afternoon sitting out there, watching as cars pulled into the backyard, as they had that morning, and settling the new arrivals into their rooms downstairs or exchanging the necessary courtesies before they left to see to their accommodation at the Royal Hotel down the road. Long, comfortable silences regularly fell over the table; they were suitable in the company of family. The breeze caused the garden shed to wobble and the plumbing whined each time someone washed their hands in the bathroom, the refrigerator hummed loudly, and the forgotten static of life (often captured on microphone recordings) simmered behind their ears.

With most of them in town a day early, Elsie had made plans to have everyone over that night in the backyard, for the chance of a get-together that could be separated from the purpose of the wake the following evening. She described the shape of the family tree and explained that many of the guests would be relatives of theirs; they were all names his mother seemed to recognize.

Nausea of unknown and distant cousins. He remembered drinking bore water at an old woman's house who was said to be his aunty and nearly throwing up her casserole, which tasted like a kitchen much different from his own. He preferred that by a certain age, relatives you didn't know were relatives you weren't going to.

But as it began, he was reminded that not all facets of adult life were revealed at once. There was much more to come for most people of all ages. He remembered fires they used to have on special occasions: timber stacked in steel drums that seemed to materialize as naturally as the guests that gathered around them. Well, they didn't just happen. In the afternoon, he carried them out from the shed with his brother and placed them at estimated lengths from each other. They started small fires early so the flames would emerge properly at about the time everyone started to get cold. Camp chairs, plastic chairs, deck chairs—out in circles on the grass. There was something about the yellow light weak from the porch, the fires distended on the grass, the glare left in the eye between images of the party and the night black behind them. Romantic scenes like this had always been kept in the amber preserve of his memory. The atmosphere hung heavily above those gathered and contained the heat, the layers of sweat on their forehead, the strength of breath he smelled on his father's words while he dashed between legs to fetch more alcohol from the fridge. He watched his daughter as he sent her off to the kitchen to do the same for him. She ran along the side of the fence, where the grass was cool under the shade of the moonlight, which seemed far in the distance from any warmth of the party. Somewhere she could eavesdrop on her mother and her friends, as any pocket of space that was not immediate to them was often forgotten by adults. Fathers drank rum, and even mothers nursed several glasses. His own parents used to chatter then as well, the moving parts in cliques and popularity contests, when he'd never realized they could have them too. They drank too much and became silly: inattentive, for the very first time. He was drunk, silly; she was watching him from under the stairs. He found himself beginning to think that it was *only yesterday I was...* And so, he learned, it happened to everyone. How did she get there? When did that happen? He must have been getting older because everything seemed so far away and yet he had not forgotten the time once that day. The hours passed at the exact rate they should have. And yes, she had been born years ago, he knew that. He was there when it happened.

They had all been swept up with each other. It was nice. The work that went behind the feeling was only noticed by a few. People wanted party and fancy and spontaneity, but that had to be arranged. It was women like Elsie and his mother who still knew people, who could be counted on to bring distant cousins together and encourage the proper sorts of ceremony for long-past-their-due dead old women in dying old towns.

"Nothing, really," he said.

"I thought you'd moved into recruitment at one stage?"

"I gave it a go for the work rate, mostly. I felt I owed something after the time off I had."

"So, you're not working now then?"

"No, I am. It's just not very interesting."

"Oh. Righto."

Kevin was one of Elsie's sons. A cousin somehow or another. He was okay, but he had a terrible habit of small talk that made him a burden in conversation. Across from Dougy, his heavy jowls absorbed the firelight and caused the age on his face to simmer.

"When did I see you last?" Kevin asked.

"I'm not sure. For Noel's funeral, I think. That was only small."

"It was. Your Mum was angry with him, even as they put him in the ground."

"She still is. I don't begin to understand that family. Most of it goes back to when they were kids—before their dad died, even."

"She took it out on Chooky that day, didn't she?"

"You're not wrong. She can be mean, my mother. I think probably prone to depression, if you wanted to put it that way. But that runs in the family."

"Well, I was going to say. I heard Nan was awfully mean towards the end, as well."

"Oh god. She was a villain, Kev. I mean something really snapped in her at the end there. Do you know she actually thought herself into a stroke? They ran tests, man. They couldn't find anything. All the symptoms, none of causes. She sat in that little unit they wanted her to trial and drove herself so mad, she went catatonic."

"I heard it was something like that."

"Oh, it was gruesome. She looked like shit. Babbling like an idiot. And she was faking the whole thing... or she faked it so well she believed it herself. I don't know how it worked. But it was all her."

"How did your mum handle it?"

"You're better off asking her, mate. She was upset but she seems fine now. I think she knows that this is where she's supposed to be. Everyone thought it would end up with her being the last one left of that family. I guess we had it right, and I'd say she's been preparing for this part of her life for a while now."

"Well, let's just hope it doesn't run too far down the family tree."

"Vote for the Greens, Kev. Assisted dying at the first sign of madness." He stood up from his chair. "Give me a second, I've got to take a piss."

He wandered the long way around all the guests who had established circles in the yard, past the trailer and the garden shed, and stepped behind the hedge at the farther end of the back fence. He spied Kevin though the branches, sitting alone at the fire. If he waited long enough, someone would sit down and take his place and he would find his way back to more immediate family members, safe in numbers.

A quiet space to piss alone. Dirt splashed on his foot. He finished the warm neck's worth of his beer and felt his breath in the back of his throat. It was comforting. The presence of something else that kept him company.

The paddocks behind his nan's place were fenced but empty; the road they belonged to led towards the bush and faded from bitumen to dirt in a gradient style that fell apart at the end of the incomplete cul-de-sac.

In the dark, he could make out two figures rustling behind a small mound of dirt and grass in the neighboring paddock. They were both whispering, laughing quietly. He recognized the voice of his older daughter and called out to her: "Isobel!"

They thought that if they waited long enough, he would forget what he had heard, or figure them for something else.

"Isobel. Come here now."

The boy and the girl followed each other into the open moonlight on the paddock and approached him as he leaned over the fence, the empty stubby dangling in the ring of his finger and thumb.

"What are you doing?"

"We were just sitting out there. Bubby was annoying us, we wanted to be alone."

"Why did you need to be alone?"

"Stop it! Not for anything. Just because we wanted to!"

"I heard your mum asking for you, Bart. Why don't you go and find her?"

He waited for the boy to head back in.

"What were you doing out there?" he asked.

"Nothing!"

"Go and sit with your mother."

He followed her closely across the yard. Cold grass under the fig tree. His piss nearby. He stared seriously at the back of her head as they walked past Kevin and made sure to appear obviously in the middle of discipline—did not have the time to sit back down just now. Her mother could see that something was wrong when she sat down in a huff beside her and she looked to him for answers above the heads of relatives, already feeling that the situation was not urgent, more than likely natural, to be dealt with sensibly, understood by a mother.

"I found her in the paddock next door alone with Bart."

"Okay, well, she's going to sit here with me now."

"You know we're supposed to be here for your nan's funeral, Isobel…"

"It's okay. Let's talk about this later. She's here with me now."

Leaving her to the women, he looked for his brother, whom he hadn't had the chance to speak with much since he'd arrived in the afternoon. He found him sitting beside the fire with Kevin. They had got onto one of those reality programs about ordinary Australians who dream of owning their own restaurant or renovating a house for auction. Judges, drama, advertisements: *And what about those*

Lebanese lesbians! He took a seat next them, studying the first pangs of back pain he had been suffering lately. Too close to the fire, it was drying out his skin. The urge was to sit there stubbornly until it got unbearable. A small hand tugged at his sleeve. It was his youngest, Bubby, who had returned with the beer he'd asked her to fetch for him, which she had gleefully taken a sip from, having spent a considerable amount of effort in twisting the metal cap from the glass.

* * *

The bedroom in the middle of the house opened into almost every adjacent room through doorways, a lean-through window, or the en suite bathroom that connected to the kitchen. Deep sleep breathed throughout the house. The girls snored on mattresses set up in the front room, pulled next to each other so they could whisper quietly without being overheard. Jill slept with her back turned to him, though they had gone to bed on good terms. Having slept well, he could lay with his eyes closed without the risk of falling asleep again, and he stayed that way for a very long time. The house settled loudly, more regularly than one would think. The iron roof expanded in the morning sun. The refrigerator leaned heavy into the floor and cracked suddenly as another year went by. The ceiling fan turned on the lowest setting, and a loose ball bearing drew a circle of razor sound in the air.

A vacation day, full and expectant. The kind that often surrounds occasions like funerals, birthday parties, indulgent weddings, or the odd Christmas that finds everyone in the right spirit. The morning was to take its time, it said. For Dougy, this first chapter had to do with becoming a person again: forgetting the dreams from last night, farthest-flung images that sat in negative on the back of his eyes, aches in his bones and muscles that felt good to ache in bed; soothed against the linen, soft calves of the morning rubbed against each other (she began to stir), sounds the mind had registered and retired to habituation, boredom that complained of the need to urinate, check his phone, stretch his legs, and listen to news breakfast updates from the television at a reasonable volume.

In the absence of her mother, it fell to his mother to play host in her girlhood home. She climbed the steps outside, causing the metal frame to wobble and vibrate through the floor of the second story, and prepared breakfast for them in the kitchen, refusing help of any kind.

"You'll only make things busy, darling. Sit down for me."

"Will we see Chook there today?" he asked.

"I don't know if he even knows. The man's a fool. I don't know where he is."

"It's better for everyone if he does come, though. So, if you see him…"

"It'll be nice to see him. Don't worry, I want him there."

Her calves were broad and strong from standing occupations her whole life. The footprints of her mother were embedded in the linoleum in front of the stove, which hers fit almost exactly, a little smaller in the heel. The veins in her legs were a deep blue green and palpable under the skin behind her knee. He stared at them while she talked over the stove and out the window: a little grotesque, he thought, sad that he could think things like that about her.

For all the years she had spent living there, the weight of his old nan was incredibly light in her house, and it had only been days since she had been gone. Everything they did felt much the same, the kinds of the things they used to do when she was alive. The family gathered here. Casual around the kitchen table. The spare rooms were at capacity. Loose children scattered over the floors. There was not the sense that she was smiling on them, that idea had soured with her sudden behavior before she died. But it was nice to honor the home for what it was: a part of the family canon, the setting for certain stories told again and again. Bacon grease shimmered in the light on the white stovetop. Breakfast was ready. The girls were fighting in the bathroom over the hair straightener they shared. The breeze outside could be felt through the lever windows and between the gaps in the wooden floorboards; the damp smell of the grass was pleasant that morning. It had been very easy for everyone to say goodbye, and that was what he sensed she was battling with, when he saw that she was crying in the reflection of the kitchen window that had been left open overnight.

"Are those girls of yours in trouble this morning?" she asked.

"My girls? No, they're all right. What do you mean?"

"It looked like you weren't very happy with them last night."

"No, that was just something silly. Stuff kids get up to. I don't know why I was upset with her. Sometimes you react to things the way you think you're supposed to. I caught her out the back with one of those boys from Atherton. I don't know what they were doing. Nothing serious, it's just what kids do."

"What's wrong with being upset about that? She shouldn't have been out there with him."

"It's not about that. No, she shouldn't have been out there. But then, yes, she should've. It's just what happens. Kids get to an age and they experiment. It's boys and girls. I know all about it."

"They're cousins, Dougy."

"Please. Fifth or sixth, they've never met each other."

Jill came in from their bedroom and sat next to him at the table. She was obviously eager to hear what they had to say (smiling carefully, the friendly eyes she used to suggest an open mind), but his mother wished her good morning and pretended to concentrate on finishing breakfast: plates, cutlery, open drawers, and busy to-and-fros across the kitchen. They got on very well, Jill and his mother, but he was aware that they had never shared a disagreement. It seemed quite unspoken between them that they should preserve that condition for as long as possible, each more afraid of themselves than the other in that scenario.

"She's getting ready first and then she'll be out," Jill said.

"Whatever she wants to do. She's not in trouble."

"I know, but it might be hard for her to face up to everyone this morning."

After breakfast was well and truly served, they called the girls to come sit at the table. They took their time and had to be shouted at about their food going cold. Jill had dressed them in mature grey dresses with black headbands that peeled their hair back from their fringe. Isobel's forehead was red with scabbed acne.

It was surprising how sad they seemed. He didn't think either of them had really known their nan. They made no secret of how much they dreaded her stays back home, which required them to share a bed with each other in order to make room. They ate their food slowly, toyed with it, and were completely absent from their grandmother's soft voice that asked them about their cousins and how they enjoyed meeting them all. He knew that it was a lot for a child to take on, and the very lost way that Bubby began to cry— gaping up at them for answers—told him that she was crying for herself, and perhaps (if she could manage) her mother and sister, as she understood that this was going to happen to everyone (or hoped desperately, for the first time, that it would not). Her sister, Isobel, tried to rub her on the shoulders but was turned away by the fleshy arm of her mother as she scooped Bubby into her chest and squeezed.

"It's okay, darling," their grandmother said, "we'll go down together, and you'll see. We're lucky today because this is our chance to say goodbye."

"I miss Nan!" Bubby cried.

"I know, darling. Me too."

At the cemetery, a small crowd gathered on the gravel driveway and shifted in conversation to make way for the slow-crawling cars in the corners of their eyes. Many of the more recent graves were unmarked, as it took quite a while for a stone to be arranged, and fewer daughters seemed to be present each year to see them through. Unfamiliar children played under the rotunda girt beneath the excess of the many mulberry trees forgotten by the council groundsman. A man in jeans wrestled one of them discretely under his arms and had him stand still against his legs. Distant friends and their immediate families kept closely together and out of the way, in respect of their status as guests, sensitive to the tiered rights of grief they sat at the bottom of: modest, solemn, and unhysterical.

Behind the thin morning air, veiled by dew misting on the horizon, singing butcher birds seemed far away in that anxious space of day that had not yet slid into its fixtures, still due to vibrate the earth and knock the sun against the back of their necks once it finally got under way.

The same plastic chairs used at the school fete and the athletics carnival were arranged in long rows back from the obvious site of her grave. A green carpet of some kind laid on the grass. The priest nearby who said he knew her well enough. The stretched apparatus used to lower her into the ground was established over the open grave. His mother made the walk to the coffin and laid her hand on the wooden polish. She disturbed the loose arrangement of flowers near the base of a framed photograph: her mother's portrait in some kind of club uniform (she used to garden seriously was all he knew). The coffin was cluttered with gifts and toys, knickknacks pilfered from her own drawers the night before, and largely written letters, after an exercise meant to keep her distant progeny of nieces, grandchildren, and removed cousins occupied had gotten out of hand.

Certain men who knew each other shook hands firmly and carried on their good mornings across the paddock as the guests made their way under the canopy and began to stand politely behind and next to one another, so that enough space to see and hear would arrange itself, now that their slow meander permitted the funeral to begin.

"Dad, can I go and sit with Granny?"

"Go on, quick."

He joined the pallbearers at the wing of the canopy. They looked like an order of knights in their finest denim jeans and mismatched black button-ups they had found in the cupboard and tucked safely under the bulge of their heavy stomachs.

When the priest began, he recalled a young couple and their intention to settle down in a small house and the two children who came along shortly after to complete their vision. It was only once he had properly started, and people's attentions began to distract under the monotone of his voice, that Dougy noticed Chook arriving late. He was talking loudly with someone; it required the priest to talk over the top of him, but he didn't seem to notice. Chook walked by rows of friends and family, shambling on the one leg he still had, winking, shaking hands, and patting the broad backs of every second man he passed.

"Chook!" he said.

"Hey, boy!"

"Here with us. Are you right?" he put a hand out to steady his arm.

"Yeah, I'm all right. Did you carry that bloody thing?"

"She didn't weigh much."

"I noticed your mum over there."

The back of her head seemed directed at them.

"She'll be glad you came. We'll talk after, okay?"

"I don't know about that, mate. I just wanted to make sure I saw the old girl off."

"Hey, Chook. Stick around, mate. I want you here. So does Mum."

Beside them, Kevin began to sob heavily. Meaty hands pulled on his shoulder, and his brother's forearm came to rest around his neck. It seemed wrong that he could not mourn his grandmother the way that Kevin mourned his aunt. Chook smiled sadly at them and began to laugh once it was clear he didn't have anything to say. A long stretch of highway carried several trucks on their way to Richmond. They could be heard groaning as they pulled out of the service station and rattled the chains left loose in their empty trailers. The priest continued, still unbothered, moving on to the brief eulogy that had been prepared by an old friend of hers who did not have the courage to read it herself. She had originally hoped that someone else close to Nan would choose to read it on her behalf, but they had all claimed to suffer from the same embarrassment, and the old priest read from the notepaper in a disembodied style that drove through obvious phrases meant fondly or to poke fun. A lot was made of her stubbornness, particularly as it pertained to her remaining for so long in Hughenden against all odds or health crises. A romance, he read, had occupied most her life with an old soldier named Douglas taken too early by a heart condition, whom she could never find it within herself to abandon and whom she was being buried next to that morning; and there was her youngest, a son she had vowed needlessly never to forget, who was nearby but not next to them, due to the logistical error he had made in not dying soon enough.

He sensed Chook beginning to lean unsteadily on his prosthetic leg, and he placed a palm on the middle of his back to spot him in case he needed it.

"Poor old Dad, off on his own over there," Chook said.

"Did you see him on your way in?"

"I'll visit once we're done."

"Mum will want to."

"God, I hope not."

The music started (country, sad, acoustic—someone had picked it out the day before), and the girls followed their grandmother up to the grave with handfuls of dirt from the pile and threw it over their drawings and letters to say goodbye. They were hysterical. They needed to be taken into the nearest car for a private space to settle down. Many of the women fawned over their sadness, said how much they missed their nanny: *Adorable!*

Dougy and Chook walked respectfully between graves several rows over, stopping at the foot of his Uncle Noel's. There was a chance, knowing Chook, that it was the first time he had come to visit since he died, and he did not know what to say.

"Poor old Dad," Chook said.

"You just start feeling bad for them one day, don't you?"

"When they get old and foolish."

"Something they had goes away..."

"Or they lose a leg and have their wife run off."

"Or they come unemployed to the last reunion we'll ever have."

"God, it's happening to us."

"Poor old dads, mate."

"It's fucking cruel."

His mother crossed the yard towards them. She scowled deliberately at the sun, taking pains to prove she was blinded by it and oblivious to their gaze.

"And they don't go easy on you for it, either," Chook said.

"Well, they don't go easy because they know better. We beg for center stage our whole lives and complain when we can't keep up the act. They don't really get to be anyone's favorite, so they learn how to get on with it. You know, I think they're humiliated for us long before we have the sense to notice we should be, and we only turn to them for help once it all falls over. By that time, they're over it."

"Good morning, Aunt," Chook called to her.

"Morning, Chooky."

"That was a lovely letter Margie wrote, wasn't it?"

"Oh, it was. I wish she would have read it. Father Pat, though, he was nice."

"Dad would have read it well," Chook said.

"He was always good for that, wasn't he? He loved to read in front of a crowd."

A cloud, must have gone unnoticed, passed away from the sun, because it became very bright again that second, and he noticed that the soft smell of body odor had sunk into the cotton under his arm. Gravel shifted underneath the grass. It was easier to pay silent respects to Noel than it was to his nan, who was still a body among them and not yet buried. He didn't know how to think of her in retrospect yet. But, for a heart urged—and genuinely hoping—to extend somber sadness onto something on a day like this, it was the perfect occasion to strike. The lump he felt building at the bottom of his throat felt like a gift he could give to Chook: to cry for the memory of his dad.

"He was a good man, mate," he said.

"He loved you, Dougy. And you too, Aunt. He never apologized to anyone in his life but god I know how much he wanted to say sorry to you."

"I know, darling. He was stubborn right to the end. We both were. It's okay. Chooky, I want you to know I'm sorry I haven't kept up with you."

"It's not your fault, Aunt. I haven't been reachable."

"But you've always known where to reach me, and I know I made you feel like you couldn't."

"Don't worry yourself, Aunt. I deserved it. I can be a mean bastard sometimes. It's in me, and it was in Dad too. I shouldn't have said those things to you."

He looked like he was about to fall forward.

"Can I tell you, Aunt?" he said. "Truthfully, I'm nearly an old man and I'm still looking up to my dad for his example. But if I think about it, the man I'm remembering half the time was a lot younger than I am today. He was only a boy when he had me. So, when I think of him. Who it is I'm thinking of... he was a young man! How was he supposed to know? And that's who I'm looking to for answers. A boy! An angry young man. He's still my father in mind... and when he got old, I was angry with him for it! For disappointing me. I was embarrassed seeing him like that. For being an old fool. But now that's all I am. So, I've got to start making my own decisions."

Once everyone had finished, they gathered in the late afternoon for the wake at the Royal. They stood on ceremony for a moment, feeling obligated to produce more toasts on her behalf, but eventually resumed the same sects of family they had gathered in the night before around their chosen tables or ends of the long bar. The family convinced his mother to share a Victoria Bitter with everyone in honor of Nan and Noel (how it had become Noel's preference was unagreed) and she proved her mettle by ordering another. Any awkwardness they might have felt about Chook had disappeared, and he was permitted to belong with them again under the secure hum of throaty chatter that belonged to family. His mother allowed Chook to hug her: largely and comedically. He kissed her on the cheek, smelling strongly like a functioning alcoholic (an obvious collection of colognes kept somewhere), and this completed their apology to one another in a way they had been uncertain of that afternoon and confirmed to the rest of the family that something positive had come from the sad occasion, which they were always looking to prove.

The open windows allowed for breeze to keep them cool but served more effectively as channels their laughter could spill through, over the veranda and across the flat earth that extended in all directions. The fissures that grew in the dirt as the earth continued to pull itself apart drank the sound of them without nourishment. A few scraps got by, small gusts that threatened whirlwinds at the edge of the highway; a car travelled through with its high beams on and that seemed to disperse the laughter against the background of night.

Hughenden, it realized, would be thoroughly outlasted. There were only a few souls left. Pam on her mobility scooter. Margie across the river. Arthur in squalor somewhere. Once they were gone, there would be no reason to remember the final days they lived, when they had already been young and strong before and made the successful impacts they were supposed to. The dry evidence of the riverbed was enough to know there was one. A new species of dinosaur had been uncovered at a dig site farther south, much larger than anything we had known before, considered a marvel for what it *was*. The last buildings that would be condemned were still occupied that night. By the cemetery, road trains roared through black space parted (each second!) by the light that lit their way, while the dirt settled in Noela's grave and restored her sanity in the minds of those who'd buried her and took her with it into the soul of Hughenden, that with each final addition, softly passed away. ■

POST-PARTUM
Kristy Nielsen

The marvel of separated breast milk:
yellow cream atop a white as blue
as come-to-dinner cloudless August skies.
I'm never easy in my mind. Shattered dawn
suffused with garnet, red like the baby's rigid gums,
and hyacinth-lavender-blue like the feathers
I glimpsed by quiet luck on the private side
of open bird-flexed wing. So now colors make me cry.

My body never quite re-pleats, the played-out accordion,
pelvis curled like a broken hand. The garlic skin
of fontanelle, the staples across my middle, scent
of blood and milk: we are prey animals, defenseless
as that boot-rolled garter snake, seam-ripped
pink-fleshed belly exposed to trailway grit
yet writhing still toward protective grasses.

IN THE NEW SUBDIVISION
Kristy Nielsen

A band of fathers kills a snake,
beheaded in the street, and flung
into the trees. I go beyond
the new-built homes, abrupting
frames and ravaged clay to roll
its gray-green muscle with my feet.

Hovering doubled dragonflies
pull milkweed silk. I tell my sister
secrets in the ferns, muffling
green, a thigh-high quilt. Witnessed
confession: scouring release.

Wild garlic border back at rawboned
tract of houses, street and bowl
of cul-de-sac. Chevrolets
and Fords on fresh-poured drives
reflect the unblocked sun. The boys
are climbing piles of dirt
and mothers measure window spaces.
Unencumbered daughter creatures
forage for another snake. Fathers
roll out virgin sod from pavement edge
to property line and stamp it into place.

BULL'S-EYE
Josh Emmons

Kyle announced his plan to run for mayor of Ambleside on the same day he closed the theater he'd started with inheritance money from his Aunt Pat, a woman who'd walked into an open manhole in Phoenix at age fifty-three and broken both legs and ruptured her spleen and received a $10.2 million settlement from the city ("I think it's too much but my lawyer says you can't put a price cap on suffering," she wrote in an email blast to the family) and who died six months later when a loose garage roof shingle hit her head on a gusty fall morning. No one could explain her luck, good or bad, in eulogies at her funeral. Instead they focused on her support for animal rights, her rich soprano, her fabulous hairstyles (from bold mullets to ombré blowouts to Empire curls), her love of late-eighties new jack swing and mid-aughts chillwave, how she pronounced *syrup* "soar-up" and not "seer-up" or "sir-up," and how she'd won hot-dog-eating contests in her thirties. There were so many ways to lead a full life. Kyle took two powerful muscle relaxants before the service—plus a horse tranquilizer during it—and later remembered the eulogies as tone poems, with the church and his fellow mourners forming a backdrop of blurred shapes, some audible and some sublimely silent.

When Kyle followed up his post about running for mayor with a post about turning Mariner Island into an eco-park and animal refuge if he won, his ex-wife left a comment under both saying that he had abused their dog, Mr. Stevens, while they were married. *I'll be haunted by it for the rest of my life,* she wrote.

"I what and she'll what?" he said, setting down his phone on the couch end table in the open living room of his spacious loft apartment, as his lower back went into spasm. A book about political debate strategies sat unopened on his lap. "Not that I think you're not ready to run for mayor," his sister had said when giving it to him the week before, "but I'm not sure you're *not* not ready, you know?" At Aunt Pat's funeral, she had introduced Kyle to a bald, badly sunburned man in a paisley-patterned dinner jacket and tight black slacks as,"My date, Lars." She and Lars had just met at a throw-your-own pottery studio and were both into Settlers of Catan and hard cider. When Lars went to find the bathroom, Kyle said, "I can't believe you brought a date to Aunt Pat's funeral," and she said, "Why not?" and he said, "Because," and she said, "Tina texted me that she'll miss being my sister-in-law, which, we're not close, but it still made me sad that I won't see you guys together anymore," and he said, "Aunt Pat bought a ticket on a rocket into orbit. Did you know that? I was gonna drive her to the launch site in October so she could go to the final frontier," and with a dozen perfumes floating in the air his sister touched his elbow and said, "You're on something. Give me one and I won't tell anybody."

Kyle reread Tina's comment about him abusing Mr. Stevens and then biked over to her duplex and asked her to delete it and say she'd been joking or drunk when writing it. She refused. Leaning against the doorjamb robed and slippered, her red hair in purple curlers, she said he would make a terrible mayor because he was bad with money ("You'd've declared bankruptcy if you hadn't gotten an inheritance.") and a bad steward of the land ("Our backyard when we were together, it was all overgrown weeds and creeper ivy choking the elm tree, and you dumped your go-cart equipment there so it rusted and chemicals soaked into the ground, and now you want to build an *eco-park* on Mariner Island? Um, no."), and she had to warn people against voting for him.

"That's debatable and not the point," he said. Behind her the Welsh dresser they'd bought on their honeymoon in Ohio seemed to glow, like an enchanted object in *Beauty and the Beast*. "Which is that you said I abused Mr. Stevens, which didn't happen."

"There are other ways to abuse animals besides hitting them," she said.

Kyle breathed in through his nose, one-two-three-four, and out through his mouth, one-two-three-four-five-six, as advised by his sensei, Juan Carlos, when summoning the strength to turn away from rather than engage in combat. "Lie about me all you want, but it won't matter because voters'll see the truth in the end."

"Oh yeah, I forgot," she said, "you live in a fantasy world," and shut the door.

Kyle got back on his bike and rode towards his apartment through the tree-lined streets of Ambleside. How was he living in a fantasy world, exactly? By thinking voters could tell the difference between truth and lies? His lower back spasmed again and a sharp twinge in his left knee made him get off his bike and sit on the curb with his leg outstretched. While massaging his knee with one hand—"The worst-designed part of the whole body," his orthopedist mother had told him growing up, about knees, "which you'll find out for yourself someday"—with the other hand he wrote a message of love and support for dogs and dog owners all over town and all over the planet. It was too bad his ex-wife so resented his initiative and civic spirit that she'd lied to hurt his chances of becoming mayor, but anyone who'd had a rough divorce or knew people who'd had rough divorces could see what was happening. One ex-spouse trying to hurt the other ex-spouse by any means necessary. As a token of his affection for that superb animal, the dog, he was going to adopt a couple of rescues from the Humane Society, labradoodles he'd name Patricia and Patrick, and make a big donation to canine cancer research. Also, on a side note, while he had been lucky to receive an inheritance several years ago and didn't have to worry about money personally, that didn't mean he couldn't balance the town's budget and grow its economy. Because he could. He could do those things. If Amblesiders wanted a solid financial base that'd help the environment for years to come, they should elect him mayor.

Deciding to post a selfie along with the message, he held up his phone camera so the sun lit his smiling face evenly, and the faint crow's feet around his eyes conveyed warmth and trustworthiness and, perhaps, a hint of sexiness.

Just as he was about to take the picture, an off-leash vizsla bounded over and started licking his cheek. Kyle laughed and laughed, and the resulting shot couldn't have more perfectly shown man and dog as loving, boon companions, but before he could post it, the vizsla saw a squirrel dart across the street, and in turning to chase it, ripped out one of Kyle's hoop earrings with its eyetooth. The vizsla's owner ran after their dog without checking to see if Kyle was okay.

Kyle was not okay. With a smile frozen on his face and his split, dangling earlobe dripping blood onto his shoulder, he watched the vizsla bark at a terrified, treed squirrel, which began to spray a mist of urine into the air high above him. A gentle breeze carried the mist towards Kyle, in whom confusion and pain and anger rose up as he glanced down at Tina's comment on his phone, its screen now flecked with squirrel urine, and pressed Like.

Then he stood up and walked his bike home stiffly, taped up his earlobe, iced his knee, took two gravity bong hits, ate a microwavable pizza topped with cool ranch kale chips, queued up a documentary about jazz or the Amish—or maybe baseball—and fell into a dreamless sleep.

* * *

In the morning Kyle woke up to a pain-free knee and texts from friends asking what the fuck he'd been thinking by Liking Tina's comment. If he'd meant to be sarcastic or ironic, it was tone-deaf and unfunny in this day and age. Animal abuse, like elder abuse and sex addiction and cockfighting, wasn't a joke anymore. Had never really been a joke. Unless—could Tina's comment be true? Had Kyle, like some guilt-haunted monster, Robert Durst or whoever, accidentally confessed on purpose? Social media responders to the Like were calling him a sick coward who deserved community service or jail time or death, and possibly all three.

Kyle wandered into his living room and looked out its bay windows at people hugging themselves in thick overcoats as they crossed the town square. It was May and still cold out, life in a northern town, and yesterday he'd been a viable mayoral candidate—more than viable, since he didn't have to work and could commit himself fully to the office, unlike the other candidate in the race, a part-time realtor—and now he was a villain.

To relax his mind and body, he did some light calisthenics and yoga and took off his shirt and turned on an oscillating fan and wondered if he could tell people the truth, that he'd pressed Like on Tina's comment because a dog had just hurt him and a squirrel had peed on him. No. Could he say that his sister's doubts about his preparedness to be mayor had caused him to self-sabotage? No, again. That his interaction with Tina had so upset him that he'd briefly lost his mind? No, again, again.

While flowing from downward-facing dog into warrior pose, he got an idea: a stranger had borrowed his phone because theirs was dead, and this stranger had Liked the comment without telling him, either by mistake or as a prank, and so, just now learning about it, Kyle was as appalled as everyone else. The idea sounded unlikely, but maybe Tina was right that voters couldn't distinguish truth from fiction, not because they were naive or undiscerning, but because the world today was even more full of shadow play than it had been in Plato's parable. Yes, maybe.

There was a knock at the front door and he opened it to see an actor from his theater, Stavros. Stavros had played the Monster in *Frankenstein* and Bottom in *A Midsummer Night's Dream*, and his prematurely white hair, usually structured into a kind of meringue on his head, stuck out in clumps beneath a green-and-yellow "Nothing Runs like a Deere" baseball cap.

"Stavros," said Kyle, "you know where I live."

"What happened to your ear?"

"Nicked it shaving. Come on in."

"It looks real bad."

Kyle closed the door behind his guest and pulled out two barstools at the kitchen counter. "Tina's post isn't true. What's happening is she doesn't want me to thrive in life. It's petty and aggravating, but I get it. If our roles were reversed I wouldn't want her to become mayor, either."

Stavros rested his elbows on the countertop and stared at a line of stone tortoises along the backsplash wall facing a Tibetan singing bowl and a stack of expired gift cards.

"I loved Mr. Stevens," Kyle said, going into the living room to put on his shirt and turn off the oscillating fan. He grabbed two kombuchas from the fridge and put one in front of Stavros. "I loved him even more than Tina did. When he scraped the pads of his feet on walks, I'd let him rest until his feet healed instead of forcing him back out in rubber socks. And when he got into grocery bags and ate all our food, I'd say let's not get mad at him since that's his nature. Tina'd yell at him and not give him treats for days. My point is that Mr. Stevens and I had good times together, excellent times, and I never hurt him."

"Who's Mr. Stevens?" Stavros asked.

"The dog I had with Tina."

"You have a dog?"

"Tina got him in the divorce and he died last year from diabetes."

"I'm sorry to hear it."

After a short pause, Kyle said, "Shouldn't you be at work right now?"

"I'm taking a mental health day." Stavros slid the kombucha away from him on the counter. "Could I have something else to drink, like a beer? This stuff is sour."

Kyle handed him a beer. "If you're here because of the theater, I kept it open as long as I could. The shows all lost money, you know that, you saw the audience sizes. But even if they hadn't, I would've closed it now anyway because I need to give back to the community in a way it'll actually appreciate."

Stavros finished his beer and got another from the fridge. This he drank as quickly as the first, then delicately tore off the label.

"You're making today a mental health day *party*," said Kyle, wanting to post the story of a stranger borrowing his phone right away.

"Mind if I have one more?"

"Yes."

"Cassie's cheating on me. I found out yesterday. Haven't slept since. Sounds're all muffled, like I just went to a loud concert."

Kyle got a third beer for Stavros and wasn't close enough to him for this to be happening. They'd never socialized together and Stavros had been the weakest link of the two productions he'd appeared in. If more people had auditioned for either play—if Kyle had had any alternatives—he wouldn't have cast him at all.

"One time in rehearsal," said Stavros, "you said you used to go to the archery range in Blake Park when you were getting divorced, to get your mind off things."

"I don't remember saying that."

"I'd like to get my mind off things. Maybe, I was wondering if you'd take me over there now and give me an archery lesson. I figure it could be the thing that gets me through this."

"Now isn't a good time. I'm dealing with something." Kyle wetted a rag and wiped the spotless kitchen counter. "Are you sure Cassie's having an affair? Maybe you're misreading the signs."

"There's naked pictures on her phone."

"Those could be artistic pictures. Self-portraits. I've got some black-and-white nudes of myself on my phone, for example."

Stavros took off his "Nothing Runs like a Deere" hat and scratched his head vigorously. "She admitted it. Said she had all this free time when I started acting and heard about an app for married people. It filled the hours, she said." Stavros's third beer was empty now. "I was gonna quit *Frankenstein* when that bad review came out in the *Register*. It hurt, you know, how the reviewer singled me out. I was done with theater. But then you gave a speech about how critics tear stuff down because they can't build stuff up. I could tell you didn't believe it, but I finished out the play because I didn't want to let you down."

In his mind, Kyle had been composing the message about a stranger borrowing his phone and pressing Like, and he was ready to type and post it quickly. "You and Cassie can get counseling," he said. "Lots of couples get past this."

"Not us. We're past the point of no return."

Kyle went into the bathroom and posted the story about a stranger, then came out and got his coat. "Let's go shoot arrows. I'll drive."

* * *

In the parking lot of Blake Park Archery Range, Kyle locked his car and watched a lobster-shaped cloud scud overhead. He wanted to check the comments under his stranger post but told himself to stay in the moment for this grieving person, Stavros, who'd had a fourth beer on the drive there and was leaning sluggishly against the passenger side of the car.

A bright-green sedan pulled into the lot and parked next to them, and six people got out wearing matching blue T-shirts with The Pham Family stenciled on the front. The youngest, a girl of ten or eleven, did a series of cartwheels around the sedan, expertly threading through relatives as they fiddled with gear and fanny packs and collapsible mesh hats.

"It's freezing out here," Stavros said, his words thick and slurred, in no condition to handle a deadly weapon.

"Let's walk some of the park trails to warm up," Kyle said, "and let these people play ahead of us on the range route, way ahead."

Slinging his quiver bag and bow over his shoulder, Kyle led Stavros to a trailhead at the edge of the parking lot, then through a grove of poplars past a small pond and into a meadow of scrub grass pocked with gopher holes and clusters of wild hydrangeas. Stavros opened a fifth beer and a giant crow took flight ahead of them, its caw as startling as a thunderclap.

When they came to a rock-lined labyrinth arranged on the ground beside the path, Stavros zipped up his jacket so it covered his chin. "You've got nipple rings. When you opened the door, I saw. Cassie thinks I don't have any piercings because I can't handle intense sensation. Maybe that's the real reason she did it."

"I doubt it." Kyle's hand grew warm on the phone in his pocket. "But maybe."

At a fork in the path, they veered left and soon intersected with the archery range course at its halfway point, the eighth target firing line, marked by a finely engraved, waist-high post cut from fresh cedar.

Stavros squashed his empty can into a misshapen cylinder. "I better go back and grab another beer, and maybe I'll sit in the car and warm up for a minute, if you don't mind."

Kyle handed him the keys and pulled out his phone in a single motion, curving his body around the device as if lighting a cigarette in the wind. He scrolled through comments, holding his breath, then slowly exhaled with relief. Comment after comment called the whole thing just another internet pile-on based on misinformation that covered no one in glory. Some people even offered to canvass for Kyle's mayoral campaign to support the principle of innocent until proven guilty. It was a beautiful reversal of a reversal of fortune.

"Hey, are you playing?" The cartwheeling girl from the parking lot stood directly in front of Kyle.

"No," he said, stepping away from the firing line. "This is all yours, I'm not shooting."

"You have your gear."

"I'm waiting for a friend."

"Want to see who scores highest on this target? Everyone in my group's back at the fourth because my grandpa's super slow. He's got a fake leg."

"You'd probably beat me."

"Please, I'm so bored. None of my cousins have done archery before and they suck."

Kyle looked towards the eighth target board, a small, particolored circle two hundred feet away mounted on a stack of hay bales. He raised his bow and in quick, practiced succession fired three arrows that made loud thwacks, though he couldn't tell from this distance where they hit the board. The girl, whose name was Bethany, and who was twelve, and whose father had taught her archery the year before, stepped to the line. Her first arrow produced a satisfying thwack. Her second landed silently on the ground. Kyle pulled out his phone to check the refreshed comments. They were all positive except for one, which cautioned that animal refuges ran the risk of being more like penitentiaries than sanctuaries, as morally suspect as zoos, and this eco-park would need to be planned with input from animal rights activists. Kyle's gaze drifted up just as Bethany's third arrow left her bow. Instead of a thwack or silence, they heard a loud, human cry.

"Oh god," he said, squinting at the target as a bright patch of green and yellow, Stavros's "Nothing Runs like a Deere" hat, slid to the ground.

"That sounded like a person," Bethany said.

Kyle took off in a sprint towards his fallen companion, with Bethany running right alongside him. "We'll say I did it," he panted to her. "That's our story. You'd already fired your arrows and then I shot one without making sure no one was there."

In a way this would be the truth, for Kyle's carelessness was the ultimate cause of what had happened. He should've noticed which way drunken Stavros had gone instead of jumping on his phone to assuage his ego. Tina was right that he lived in a fantasy world, as she'd been right a year earlier when she said that Mr. Stevens's diabetes had resulted from Kyle giving him too many treats and not walking him enough. Carelessness and irresponsibility were Kyle's defining characteristics, and he'd been foolish to believe otherwise, to think that muscle relaxants and horse tranquilizers and running for mayor could disguise or change the facts.

Kyle and Bethany came to a stop at the target just as Stavros was rising shakily to his feet and dusting himself off. On the ground a few feet away lay a mountain lion with an arrow sticking out of its side.

"It was gonna attack me," said Stavros, paler than when, as Frankenstein's Monster, he had prowled a stage designed to be open tundra, an outcast from the world of the living. "It was coming for me. But you shot it. You saved me. Thank you."

"No problem," said Bethany.

Stavros ran his hands over his face and made a high-pitched sound and looked at the girl. "It was you who shot it?"

She nodded, her face expressionless.

"Then you saved my life. You're a hero."

"I guess."

"How old are you? I owe you a reward." Stavros said to Kyle, "Take a picture of me and her with the mountain lion in the background. She's a hero."

"Yeah!" said Bethany, becoming animated now. "Take a bunch, and a video."

Kyle took a series of pictures of Stavros looking grateful and Bethany looking excited and the mountain lion looking dead, then a video of Bethany and Stavros narrating the events that led up to this moment. They were giddy and Kyle heard their words as varying pitches of gibberish. He felt faint as Bethany ran off to tell her family.

"We'll post these everywhere," said Stavros, selecting images on Kyle's phone. "That girl saved my life. We'll get the *Register* to write an article about it and she'll get the key to the city. The mayor can give it to her."

Kyle stood next to the mountain lion, whose coloring resembled that of the tabby cat his Aunt Pat had had when he visited her as a kid, Ms. Golightly. He'd sat for hours with Ms. Golightly on his lap, reading aloud to Aunt Pat from whatever book she had going at the time: *Jane Eyre*, *The Silence of the Lambs*, *The Autobiography of Malcolm X*.

"Let's observe a moment of silence," he said. Stavros took off his cap and fluffed his hair to give it volume. As blood trickled down the mountain lion's tawny belly and stained the dirt beneath it, Kyle whispered, "I'm sorry."

"I'm going to make it work with Cassie," Stavros said. "I'll get nipple rings. Maybe a few pairs and see which ones she likes. Does it hurt much getting pierced there?"

Kyle watched the first fly land near the mountain lion's suppurating wound and then rise up into an atomic zigzag pattern in the air. *Does it hurt much?* Getting a ride from his sister to his hotel after Aunt Pat's funeral in Phoenix, Kyle had seen a tattoo and piercing parlor in a semi-residential neighborhood with an "Open 7 days a week" neon sign and asked to be let out in front of it. His sister pulled over and reached a hand back to squeeze his knee, and Lars turned around to shake his hand. Kyle said he hoped they got a good board in Catan that night. Inside the parlor a young woman told him that the main artist was at home sick, so if he wanted an intricate design he'd have to come back later. He said was there for a piercing. "Let's say I was on some heavy medication right now," he said to the woman. "Where would I feel a piercing the most, besides the obvious place?" She said, "Take off your shirt," and five minutes later he looked down to see two silver bars sticking out of his nipples. The pain in each was as dull as an old bruise and as acute as a bee sting, and as he walked back to his hotel shirtless he fantasized about taking Aunt Pat's ashes in a jar to the rocket launch site in October and placing that jar in the seat she'd paid for. With any luck, the rocket would go up into orbit and explode and she would become what he'd always known her to be, stardust. Walking along the uniform blocks of Phoenix on a sweltering day, his skin turning an alarming shade of red, he smiled, and his smile turned into laughter, for even if no one could identify whether it was good or bad, Aunt Pat's luck had always been a pure, eternal truth. ∎

UNTELLING EYES
Amy Marques

TINTED LENSES
Amy Marques

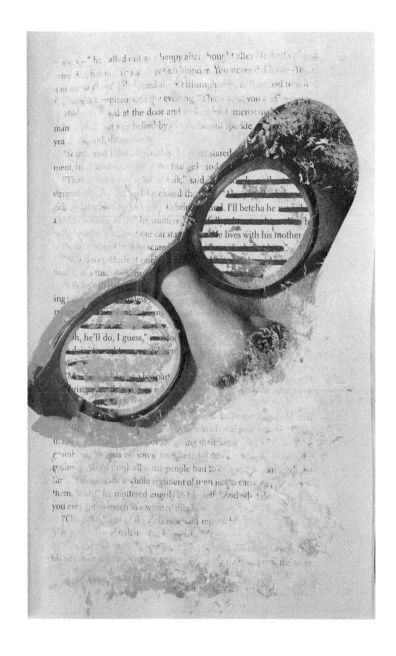

IT DID NOT SIT WELL

Amy Marques

DIVING BENEATH THE DEAD
Melissa Pritchard

Ospedale della Pietà
Riva degli Schiavoni
Venice, 1703

O*n the day of his ordination, the girls of destitution cloister themselves behind an iron screen. Abbe Vivaldi has never seen his foundling choir, his illegitimate instruments—soprano, tenor, alto, bass. Cattarina dal Cornetto, Anneta del Basso, Prudenza dal Contralto, Madalena dal Violin, Paulina dal Tenor, Lucretia della Viola, Luciana Organista—bastard voices he conducts but never sees. Brats like his own frantic scores, heads black top notes, bodies like slim, slanted staves arranged, never forced, into impeccable, sylvan sound.*

Before it was a subdivision in Phoenix, Date Palm Manor was a palm grove, its trees imported from Algeria, Egypt, Morocco, Iraq. From the steps of her saltwater pool, facing west, she repopulates, reinstates, imagines row upon row of feathered, regal palms, their amber fruits protected by muslin shrouds, ripening to a violet tinge before being harvested and railed east. In her garden, queen palms stand sentry around the pool where she swims naked, as *The Four Seasons* of Il Prete Rosso, the red priest, glitter out from the flung-open doors and windows of her house, each note a sequin in his masterpiece. She floats faceup beneath these she-palms, their topaz clusters chandeliered beneath dusty fronds, gray-green fireworks. The pool, shot through with desert sun, is Mediterranean blue. Mourning doves, Aladdin's lamps, swag between the palms, feasting on syrupy, oblong fruit.

Her secret wish had been for solitude. Peace. Now she has it and finds it terrible. Two grandfathers dead, two grandmothers, then Father, now Mother, six months, a pricking nimbus of memories, guilt, regrets. Hours after her mother's death, a hummingbird had whirred around her bedroom window, looking in, looking in, an iridescent, electric messenger. Now pale doves swoop the yard, drunk on the fruits of Babylon, daring the air's monastic dryness, all highwire.

House composer, violin teacher, Abbe Vivaldi reveres one girl's soprano above the rest for its seraphic purity. He cannot know or see its owner, female spawn of the befouled, bruised waters of the Canale di San Marco.

Two weeks after her husband was deployed to Baghdad, she'd come home to find a little parrot, Paraguayan green, fastened like an omen to the oval knob of her front door. As she came near, it swiveled its squat neck and stared so vilely, she let herself in by the back door. By morning the parrot had gone, though she'd dreamed of being trapped in a cage made of parrots, thousands and thousands of them sealing her in, suffocating her with the blurred, beating fronds of their wings. Most nights she steps from her salt pool ringed by palms, the pavement cobbled with their purplish-amber beads, their scent a smoky, sweet musk. Cockroaches scuttle over her naked feet, searching out the sticky, darkening fruits. In the morning are the striped honeybees and mourning doves. In the darkness, cockroaches, a barbed, translucent scorpion.

Her two daughters are distant women now, mottled with secrets. As children, they kitten-curled around her, begging for made-up stories, kisses. Detritus of those lives boxed up, photographs, old toys, crayon art, babies' silver cups engraved with family names. One gone east, the other west, one calls, one doesn't, their mother's womb a painted gourd for birds, stuffed with straw.

Vivaldi is ill, he can no longer serve mass. He is still music master to his little errors and longs to know the nightingale. Which is she? He waits outside the chapel one day, watches them file in, plain gowned, mute, wearing diminutive white caps. Each one misshapen, smallpoxed, homely, cast off. How can he know which is his nightingale? He turns to the music, coaxing sweet female airs from behind the screen, sounds embellished with sin. How they hurry to leave when he is finished! Rush to escape their choirmaster, his red hair repugnant, a devil's cap, Prete Rosso, leaving only a faint residue of their voices. But look how helplessly and well he loves the waterways and canals, the broad, sonorous sea, veils of light settling over its deceptive, mutable face, gilding the little island of San Giorgio! A world that will pierce and kill him.

In Iraq, the *nakhla*, date palm, is sacred. In the Koran, Archangel Gabriel spoke to Adam, "Thou are created of the same material as this tree, which henceforth shall nourish you." Mohammed named the date palm "maternal uncle, one blessed, as is the Faithful Muslim among men." During the years he lived in Medina, a poor man, he lived on dates and water, his favorite sweet the *khabis*, a confection of dates, honey and butter. Pollinated in April, the *nakhla*'s fruits are harvested in September. "Bread of the desert," they are dried, pressed with sesame seed into cans, sealed, saved for winter months. Words used in relation to the *nakhla* derive from Babylonian. To harm a date palm is a crime. "Do not kill a woman, a child or an old man. Do not cut a tree," the guideline for Islamic troops. In the southern Basra region of Iraq, thirty million date palms once flourished in irrigated orchards. During the Iraq-Iran War, many of these were "beheaded," left to die. On the road to Baghdad Airport, one sees where thousands of *nakhla* were bulldozed, for security reasons, by American soldiers. In the Koran, the *nakhla* is the Tree of Life. In the pool, saline wings surge, melt over her naked shoulders. Hot summer nights make her think: *Egypt*. The cockroach becomes a holy scarab, her suburban pool a widening bend in the Nile. In darkness, insects breed, die. Honeybees, lured to the date's dark sweet, then the coolness of water, drown. Mornings, she scoops them from the pool, marveling at the stripes around their long abdomens, how, inside, like a series of golden belts, she can see their honey. Scoops out white moths like tiny triangular kites, beetles taffeta green and humped, and always the cockroaches, sable brown, dying or dead, on the water's salt blue surface.

He is fighting in what was once Mesopotamia, Assyria and Babylon, now Iraq. For too long, she has had no news, no word from him. On the day a pair of Army officers appear at her door, afterwards, she hurtles, white arrow, through the water, hitting no mark, only turning and traveling back, Vivaldi's *Gloria* thundering out the opened doors and windows, her underwater rage, sonar keenings, lost to Persian seas. The queen palms are elegiac, the ground a rotten litter. Swimming beneath the latticed palms, thrashing water as bees, doves, fruits from the *nakhla* fall, then turning on her back, half-dead, to gaze beyond the stoic faces of female palms as the male palms, farther off, cast clouds of soft pollen over the dying grove.

Vienna, Austria
28 July 1741

The Abbe's death (internal inflammation) is marked by paupers' bells. Six pall-bearers, six storm lanterns, six choir boys from St. Stephen's (young Haydn among them) lug the corpse, hammock of wax cerements dusted with quicklime, drop it into a hastily dug grave in Bürgerspital-Gottesacker, while in a faraway chapel, a song-bird, cloistered nightingale, sings her ruddy priest—"Cum Sancto Spiritu"!— into a clamorous, empyrean sphere. ∎

WINESBURG DAYS
Michael Downs

"Adventure"

We arrived in Clyde, Ohio, on a midafternoon in late December, one of those inert, gray days wedged between Christmas and New Year's. The cold air bit, the sky looked hard as a sidewalk. We were a husband and wife on an adventure and confused about it. Behind us, to the west, was the home in Montana that she loved and never wanted to leave, mountains and clear water. Ahead lay Baltimore, a spirited eastern city that was also the ruin of a city, and yet another career for me: a fresh start as a forty-three-year-old writer who had some months earlier published his first book. We drove a white four-door sedan, bought used, the best car we'd ever owned. In the back seat stood a big dog we held dear. Ozark, a Great Pyrenees mix, balanced on her three good legs. A cancer had dissolved the bones of the right fore, so it dangled useless as a stocking filled with broken sticks.

Though Clyde looked to have buttoned itself tight against the cold from the great lake ten miles north, we lowered the car's back windows; Ozark wanted the rush of air against her face. We'd come to this town of some six thousand souls because the writer Sherwood Anderson grew up there, and out of that life he'd written a book of tales called *Winesburg, Ohio*. No, that is not quite right. We'd come to Clyde because that previous summer I'd read the book for the first time, and it had made something in me want to be closer to something in Sherwood Anderson. I wanted to know Clyde so I might better know the writer and how their alchemy made *Winesburg*.

Winesburg is an old book and a famous one. Writers, especially, admire its example. Anderson's characters imprint themselves on one's imagination. If you have read the book, you know what I mean. Few can forget twitchy Wing Biddlebaum with his amusing name and terrible past. Or the Reverend Curtis Hartman, who peeps through broken stained glass at an undressed woman. That same woman, Kate Swift, scandalously smoking cigarettes while reading books. And especially memorable: the young newspaperman George Willard, to whom people reveal their deepest selves as best they can. Yet no matter how many secret truths they confess, no matter the strength of their yearning for rapport and shared sympathy, the people of Winesburg remain apart from each other and terribly alone.

It's uncertain when Anderson left Clyde, but the biographers say 1897 seems likely, two years after his mother's death. He would have been twenty. The time of which I now write was the year 2007, its last days. That morning we, wife and husband, had left the comfortable house of her niece and the niece's family in Indiana. We'd since driven the turnpikes and become numbed by their uniformity, the Burger King at this plaza, the McDonald's at that one, the Michigan drivers all too fast. I'd looked ahead and noticed that Clyde lay only a few miles off our main route. A detour toward a different adventure. A distraction from my wife's sadness about our move. "We'll have fun," I said to Sheri. "Clyde will have a Sherwood Anderson museum, and we can spend the afternoon there, enjoy a nice dinner and stay over at some mom-and-pop motel." She agreed. We were and still are people who chart our lives by the twin stars of chance and discovery.

Trusting, as we did, in the old technologies, we found our way to Clyde using a printed road atlas. Behind the wheel, I glanced about. An urgency propelled me, as someone intent to rectify a mistake. Having read *Winesburg* so late in life, I lacked longevity with the book and wanted immersion to take its place. On Route 20, on Clyde's outskirts, we passed a training center for Whirlpool employees and a Whirlpool distribution center, which all could be reached by an avenue called Whirlpool Way. Even this put me in mind of Winesburg, the fictional town, where people struggle to make lives in an economy turning from handcrafts and farming to factories. Anderson's own father had suffered in Clyde when his work, harness making, became industrialized and he redundant. Here now in Clyde was a maker of refrigerators and washing machines. Victory for the conveyor belt.

We drove on. Were I a character in *Winesburg*, Anderson might have called me bespectacled, then noted the salt and pepper in my scanty beard, the eager darting of my eyes as I sought signs of the famous writer. I wore a ball cap, because to protect my balding head against skin cancer I always wear a ball cap. Beside me, Sheri wore sunglasses in her thick blonde hair, ready should the clouds break, prepared as she ever is for a better turn from the events of a moment.

And here came a good turn. A Winesburg Pizza. And a Winesburg Motel. A sign with an arrow directing us toward

"America's Famous Small Town." The citizens of Clyde, it seemed, knew we were coming. How much more would we discover once we reached the town's heart! We turned onto Main Street. My copy of *Winesburg, Ohio* comes with a map, which is very much a map of Clyde. In worlds real and fictional, Main and Buckeye Streets cross near the center of the old part of town, so I had a good sense of where to look for a coffee shop, or a bookstore, or a Sherwood Anderson museum.

Yes, here now were broad sidewalks and storefronts for insurance agencies and law offices, a hair cuttery and a bank, street lamps and small, leafless boulevard trees. Here is where we came upon a wind-battered banner, strung from one side of Main to the other, announcing a celebration called Winesburg Days. The banner hung tenuously, folding over itself in the wind, but we could make out the words in red letters and two piney wreaths depicted, one on each end. Alas, we'd missed the party. The festive weekend had occurred some half month before, part of the secular advent that leads to Christmas. The news of Winesburg Days gladdened and confused me. True, Clyde acknowledged its literary heritage. But I did not remember *Winesburg, Ohio* as a book concerned with the Nativity. In fact, the book's memorable line involving Jesus invokes not Christmas but the cross, when a character named Dr. Parcival declares to George Willard that "everyone in the world is Christ and they are all crucified."

We continued along the length of Main Street, scanning storefronts and signs for other evidence of Sherwood Anderson. But we cleared the three blocks or so of Clyde's downtown having seen nothing more. Finally, a half mile south of Buckeye Street, we stopped at an elementary school, closed for the holiday. Ozark needed to sniff and squat.

I'd like to report that the school was called Sherwood Anderson Elementary. It wasn't—though "Clyde Elementary" comes out of a sensible logic. Ozark limped over the beaten-down grass of the schoolyard, and I felt disappointed and silly that we'd driven so far for Winesburg Pizza and, perhaps, nothing more. No Sherwood Anderson Museum. No Kate Swift Bookstore. No Willard Inn, named for the hotel George Willard's mother owns in *Winesburg*.

"Nobody Knows"

To return to the turnpike, our most direct route would send us back along Main Street. "We should look one more time," Sheri said, her sentiment unsurprising. Like George Willard, she and I had both worked as newspaper reporters. If Winesburg existed in Clyde, we would find it. We'd knock on doors. We'd ask questions. Now we drove slower through town, peering down side streets and up alleys, unconcerned whether our puttering inconvenienced drivers behind us. There were few of them anyway, and fewer pedestrians, owing to the many storefronts closed between Christmas and New Year's. A city government building, though, looked open, so I parked by what appeared to be a town green. "Look over there," Sheri said, pointing out an Ohio Historical Marker that extolled Sherwood Anderson and his contributions to literature. I left the car to snap a picture. Placed in 2003, the plaque did not have much to say that I didn't already know, though in proclaiming that Sherwood Anderson "gave up a successful business career… to concentrate on writing" it glossed over the dramatic circumstances, which Anderson himself once described as "went nutty—had nervous breakdown—slight suspicion have been nutty ever since. Started writing for the sake of the salvation of my soul." The plaque did note that Anderson had influenced the likes of Faulkner, Hemingway, and Steinbeck. Faulkner, it is true, called Sherwood Anderson "the father of all my generation."

Across the street stood the Clyde Municipal Building, a handsome brick structure with a clock tower and a look that fancied a railroad station. Sheri said she'd stay with Ozark while I visited. Inside, I met the police dispatcher/city hall receptionist, who sat on the other side of what I took to be a bulletproof window. She said she'd never heard of Sherwood Anderson. My heart surprised me, so quick its heaviness at her answer.

"Respectability"

But a second woman who passed within earshot interrupted to tell me she knew who I was talking about. There was a brochure upstairs. She could show me.

"You know," she said, as we climbed to the second floor, "he wrote a book. I didn't care for it. It's kind of crazy. Depressing. A guy looking at women through windows and things."

It is true that when *Winesburg* was published some critics called it "filth" and a "sex book." Though the book's references to masturbation and carnality are coy, they are clear; also less threatening now than they were in buttoned-up 1919.

I told the woman that I'd also read the book. It's why I'd come to Clyde. She then showed me a display of brochures, including a flashy colorful one touting Clyde "for a visit or a lifetime." A photograph of a chubby-faced, pink-cheeked boy clutching a small American flag graced the cover. "Residents enjoy an award-winning water system," the brochure told me, "low utility rates, well-maintained streets, an excellent public library, and one of the state's top school districts... Clyde's parks and public facilities offer swimming, tennis, ball diamonds, fishing and boating."

The brochure also nodded to history buffs, extolling the life of General James Birdseye McPherson, a Clyde native who served at Vicksburg and was killed by Confederate troops outside Atlanta, making him one of the highest-ranking officers martyred for the Union cause. Interested parties could tour his home and its veranda or admire the monument raised to honor him. Sherwood Anderson received less billing, a bare mention that he'd written several books and that "each year Clyde hosts the Winesburg Christmas Weekend including the Friday evening Santa parade."

I learned that the weekend also included trolley rides. The accompanying imagery suggested penny candies and scented candles for sale, which have nothing to do with *Winesburg, Ohio* or with life in Clyde at the time Anderson lived there. In fact, Anderson's Winesburg is home to lonely oddballs, drunks, gamblers, itinerant salesmen, domineering husbands, libidinous teenagers, violent farmers, and a night watchman who hopes for a new career raising ferrets. Filth and sex—what Anderson knew to be the reality of Clyde. I did not judge. After all, why would the Clyde Business and Professional Association, sponsors of the Christmas weekend, want to claim Anderson's depiction of his hometown? Understanding, however, did not erase my disappointment. Winesburg Days! It recalled the author's own description of Winesburg's harvest fair: "An American town worked terribly at the task of amusing itself."

But I digress. The woman at the Clyde Municipal Building handed me brochures, and I took them, along with an understanding that she and other townsfolk wanted the world to know that Clyde was not Winesburg and Winesburg was not Clyde. We're not like that small town in the book, was the message. We're a place of steady, happy neighbors, quiet and safe. A community in which to raise kids. With a past that can be grand or quaint—however we want—and present that is comfortable and workaday, a future so shiny bright.

"An Awakening"

Among the brochures was one printed in black and white, made by photocopy on a sheet of plain paper, double-sided, then folded. It had been published by the Clyde Historical Society some twenty years earlier, and it was called "The Anderson Guide." In it was a hand-drawn bird's-eye view of Clyde and its outskirts. Numbered spots indicated sites of interest that pertained to either Sherwood Anderson or *Winesburg, Ohio*. This was it. I held the treasure map.

In the car, Sheri navigated while I piloted. Our first stop, the town historical society, was closed, and though I peered through windows and observed references to General McPherson, I saw nothing of Sherwood Anderson. Outside a church said to be the one out of which Reverend Curtis Hartman spies on naked Kate Swift, I took photographs with our camera. Kids on bicycles in the parking lot stared at me, curious. We saw two homes in which Sherwood Anderson had lived as a boy. The first now had a two-car garage that had been converted into Bill's Upholstery, though an *L* was missing so it read "Bill's Upho stery." The second house was small and tidy. Neither home announced its literary legacy: not a historic marker or yard sign. I wondered whether the people who lived there even knew. And if they knew, how did they react to the history? Did the homeowners embrace the ghost? Own copies of all Sherwood Anderson's books? Invite tourists in for tea and literary conversation? Or were they annoyed by the occasional stranger who came to the door? I'll never know, because I didn't knock at either place. Even with my experience as a journalist, having knocked on many doors and often under worse circumstances, I now felt uneasy at the prospect. Why trouble poor Clyde over the famous son they seemed content to acknowledge but not to celebrate? Why strike again at my already dashed illusions?

By this time, we needed a bathroom. So we made our last stop the public library, an elegant building constructed with Carnegie dollars in 1905—a decade or so after Sherwood Anderson fled town. Outside along the highest parts of the walls, names of famous authors stood in relief: Whittier, Longfellow, Holmes. Not Anderson, of course, who was not yet famous when the town raised the building. Inside, high, clean windows made the dreary day seem brighter. The library bustled with patrons, especially children and teens on winter break. A few read books but most availed themselves of the library's large DVD collection. Sherwood Anderson, I knew, had a complicated relationship with this library. In his later years, he read a story about himself and the library in a student's thesis, and that story dumbfounded him. He sent a note to an old friend in Clyde.

"She also says in her thesis," Anderson wrote, "that later the Clyde library wrote and asked me for copies of all of my books to put on their library shelves and that I answered by writing a rather impertinent letter telling them that if they wanted my books they should buy them. I wonder, Herman, if this story is also true as I have entirely forgotten the incident... I would have liked particularly to know because if the library there in my hometown really wants my books I would be glad to arrange to have them presented to the Clyde library."

Sheri and I explored. We learned that the public library in Clyde did, indeed, keep a Sherwood Anderson collection for researchers, including letters, notebooks, and other ephemera—and perhaps copies of books he'd presented himself. But access to that history required an appointment. Lacking one, Sheri and I satisfied ourselves by studying framed pen-and-ink sketches in an anteroom, which depicted Clyde at the time Anderson lived there. In the stacks, I looked for his books and took a photograph of what I found. Though he published more than two dozen in his lifetime, here, only, was *Winesburg, Ohio*: four paperback copies.

"The Untold Lie"

It is valuable, sometimes, to learn that your passions are not shared by some others. At first this feels crazy, depressing. But it is also called perspective. What mattered more in my life that day than how Clyde treats Sherwood Anderson was that Sheri and I were in the midst of our own life adventure. Everything was about to change, through chance and discovery. We would long for one former home and come to love a new one. This was our habit. The move to Baltimore was one of several by which we had taken turns following each other's passions. I followed her to Montana, her dream; she came with me to graduate school in another part of the country; we returned to Montana for her; then to Baltimore for me. As I write these words, it is her time again, and who knows where that may lead us?

Ozark the dog died a year and a half after we visited Clyde. Sheri believes we kept her alive too long, and maybe we did. It is impossible to know when to let a dog go, I say, and she says yes, but we waited too long.

You can see that in the great ongoing of our lives, our day in Clyde has little consequence. Yet I've not stopped thinking about that odd afternoon. The hours there gave me a problem I couldn't solve. Clyde's response to *Winesburg, Ohio* and to Sherwood Anderson still seems wrong, even unjust. I want to say, "What's wrong with you, Clyde?" And then I wonder, what is wrong with me that I care so much? Sherwood Anderson doesn't need me to defend him to good people who busy themselves with lives in a place he gave up on more than one hundred years ago.

But because I could not let Clyde go, because I remained curious, years later I did return in a manner of speaking—through the internet. I learned that since we'd visited, Clyde had come under scrutiny from the United States and Ohio environmental protection agencies. In town and in the area, an unusual number of children had been stricken with cancer. News stories called it the Clyde cancer cluster. Suspicions were that Whirlpool left polychlorinated biphenyls—or PCBs, which the EPA calls "probable human carcinogens"—in soil in various spots around Clyde. Most attention had gone to a children's park that Whirlpool built for the community in 1950, with a basketball court surrounded by dirt filled with PCBs and a swimming pool that might have been deadly. The pool drew its water from a pond at the bottom of a slope. The slope was also found to have PCBs in its soil.

Sherwood Anderson first intended to title his collection of tales *The Book of the Grotesque,* and a remnant of that intention remains as *Winesburg*'s introduction. There, Anderson writes about truths, and about how there are many in the world, but sometimes a person takes a particular truth and believes in it, and that truth becomes fixed in the person's life. There's comfort in thinking you've got things figured out, that every village must celebrate its famous literary son. Or that our town is a good place to raise kids.

At best, such a fixed belief closes the paths to chance and discovery. At worst, the belief stays too long fixed. Then, it's likely—over time—to be proved a lie. If accepted, the falsity of that belief creates misunderstanding and grief. Worse, though, is this: held to despite all, the lie turns a soul grotesque.

"Departure"

As we left the library that long-ago afternoon, we'd already decided, without saying much about it, that we wouldn't stay the night in Clyde. Neither the Winesburg Motel nor the pizza parlor offered enough to keep us. We'd given maybe an hour in all searching for Sherwood Anderson, and with what the day still offered we could cover many miles. So we drove away, listening to the radio and learning that the leader of Pakistan had been assassinated. That news took our attention until, tired and hungry, we arrived at a motel outside Pittsburgh, one that allowed dogs. ∎

MAN OF LA MANCHA
Markus Kirschner

I didn't want anyone to know
my father was a high school janitor.

He cleaned our graffitied toilets.
He carried leaking garbage bags.
Thankfully he worked nights.
For three years, I avoided exposure.

I was our symphony orchestra concertmaster.
At a reception after a performance,
I held court in a rented tuxedo.
Suddenly my father arrived
wearing his pale blue poly-cotton uniform,
on break from his work elsewhere in the building,
his surprise gesture of support
overshadowed by his Americanized name
hovering over his heart in embroidered cursive.
I wanted him to disappear.

In accented English
he introduced himself to other parents.
He made a joke that didn't land.
He excused himself to get back to work.

After the reception,
on my way out of the building,
I discovered my father
in an empty hallway,
tethered to one of those large
metal buffing machines,
polishing the linoleum.

Above him, a hand painted paper banner
hung across the width of the dimly lit cave
announcing that year's prom theme.

SURVEILLANCE
Ernie Wang

E merick Schuster's body aches in these final hours of his shift at Let's Fly!, but ever the professional, he conceals his fatigue and doles out enthusiastic words and high-fives. Seventy-five-year-old Mabel Rogerson—Emerick's and his son Reid's first-grade teacher at Southeast Dayton Phase Two Elementary School—is next. She is petite, and Emerick has fit her in a child's skydiving suit and helmet. The orange goggles cover half her withered face.

"Are you ready, Mrs. Rogerson?" Emerick shouts over the roar of the wind tunnel. So far it has been uneventful with this group of eight schoolteachers, who booked the standard flight package and were attentive and courteous during instructions, and who endured his terrible stock flight jokes like champs.

He frowns. Mrs. Rogerson has latched on to the ledge rail. Her face is etched with terror, and she refuses to let go.

Her friends yell reassuring things at her.

"You can do this, Mabel," Erika Einhorn, Emerick's fourth-grade teacher, exclaims, though she herself has yet to take her turn, so her words feel a little dampened with uncertainty. She places her hand on Mabel's shoulder. Mabel snarls. Erika quickly withdraws her hand. *I'm sorry I'm sorry*, she mouths, then gestures at Emerick helplessly.

Emerick stoops down. "Mrs. Rogerson," he says. "I can lower the wind strength, so you'll be just barely above the ground. In fact, you'll be able to reach down and touch the floor, if you want to."

Mabel turns. Her arms remain shackled to the rail. "You can do that?"

"Of course." Emerick motions at Ace, the wind operator behind the plexiglass, and jerks his hand downward. Ace gives a thumbs-up, and the roar of the wind diminishes.

She hesitates, then unlatches herself from the rail and clasps Emerick's extended hand. He leads her to the wind tunnel while the other teachers applaud. She looks up—she reaches no higher than his sternum—and waves bravely at her friends.

Emerick motions again at Ace. *Less*, he mouths, his finger pointing downward. Ace obliges. Emerick is one of the most knowledgeable flight instructors here at Let's Fly!, and if he says less wind, then it shall be so.

Emerick steps into the wind tunnel first, then beckons Mabel forward. She takes a shaky breath, then gingerly steps inside. She closes her eyes and raises her arms, as though to surrender to the Lord. Emerick places his hands on her shoulders and waist, then leads her to the center and carefully lowers her into position.

The surge of wind lifts her off her feet and propels her body. She is flying. She extends her arms and legs. She is a condor. She is Superwoman. She cries out in wonder.

"You're doing it," Emerick shouts. And though Mabel hovers at the height of Emerick's knees, he crouches way down, to where his back twinges, and adjusts her torso so that she is positioned comfortably.

"I'm flying! Whee!" Mabel laughs, and her friends standing outside the glass wall cannot help but feel a burst of emotion in witnessing her exhilaration.

"Higher! Higher!" Mabel cries, and when Emerick bends farther down and says, "Are you sure?" she shouts, "Yes yes, higher!"

"Okay!" Emerick motions to Ace and sweeps his hand up.

Moments earlier, Ace's phone buzzed with the arrival of a text. His eyes widened and his heart pounded. The text was from Crystal, who moved out of his studio apartment two months ago. He has been unable to think of anything or anybody other than her since. He breathlessly opened the text. It contained three words.

I miss you

He exhaled. He had been praying for this text every day, and here it was, finally and actually, here on his phone. His heart soared.

So when he sees Emerick from the corner of his eye motioning at him to adjust the dial a little, and feeling distracted from imagining what will surely be a passionate reconciliation with Crystal, he absent-mindedly twists the knob to maximum power.

Mabel is instantly catapulted to the top of the wind tunnel, a mere few feet from the ceiling. Her friends gasp and cover their mouths.

"Maaaabel!" Mrs. Einhorn shrieks, thrusting her arms high in the air.

"Help!" Mabel commands from above, barely audible over the rush of wind. "Help me at this very moment!"

Emerick leaps and futilely grabs for Mabel's legs. "Ace what the hell?" he yells. "Turn that down!"

Oh my god oh my god oh my god, a panicking Ace mouths behind the plexiglass. Emerick sees Ace reach for the dial and twist it aggressively, and he knows what will happen next. He braces himself and thrusts his arms forward in a cradle.

Mabel comes crashing down, squawking like a smushed cat. Emerick steps slightly to the left, then raises his arms and catches her in his arms. He swings her to one side, then plops her safely on her feet.

Ace has shut off the wind, so this moment is met with a stunned silence. Erika Einhorn has begun to cry.

"Are you okay, ma'am?" a shaken Emerick asks.

After finding her footing, a smile creeps onto Mabel's face. Her heart pumps life and adrenaline and vigor through her trembling body. She is exhilarated. This is the most fun she has had in decades. She wags her finger sternly at Ace. "You're a bad, bad boy," she says.

Ace squeaks behind the plexiglass, terrified and relieved and, quite astonishingly, thinking about Crystal. He is happy that Mrs. Rogerson is safe, but he is certain he will get laid tonight, and he is very, very happy about that.

The next day, Emerick walks in on his son, Reid, having sex with his secret boyfriend, Hannon. A building-wide mechanical failure at Let's Fly! resulted in Emerick coming home unexpectedly early. For a moment, Emerick, who until now was not aware that Reid even had a boyfriend, is hurt that Reid never mentioned anything, and then he considers the possibility that maybe Reid did tell him about Hannon and Emerick forgot about it, and this really concerns him if so, so he says nothing and instead clears his throat.

"Dad, I can explain," Reid says in the ensuing silence.

Hannon has dived underneath the bed covers. His arm protrudes and probes like a tentacle, and coming upon a pair of jeans, snatches it, and Emerick and Reid turn to observe his outline thrash and wrestle on the jeans. They are Reid's and several sizes too small.

Standing in the doorway, Emerick, who could not care less whom his son shags, is curious what excuse Reid could possibly come up with, so he says, "Go on then."

"He's. Um." Reid panics. "He's paying me for my body."

Hannon's head shoots out from beneath the cover. "*What?* You ho, you know that's not true."

"It totally is," Reid snaps, red-faced, his eyes pleading with Hannon, but Emerick, who musters all of his self-control to refrain from laughing, knows that any chance for collusion between these two disappeared the moment his beautiful, lying son placed the blame on his poor boyfriend.

"I'm starving," Emerick announces. "Are you fellas hungry?"

They are, despite their sullenness. At eighteen, they are always hungry.

At Applebee's, Reid and Hannon's moods improve noticeably. After they devour platters of fiesta lime chicken and oriental chicken wraps, Emerick feels brave enough to begin prying.

"I just want to know you guys aren't getting any grief at school." Emerick realizes this is not the same Dayton High that he attended two decades earlier, but this is his son, and he can never be too sure, and he is already fond of Hannon. He sees how Reid's eyes soften when Reid looks at Hannon.

They shrug. "No one really knows about us," Reid says.

"Okay," Emerick says. "And does this—" and here he hesitates. He clears his throat. "Do you still intend to go through with your plans for after high school?"

After months of torturous deliberation, Reid made the decision to enlist in the Air Force. He is scheduled to leave for Lackland in five weeks.

"Of course, Dad. Why wouldn't I?"

"Okay, great." Emerick hopes he masked his disappointment. Given their socioeconomic status and Reid's grades, both of which are heavily underperforming, they know this is perhaps Reid's best chance at making something of his life, though everything about this saddens Emerick. But the only thing that would sadden him more is if Reid ended up stuck in Dayton with a dead-end job like his own. Even still, he often imagines the scenario in which Reid changes his mind and remains here, maybe working with him at Let's Fly! and, in these moments, he feels a surge of longing and hope.

"*I'll* join you at Applebee's any time, sir," Hannon says, as if to read Emerick's mind.

"Huh?"

"I mean if you ever want company after Reid leaves," Hannon says quickly.

Emerick smiles. "I appreciate your kindness," he says, and he means it. He wonders if it's obvious that he looks lonely already.

Three weekends later, Hannon asks Emerick if he wants to join Reid and him for their day at the state fair.

"If you're not busy, of course," Hannon says, quickly, when Emerick and Reid look at him in surprise.

Emerick is never busy outside of work. He sneaks a glance at Reid, who nods cheerfully.

"I'm leaving soon," Reid says. "I'd love to spend as much time with you both as I can."

Reid and Hannon were still children the last time either of them visited the fair, and they chatter excitedly during the drive to Columbus and try to recall what memories of the fair they retain. They head straight for the wild mouse coaster, where Reid and Hannon take the front seat. Emerick takes the back. Hannon shrieks in terror from the moment the coaster begins its series of unbanked turns.

"No, we are *not* going to die," Reid yells over the roar of the coaster and Hannon's screams. "Get a hold of yourself!"

Hannon does not get a hold of himself, and Reid resorts to lowering his head and covering his ears. Emerick leans forward and offers his hand to Hannon, who grabs it and holds on for dear life. A wave of familiarity and sympathy washes over Emerick: the former because his customers at Let's Fly! often display a similar fear, and the latter because no person should ever feel this way.

"No more scary rides," Hannon blubbers afterward, and Emerick and Reid think if that was considered scary, they'll be shooting squirt guns and eating corn dogs for the rest of the day.

They take a different approach at seeking thrills and head for the haunted mansion, though from the outside, it looks less like a mansion and more like an old shipping container. Emerick notices the rust on the tracks and the walls, and what really scares him is the thought of Reid or Hannon contracting tetanus.

This time, Emerick takes the front seat, and Reid and Hannon the back. The cart lurches forward on the dilapidated track, and they pass through swinging doors and enter the darkness.

Hannon screeches good-naturedly when the cart swivels to reveal a featureless face. And then the ride descends into a bit of monotony, and Reid and Hannon go quiet in the darkness. Emerick considers stirring things up and jumping out of the cart and accosting them around the next corner, but the thought crosses his mind that maybe they are enjoying a private moment, and this reminds him that Reid and Hannon will have to say goodbye to each other soon enough.

More than anything, he wishes for Reid to enjoy these final days in Ohio. He tells himself to stop worrying over Reid's safety. His friends who are military parents have dismissed his concerns. Reid will be fine, they said. The Air Force will keep him healthy and busy and well-fed.

A flash of red light in the next room reveals a scowling ogre. Emerick chuckles. He is less sure whether he himself will be fine. On his bad days at work, when his shift was filled with insufferable customers, he could look forward to coming home to Reid, who never failed to remind him of what really mattered in life. Soon it will be just himself. He can date again—he *should*—but for the last eighteen years, his sole focus has been to raise Reid, and he has long forgotten how romantic commitments work.

He is aware that the process of meeting romantic partners has shifted to online dating platforms. He wonders if the women online will see him not unlike this ogre: faded and outdated and trying too hard to impress. "Hang in there, buddy," he says, nodding sympathetically at the ogre, before they move on to the next room.

Imagining his future, Emerick is hit with a jolt of loneliness. An empty ache fills the cavity of his chest. So he is surprised when he feels a hand squeeze his shoulder as they turn the final corner and out of the haunted mansion, as sunlight floods their squinting eyes. He turns around and sees Hannon smiling at him.

"That wasn't terrifying," Hannon says.

"No, it wasn't," Emerick responds.

Emerick figures this is a good time to give Reid and Hannon some time alone, so he excuses himself for a couple hours. He'll meet them later at the food court.

He passes pedestrians shuffling to the next ride. Up ahead, a crowd has gathered around a mechanical bull. A thin man, resplendent in his ten-gallon hat and shiny boots, leaps onto the bull. The crowd quiets. They know he means the business. The bull begins to spin, and sure enough, the man easily handles its gyrations with swagger, at one point releasing one hand into the air and finger-pistolling the crowd. The bull's swerves intensify, but the man shifts his weight from one side to the other, comfortably maintaining his balance. The crowd applauds.

The bull begins to slow. The whirr of the bull's engine diminishes, then stops completely. The crowd goes silent. The man squints, then taps the bull's foam flank. "Slap it harder!" a woman calls out from the crowd. The man cocks his head, then raises his arms in a mixture of confusion and exasperation.

The whirr of the engine inexplicably, suddenly returns. The bull bucks violently and flings the man high into the air, a potato cannon doing God's work. The crowd gasps. The man screeches before landing clumsily on the padded inflatable. The bull stops once again.

Emerick feels sorry for the man, and all of this reminds him of the time Mrs. Rogerson was flung into the air on his watch, so he continues down the street. He takes a seat on a bench. Above him, sky gliders whirr and transport couples from one end of the fair to the other. It is a gorgeous day.

"We're flying! Whee!" a young girl above cries, sandwiched between her youthful parents.

When he was still young, before he outgrew it, Reid would beg Emerick to take him to Let's Fly! on Emerick's days off. Emerick happily obliged. Reid suited up, and they waited for an empty wind tunnel, and then off Reid went, his arms and legs splayed like a little flying carpet, his baby cheeks flapping with the rush of wind. They went one Halloween with Reid dressed as Ironman. After heated negotiations regarding safety and protocol, they settled on Reid retaining his full costume but swapping out the Ironman helmet for a skydiving one. After an extended flight, Reid deftly landed and removed his helmet. His eyes sparkled so intensely Emerick feared his heart would explode.

"How was that, son?" he asked.

"This is the best day of my entire life," Reid said solemnly. This was probably the best day of Emerick's entire life, too.

Emerick watches families amble by, their hands linked, their laughter in sync. An elderly couple shuffles past Emerick. Their pace is glacial, but their smiles are carefree. From the other direction, four fraternity brothers from the Ohio State University meander in matching sweatshirts and baseball caps. They do not look much older than Reid. Emerick wonders if these kids realize how fortunate they are. The elderly couple notices the letters on their sweatshirts and flags them down as they pass by, and the six of them chat comfortably and familiarly, as if they have been friends all along.

Emerick checks his watch. He wonders what Reid and Hannon are up to. Wherever they are, he hopes they are enjoying this beautiful day. He hopes Reid is not worrying about his future. *Leave that part to your dad, son,* he thinks.

And as though by way of answer, he hears Reid call out, "Hey, Dad!" from above. He looks up and sees a waving Reid and Hannon sailing by.

He laughs and nods back. "Fellas," he says, and his heart is full and warm. He watches them disappear before a line of trailing gliders. He smiles. Of course they would choose to ride the sky glider.

The day has come. Reid's bag is packed and sits by the front door. He is leaving virtually everything behind. The Air Force is explicit on what little he can bring. Emerick has taken the day off from work to drive him to the airport in Columbus. He already looks forward to the day he will pick Reid up again, whenever that is. He hopes it is soon. He imagines Reid appearing through the airport security exit, no longer a boy, his body filling out his fatigues, his eyes weary and wise and displaying the first sign of creases when he smiles, as though he has experienced more in his brief time in the Air Force than in all his years growing up in Dayton.

Reid and Hannon emerge from his bedroom. Reid's expression is inscrutable. Hannon wipes his red eyes.

Emerick stands from the couch. "You fellas ready?" he asks. He himself is not. Nothing would have prepared him for this day.

They are not ready, either, but they nod. Emerick picks up Reid's bag. He is struck by how light it is, but he reminds himself that the Air Force will take good care of his boy.

It is early, and there are few cars on the road. They are silent in the truck. Emerick resists the urge to engage in conversation. He wants to fill the space with the sound of his son's voice one final time, but he lets him be. Emerick, in his shoes, would have wanted to be left alone as well.

"Hey, Dad? Can we swing by Let's Fly! one last time?" Reid breaks the silence.

Emerick cannot recall the last time Reid asked to fly. He checks his watch. He has building keys and free rein. They don't open for a couple hours. "You want to get one last flight in?"

"*I'm* not doing it," Hannon says. "I will die."

"I'll teach you one of these days," Emerick says.

"He's a damn good teacher," Reid says.

Emerick boots up the building lights and thermostat and wind system as Reid changes into his jumpsuit. He enjoys opening Let's Fly!, which he has done hundreds of times. The building is wired mostly with incandescent lights, and in the winter, when it would still be black outside, watching the room emerge from darkness and feeling the cold cede to the first tendrils of warmth made him think of the world being reborn.

In a burst of inspiration, Emerick realizes that Reid has not experienced virtual-reality skydiving, a technology Let's Fly! has just recently incorporated. He rushes into the office and retrieves a pair of goggles.

Reid is waiting by the wind tunnel when he returns. Hannon has taken a seat close by. Reid looks up curiously.

"What's that?"

"Put these on," Emerick says. "You're in for one last treat." Emerick stands behind the computer screen. When the options load, he hovers the mouse for a moment before selecting Swiss Alps. He enters the wind tunnel, then helps Reid fall into position. Moments later, hovering midair, Reid gasps when the scenery kicks in. Emerick has experienced Swiss Alps many times, and he knows what Reid sees. "You like that, son?" he murmurs, and though his words are swept away by the wind, Reid's wondrous smile says it all.

Reid spreads his arms out, just as he did ten years ago in his tiny Ironman costume. "This is *awesome*," he yells, and Emerick thinks of himself as the best father in the world. And though Reid needs no help, Emerick cannot resist placing his hands on Reid's arched, swaying figure.

Emerick closes his eyes and feels the rush of cool wind sweep past his face. As if standing at a distance, he vaguely hears Reid's excited cries. He imagines his son soaring through the Alps, through the freezing countryside air, but Reid is Ironman, impervious to the elements, safe from harm, the perfect airman.

And now Emerick himself is gliding through the jutting Alps. Trees are tiny specks miles below. Entire forests disappear. He soars into a blanket of cumulus clouds and tastes the cool, wet drops of condensation. Emerging above the clouds, now an ocean of billowing white below, he ascends into the vast sky, a beautiful pink that paints the universe. He cannot tell if the sun is rising or setting.

* * *

Airman First Class Reid Schuster of Dayton, Ohio, sensor operator for a fleet of remotely piloted aircraft at Creech Air Force Base in Indian Springs, Nevada, is celebrating his twenty-second birthday at the Phoenix, the gayest bar in all of Las Vegas, when, exiting the men's room, he bumps into seventy-nine-year-old Mabel Rogerson, his first-grade teacher. His damp hands freeze on his pants midwipe.

"Oh my god, Mrs. Rogerson, how is this even happening," he blurts out.

Mrs. Rogerson shrieks and embraces Reid, though she reaches just above his chest, and that is with heels. A purple boa snakes around her shoulders and extends nearly to the ground, and she rocks a tidy orange-and-white floral print dress from the 1970s. She looks as though she has belonged here at the Phoenix her entire life, while Reid still finds himself feeling intimidated and out of place here, *here* referring to both a space and a concept larger than the Phoenix. At any rate, Las Vegas seems like a megapolis as vast as the Mojave Desert itself compared to the inconsequential pocket of Dayton in which Reid grew up.

"But why are you here?" Reid asks weakly.

Mrs. Rogerson lifts her arm as though to deliver a karate death chop. "I've come to give you a Vegas spanking, Reid. Bend over."

"What?"

"Fear not! I'm kidding. In fact, a dear friend is celebrating his fiftieth birthday." Mrs. Rogerson brightens. "And he wanted to celebrate here, so *here* we are." She raises her palms toward the ceiling, an amalgam of praising the Lord and raising the roof and dismissing the surreality of it all.

"You came all the way here for a friend's birthday?" Reid asks incredulously.

Mrs. Rogerson clucks. "When you get to my age," she says, "you do everything you can for the people who matter to you. Anyway, what brings *you* here?" She twirls one end of her boa. "Other than to ogle these gorgeous men." She sighs. "Although that's more than enough reason in itself."

"It's my birthday, too," Reid mumbles, but before he can finish, Mrs. Rogerson shrieks again and seizes his arm and pulls him through the sea of men toward the bar.

"Move it! Hot birthday boy coming through," Mrs. Rogerson hollers over the din. The crowd parts obediently.

"Mrs. Rogerson, please stop."

"I shall never. Excuse me, boys, coming through, thank you. Now *you* two behave."

"Oh god, Mrs. Rogerson."

"I *know*. Come now."

At the bar, Mrs. Rogerson slides Reid a flight of colorful vodka shots.

"Happy birthday, Reid." She pats him on the shoulder. "It's been a pleasure knowing both you and Emerick."

A jolt of nostalgia rips through Reid at the mention of his father's name. He raises his glass. He tilts his head back, and the vodka sluices past the back of his throat.

Mrs. Rogerson ignores Reid's grimace and excuses herself, tells Reid she must return to her friend.

"You're grown up now," she chides him. "Use your powers for good, okay?" They embrace for a final time, and then she is gone.

Back at his table, Reid reunites with his friends Dallas and Mohammed, both of whom work as blackjack dealers at an off-Strip casino and who have been biding the time by snogging and taking sips of the Lagavulin scotch they got for Reid's birthday. A year earlier, Dallas and Mo stumbled upon a cowed Reid—still new to the city—alone in a corner of the Phoenix clutching his seltzer as though it were holy water, and they quickly took on the role of his older brothers.

They themselves discovered each other years ago, in Provo, where they were caught making out at Mormon summer youth camp, then sprinted south to Las Vegas the day after graduating from high school, never once looking back.

Mo and Dallas look past Reid, at the shadow Reid senses towering behind him, and wave tentatively. "Look who's finally here," Dallas says, his voice high and forced.

Reid's heartbeat quickens, right before Arjun painfully squeezes his shoulder. Reid tilts his head back and kisses Arjun, whose lips feel as heavy as his hand. Arjun has changed out of his work uniform into jeans and a tank top, displaying his powerful physique. Rail thin, Reid is too self-conscious not to wear layers of clothing himself.

"You should have waited for me to open the Lagavulin," Arjun says gruffly, snatching the glass that Mo hands him. The three murmur apologies. "I'm kidding," Arjun says. Their laughter dies down almost as quickly as it starts. Arjun downs the shot, then scoops up Reid with one arm and draws him closer.

"Happy birthday, kid," he says. Reid submits to Arjun's strength. He places his hand over Arjun's stomach, just in time to feel it rumble.

"You haven't eaten?" Reid says. "I'll get you food."

"I need a steak quesadilla and onion rings," Arjun says.

Mo stands. "I'll get it," he says, brightly. "Let the birthday boy spend quality time with you."

"Reid will get it," Arjun answers. Mo sits down stiffly.

Reid smiles reassuringly at Mo before he turns and wades through the swarm of sweaty bodies and fights off the feeling that he is tired and a little despondent, and that he does not really want to be here anymore. On most nights, he finds Arjun's display of dominance intoxicating, but something feels off-kilter tonight, as though he wishes Arjun would for once attempt to be civil with him and his friends. He thinks of Hannon, his ex, back in Dayton, who, despite his occasional penchant for hysterics, did not once treat Reid as if

Reid were inferior in any way. And he thinks of his father, the most level-headed person he knows, and how he wishes he had not taken for granted his time with him. Running into Mrs. Rogerson tonight has ushered in a wave of homesickness for Dayton, though that, too, he tries to push away.

When he reaches the bar, he realizes that he has forgotten whether Arjun wanted the steak or chicken quesadilla, and in the ensuing panic, he also forgets whether Arjun wanted French fries or onion rings. So he orders all four and figures he himself can eat the other two. He should be eating more anyway.

He balances the tray of food through the throng. He emerges from the crowd and halts when he sees Arjun facing off against an equally burly man by their table. Arjun's chair has been kicked to the ground. Their taut faces are inches from the other, and they both yell furiously, though Reid knows Arjun is not listening to anything the other man is saying. A woman is attempting to pull the other man back, but the man does not budge. Dallas and Mo are standing behind Arjun, their arms crossed, unwilling or afraid to attempt to restrain him. Reid sees the mostly empty bottle of Lagavulin scotch resting on the table and knows why Arjun is throwing a tantrum.

In an instant—so quick that to Reid it is all a blur—Arjun cocks back his fist and strikes the man, who stumbles backward, knocking both him and the woman onto the ground. Reid is not surprised by witnessing the force Arjun is capable of, but he is surprised that this is happening at all, as if he was hoping all along that Arjun would behave on his birthday.

"Arjun, what the hell?" Reid yells, but two beefy security guards have materialized, and they wrench Arjun, who has drawn back his arm back for his next strike, and drag him toward the exit. Reid watches as Arjun is swallowed by the crowd.

Reid turns to Dallas and Mo. "He drank too much?" They remain silent. "Of course he did," Reid answers himself.

"The other guy bumped him by accident," Mo said. "But you know Arjun. I'm sorry, Reid. The Lagavulin was meant for you. Anyway. You should go make sure he's okay."

Mo is right. Tonight is done for, and Reid admits to feeling relieved.

"Happy birthday, beautiful," Dallas says wistfully, then embraces him, then so does Mo, and for the final time tonight, Reid wades through the crowd and toward the entrance. The doors close behind him, muffling the pulsing music. He looks to both sides. Arjun is nowhere in sight. He scours the streets, one endless block after another. He knows that Arjun will be fine—he has never known him to not be fine—so he calls for an Uber after searching futilely for twenty minutes. Reid will report to work in nine hours, and he is exhausted.

Back in Dayton three hours earlier, Emerick Schuster, sprawled out on a mint floral couch, watches twitchy video tapes of Reid he shot with a handheld camcorder in a time when phone video cameras did not yet exist. The living room lights are switched off, the blinds are drawn, and Emerick's face is awash in the green glow radiating from the television screen. Here is Reid, still a toddler, in the backyard dodging the arc of the water sprinkler and shrieking like a banshee, before he dashes to Emerick and tugs on his shirt. A moment later, he poops in his diapers and looks up proudly toward Emerick. Here is Reid a few years later, on his first day of preschool, tearfully waving Emerick goodbye and asking if they will ever see each other again. Emerick nearly shut off his camcorder and flung Reid back in the car and drove them straight home.

Reid has been gone for three years, and now every passing car at night jolts Emerick awake. Each morning he wakes up groggy and disoriented. It takes him a moment to remember that Reid is not sleeping in the next room over. He hates how quiet the home has become. He hates conceding that he is lonely. Last week, he signed up for bowling league, and he hates that.

Everything is great is what he texts Reid when Reid asks. *I want to know how you are doing.* Hearing the amazing things Reid is doing—the parts Reid can disclose, anyway—confirms his son is destined for something larger than the sum total of Emerick's life, and this makes it infinitely more bearable that his own ship has sailed.

Here is Reid during his first-grade graduation ceremony. Reid is all smiles, until he trips on the stage right before accepting his diploma and bursts into tears. And here is Mabel Rogerson, his teacher—Emerick's, too, way back when—rushing to lift him back to his feet and, since why not, grabbing his hands and engaging him in a kind of ring-around-the-rosy, which further embarrasses Reid. There is something about the graininess of the video that makes Reid and Mabel look timeless. Emerick realizes he was twenty-three when he recorded this, nearly Reid's age now, and for a moment this takes Emerick's breath away.

The other day at the grocery, in the aisle with dry pasta, he heard a voice call out, "Mr. Schuster?" and when he turned it was

Hannon approaching him unsurely. Emerick extended his hand, then, changing his mind, scooped Hannon into a hug.

"How is Reid doing these days?" Hannon asked after they exchanged pleasantries, and that was when Emerick realized Reid had been keeping from him that Reid and Hannon were no longer together.

"I'm still around if you want an Applebee's dining partner," Hannon said wistfully as they parted, and he looked so starved for company that for a moment Emerick forgot about his own state of solitude.

Tomorrow, after work, he and Stacey will have dinner at Fleming's Prime. They have been together for just over seven months, after having met at Let's Fly!. Stacey is a professor at the law school at the University of Dayton. She lives in Pheasant Hill and drives a BMW and dresses as if she belongs in New York or Paris. She is brilliant and well-read and has complex opinions about the countries that Reid's drones surveil, and it can take her quite a while to fully explain these views, so Emerick doesn't bring up Reid and his drones anymore.

They will order wine and Bibb lettuce salads and desserts, and Stacey will pay for it all. She insists it's not a problem. He is just as fine with Texas Roadhouse, but he keeps this to himself.

Back to the television. Here they are at the state fair in Columbus. Reid, in a kiddie car attached to a revolving spoke, appears from around the corner. He waves into the screen excitedly. He waves again when he reappears moments later. And then again. A happy reunion every twelve seconds. When the ride ended and Reid skipped over the platform back to him, Emerick felt something that resembled grief.

"Do you want to ride this again?" he asked, but Reid was already pulling him toward the next ride.

He knows he is incredibly fortunate that Stacey is interested in him at all. He tries to speak in more complete sentences these days, and he is more careful about his attire outside the house. When Emerick was in high school, the drama class had put on a production of *Pygmalion*, and he recalled feeling resistant toward the play's message that poor people would not hesitate to sacrifice their integrity for a chance at upward mobility. The following week during lunch, he overheard two of the actors argue about the play's original ending, an ending where the heroine walks away from a life of wealth and instead chooses independence, and he felt that ending was much more sensible, and now he occasionally wonders whether Stacey regards him as her own Pygmalion project. *Stop it.* He was being silly back then, and he is still being silly. *Stop it now.* Here is the clip that Emerick meant to record over. It's Reid's birthday, and when Emerick asks him, through the camcorder lens, what he is wishing for, Reid hesitates before he says, reluctantly, "I wish I had a mom." Here is Emerick struggling to come up with a response, and in the end, remaining silent. Reid's gaze is downcast, the candles on the cake flickering in his reflection, and it is as if Reid was feeling guilty for speaking his mind, and that's what hurts Emerick the most. Later that night, Reid crawled into Emerick's bed and said, "You're the best dad in the world," and for a little while that had made him feel better.

"Happy birthday, son," he mumbles, then closes his eyes for a moment.

The screen is flashing the white-and-gray test pattern when he wakes up in the middle of the night. He groggily switches the television off, then closes his eyes once again. He remembers he must iron his slacks and shirt for tomorrow's dinner, which, at the moment, does not feel worth the effort.

The following night at Creech Air Force Base, in the cockpit—a large converted metal container—twenty-eighty-year-old pilot Captain Arjun Joshi, his gaze fixed on the panel of screens before them, expertly steers the drone over the sparkling Persian Gulf. Arjun's sensor operator, Reid sits to his right and controls the movement of the drone's camera. Arjun's thick forearms rest on the steering yoke at the edge of Reid's periphery, and Reid cannot help but worry about whether Arjun is angry at him. Arjun has made no mention of the previous evening—in fact, tonight he has barely acknowledged Reid's existence—and though this is more or less to be expected while they are at work, Reid is an enlisted airman and Arjun is an officer, Reid does not think that it has to be as austere as this. He simply wants to confirm that Arjun is fine. But asking this would anger Arjun, even if they were not at work. Arjun would interpret that as Reid questioning his manhood. So instead he focuses on the screens.

Thirty-two-year-old Tarek Ibrahim, suspected financier and mastermind of the bombing of a military base two years ago, which resulted in the death of twelve American soldiers, is knocking back a bottle on the bow of his yacht fifteen miles off the coast of Bahrain. They have been surveilling Tarek for the last twelve days, during which time Reid has learned that Tarek really enjoys his libations. Dressed in board shorts and a hoodie, Tarek looks every bit the wealthy playboy, though Reid knows, of course, he is not. A breeze sweeps past the yacht, sending Tarek's hair into a flutter. Tarek's daughter has emerged from the cabin. Wiry and lanky, like her father, she is wearing a pink Dora the Explorer T-shirt and purple Crocs. Her cheeks are streaked with tears.

"Zoom on target," Arjun says, his eyes unblinking. Under the dim cockpit lighting, and other than a pale bruise on his cheek, hardly distinguishable, he displays no signs of a hangover or any side effect from the events that transpired last night. Reid wonders if Arjun feels a smidgen of remorse for cutting Reid's birthday night short. No, Reid does not wonder that at all. Arjun has never once apologized to him. He feels himself get simultaneously irritated and horny.

Reid twists the knobs. Tarek's pixelated face enlarges on the screens and zooms into clarity. He is drinking Lagavulin, the same scotch Dallas and Mo got for Reid last night. Tarek's eyes crinkle upon greeting his daughter. She presents to him her stubbed thumb, which he clasps with both hands, then smothers with kisses. The wind rustles, and Tarek's skin glistens. He wipes her smudged cheeks.

Reid leans forward. Now Tarek is blowing raspberries on his daughter's thumb. A smile breaks out on her face. He pats her on the shoulder, and she shuffles back into the cabin. Tarek pours himself another glass. Reid imagines if it were himself on the yacht, how it would be silent except for the sway of the ocean and the burst of the wind, with no land in sight, just water and sky and salt and spray.

Arjun snorts. "That girl better be enjoying her time with Daddy. In a week she won't have one."

Reid looks up, surprised, if relieved that Arjun has said something that resembled the start of a conversation. "You got the orders?"

Arjun shrugs dismissively. "It'll happen. We've been on this motherfucker for weeks."

"I thought this was just surveillance," Reid lies.

"Don't be ridiculous," Arjun says.

Reid, of course, is not unaware of the possible fate of their surveillance targets—he is aware of whom he is working for in the first place—but now in his fourth year in the Air Force, he is every bit as uncomfortable with why they do what they do as he was when he was first assigned to Creech. He wishes he could ask all the questions.

Are there not any less severe ways to punish Tarek? Will his entire time with the Air Force consist of one hit job after another? Are relationships between officers and airmen really that terrible? He thinks of his dad, whom Reid, as a kid, would spend entire afternoons pestering with a dizzying array of questions. Never once did his dad shunt him away, instead answering his every question with infinite patience.

Arjun yawns. "I need coffee," he says.

Reid stands quickly. "I'll get you some," he says.

"Make it quick."

On his way to the dining facility, he wonders if Tarek's daughter asks Tarek questions endlessly, too. He wonders where his next assignment after Creech will be. There's Ramstein in Germany, Kadena in Okinawa, Aviano in Italy. He'll take any of those. But what he really wants is an assignment close to Dayton, close to his dad, though he knows he is at the mercy of the military, which will decide his fate for him.

He hears a squeak in the darkness. He stops in his tracks and retrieves his penlight and shines it into the night. On the dirt ground, a tiny desert mouse stands upright on its hind legs and peers into the shine of his light, its nose sniffing the air.

"Hello, Mr. Mouse," Reid says, quietly. It continues to stare at him curiously. "Or maybe it's Mrs. Mouse," he says. "Sorry, I can never tell with your kind."

It ignores his equivocation and quivers its whiskers.

"I'll be on my way now. The king needs caffeine," Reid explains, embarrassed for actually feeling apologetic, then snaps off the penlight and continues on his way.

The dining facility is serving midnight meals, so he picks up a burrito and a salad for Arjun as well. Back in the cockpit, Arjun inhales the food, then they quietly wrap up the rest of the mission. The sky is just beginning to brighten when they step out of the cockpit. Reid heads for the shuttle bus the base provides for its airmen back to Las Vegas. Arjun drives. He has not once offered to drive Reid back, though this, too, was to be expected.

"I'll see you later," Reid says, guardedly. Arjun grunts, then heads for his car. From the window of the shuttle bus, Reid watches Arjun's car disappear around the corner. Before the shuttle bus leaves the parking lot, Reid has fallen asleep.

At Fleming's, Emerick sits quietly while Stacey and the sommelier engage in a spirited discussion over tonight's selection.

Stacey mentions the vineyards in Italy she visited three years ago, and this excites the sommelier. Their discussion drags on. They talk about their favorite off-the-beaten-path European cities and squeal when they discover one in common.

Emerick should be accustomed to this by now—both being ignored and listening in on stodgy conversations—but tonight he feels his lack of sleep finally catching up to him. He acknowledges he does not know squat about vintage and tannins—Stacey and he both know he'll drink anything—but he has been unsettled since ten minutes earlier, when the server spat out "*tap water*," taking Emerick's response and twisting the words into something vulgar. "You'll have the *tap water*?" ("We'll have the sparkling," Stacey quickly interjected, trying to defuse the tension, though to Emerick, it felt as if she were taking the server's side.)

His sour mood deepens when he responds to the next server with "medium rare" when asked about his steak's preparation. Emerick was a lifelong medium-well guy, occasionally a well done. "Does that embarrass you?" he asked Stacey once, surprised that the thoroughness with which he enjoyed his meat cooked could actually offend somebody, and after a prolonged moment, she carefully said, "Of course not," but he took the hint and has ordered his steaks medium rare ever since when dining with her. The server nods dismissively, as if medium rare is not rare enough, as if Emerick will always be out of his league here, and when Stacey smiles at him encouragingly, he does not smile back.

After they are finally done ordering, Emerick asks Stacey what she has been up to at the university. She launches into a lengthy explanation and uses a lot of complicated jargon, and by the time she reaches the part about a potential new opportunity at the law school—greater responsibility *and* compensation—he has begun to tune out, though he continues to nod enthusiastically.

After their Bibb lettuce salads arrive—he bristles a little; it's the server who served the *tap water*—Emerick asks if Stacey has finalized her summer travel plans. An adventurer, Stacey's last two trips took her to Myanmar and New Zealand, where she parasailed, cliff dove, went spelunking, surfed, and rock climbed. Emerick's only trip in the last five years, which he took a month after Reid left, was to Myrtle Beach, where he fell asleep on the beach every morning and got sunburned.

Stacey lowers her fork. "I've been meaning to ask you."

"Ask me what?"

"Whether you'd like to join me for a week in Monaco this summer?"

"*Monaco?*" Emerick does not know whether Monaco is a country or a city, or something else entirely, much less which continent it is on. Whatever and wherever *Monaco* is, Emerick is certain the servers there will question his choice of drinking water. He is suspicious of *Monaco* already. Hell. There wasn't a city in the world he could afford traveling with Stacey to. Hell. He could not even afford date night here in Dayton.

Stacey's smile falters, and Emerick wonders if he said *Monaco* the way the server spat out *tap water.*

"You don't have to join, of course," she says, quickly. "I thought it'd be fun if we traveled together."

"It sounds pricey."

"I'll cover the costs," Stacey says, then shrinks when Emerick deepens his scowl.

It occurs to him that he and Stacey have never had dinner together at Applebee's. He is quite certain that he has shared with her, on more than one occasion, how comfortable he feels at a place like Applebee's, and explained that the familiarity of the restaurant is what elevates the passable, if predictable, food into something delicious.

"I don't know. I've never really considered visiting Monaco."

Stacey's expression is a mix of surprise and disappointment. "What would you rather do?"

Emerick looks around the main dining room, the mahogany, the rows of silverware, the wines in the showcase with their special vintages and expensive tannins ready to be brought out and brandished like trophies, the servers in tuxedos, who he is convinced gather in the back and wonder out loud what someone like Stacey could possibly see in him.

He lays down his salad fork. "I want to go roller-skating." He does not *really* want to roller skate. He cares for skating as much as he cares for Bibb lettuce salad. It is just that Skateworld is cheap, and for once he can afford to pay, and he knows that if they continue to dine exclusively at Fleming's and travel together to places like Monaco, he will one day soon feel compelled to choose how this ends, and he does not want to make that decision anytime soon.

A year ago, Reid was so distraught with the death of his first-ever surveillance target—the subsequent missile strike resulted in the demise of the target's entire family and their two coffee Labradors—

that Dallas and Mo rushed to Reid's apartment that night, armed with pizza and Dallas's PlayStation and terrible jokes, none of which involved reference of harm to any person or animal. More than anything, it was how unsuspecting Reid's target had been—how on the surveillance screens, he had gone about as if this were any other day, how he had shopped and met with his friends and jogged through the city with the certainty of routine and the expectation that he would do it all again tomorrow—that haunted Reid the most.

"You watch them day after day and eventually you feel this connection with them," Reid blubbered, and Dallas shushed him and said there was no need to justify his reaction; who *wouldn't* react the way he did?

"Arjun," Reid answered, and Dallas and Mo had no rejoinder. In fact, earlier that night, Arjun—smug and satisfied—had invited Reid to celebrate the assassination with him and the rest of their unit. Reid had feigned stomach illness.

"Are you guys still together?" Mo asked hesitantly.

Reid nodded. "He's complicated, but he has his virtues," he said, unsure as to why he felt so defensive.

"Of course he does," Mo said, quickly. Then he added, "Plus he's so hot." And they all looked sad, as if coming to the conclusion that Arjun's hotness was his sole virtue.

They fell silent, each thinking their own thoughts, before Mo said, "We need to get you out of the house."

After a minute of brainstorming, Reid asked, "You guys aren't down for bowling, are you?"

Mo and Dallas's eyes widened. They were always down for bowling. They may have lived in glitzy Las Vegas with its twenty-four-hour neon lights and never-ending streams of tourists, and occasionally loved the decadent Strip pool party with the celebrity disc jockey, or the wild night at the Phoenix, but in the end, they'd grown up in small towns, and for them, there would always be an inexplicable comfort in returning to the things that were best done away from the big cities, like spending hours at the crumbling bowling alley and snacking on nachos slathered with cheese-equivalent sauce, which at the moment sounded more delicious than anything.

Mo stood. "Did you know, young Reid," he said, "that you are talking to the former high school bowling champ of Pleasant Grove, Utah?"

Dallas stood. "Don't worry if you suck," he assured Reid. "I can't bowl if my life depended on it."

Reid wanted to thank them, but what he wanted to thank them for was much larger than the pizza and the nachos, beyond their friendship, even. He could not quite put it into words, this gratitude swirling in his heart and pushing out his anguish from earlier tonight, but based on the way Mo and Dallas were smiling back at him, he figured they pretty much knew already whatever it was he wanted to say.

Stacey, it turns out, was a childhood roller-skating prodigy, one of Dayton's finest, and at Skateworld, under the revolving strobe lights and the pulsing jams of the eighties—and still dressed in her Fleming's finest—she captures the attention of the other roller skaters with her elaborate twirls and pirouettes and, when they bring out the limbo bar, her outstanding limboing, in which she contorts into impossible shapes and slides easily under the perilously low bar.

At last, Emerick concedes that he cannot keep up. Her speed is too great. Her limbo contortions defy the laws of physics. They can start together at the same position, but thereafter, the only subsequent times they skate together is in the moments when she catches up after lapping him, before she speeds off once again. When she slows down to skate with him, he knows he is holding her back, and Stacey is too competitive—too filled with a passion for speed, for adventure, for something larger than Emerick could ever be—for that.

So he skates off the rink and leans on the rail and watches Stacey whizz by at her breathtaking speed. Stacey, in her cashmere blouse and work pantsuit and her grimy roller skates that must be as old as Skateworld itself, looks as though she has belonged here her entire life. She is beautiful.

So he retrieves his phone and begins to record Stacey skating around the rink. A farewell memento, perhaps. By the next lap, Stacey realizes that Emerick is recording her. With her every return, she smiles and waves into his phone. This time, she leaps into the air and spins and sticks her landing. When she straightens, cheers and applause erupt from across the rink. This time, she skates by while flailing her arms like a windmill out of control. This time, she sticks out her tongue and crosses her eyes. As she passes by, her head rotates so her gaze remains fixed on Emerick, a trace of concern etched into the fine lines on her face. This time, she looks past the camera and at Emerick, and she smiles this faint smile. This time, she waves gently at the camera, as though she could be saying hello, or goodbye, or I am still here. This time, she slows to a halt before Emerick and lowers his phone, then reaches for his arms. "Join me?" she murmurs, and

Emerick considers this.

His daughter is seven and her name is Sacha, and tonight, Tarek and Sacha are at a park that reminds Reid of a cross between an American state fair and a rural amusement park. It is dark, and the night is lit with lightbulbs strung between tall poles. Tarek and Sacha amble from one booth to the next, their hands clasped and swinging, singing some song Reid thinks he could recognize, if he could hear it.

It is early afternoon in Nevada, scorching under a cloudless sky, but inside the cockpit it is quiet and dark, save for the glow of the screens and control panel and the dim lights shining from the recess of the ceiling. The air conditioners struggle to keep up, and Reid is uncomfortably warm. To his left, Arjun cheerfully steers the drone. "Guess who got orders?" is how he greeted Reid at the start of the shift.

Reid stopped in his tracks. "For when?" he whispered.

Arjun's grin widened. "Soon enough, my friend," he chortled.

"Is it tonight?"

Arjun ignored his question and leaned forward and whispered into his ear, "I'm going to plow you so hard this weekend, kid, you won't be able to get off the floor," before nonchalantly plopping into his pilot seat.

That was an hour ago. Once again, Reid cannot help himself from casting glances at Arjun's forearms, wide and round like ham hocks, a network of veins running just under the skin, capable of destruction and sensuality. Today, however, he finds them repulsive. Arjun's sheer physicality is what drew Reid to him in the first place, but the world's axis has shifted.

On the screen, Tarek helps Sacha climb onto a stallion on a glittering carousel. Sacha squeals, then leans forward and kisses her father. Tarek's face is so tender that Reid nearly sighs. The carousel begins to rotate, slowly at first. Tarek stands by his daughter's side, gently placing his hand on her back as the carousel quickens and her stallion rises and falls to what Reid imagines is the cadence of the carousel music. Sacha has clasped the brass post, and her head remains steadfastly fixed on her father. Reid closes his eyes and fills in the sounds himself: the carousel calliope music, Sacha's peals of laughter, Tarek's soft words, the distant roar of the roller coaster, the sway of the breeze carrying the heat of the night.

The drone hovers in a fixed position high in the invisible sky. Tarek and Sacha disappear to the other end, then reappear moments later, Sacha's smile remaining plastered on her shining face, Tarek's hand caressing her small back.

"Zoom on target." Arjun's voice comes from thousands of miles away.

Reid twists the knobs so hard and Tarek's face enlarges so abruptly that it is as if the pixelation struggles to keep up. For the first time, Reid notices how haunting Tarek's eyes are. Green, perfectly set in his narrow, symmetrical face, the weight of his life creasing the edges, filled with love for his daughter. Filled with longing. And his smile, as though he possesses a kind of joy and sadness Reid will never know.

"I said, can you hear me?" Arjun's distant voice snaps Reid back to the stuffy cockpit.

"*What do you want?*" Reid's voice is sudden and large and distraught.

Arjun jerks his head in surprise. "What was that, kid?"

"Yes, sir, I can hear you."

Arjun cocks his head and studies Reid. "You all right?"

"Yes, sir." Reid backs off in volume, if not in rancor.

"What's gotten into you?" Arjun barks.

Reid is turned away from Arjun. He knows that Arjun's surprise at his insubordination will morph into rage at any moment; he is surprised Arjun has not angered yet.

They are interrupted by a squeak emanating from somewhere between them. They pause and look down. On the control desk, a tiny desert mouse crouches in the space that separates Reid from Arjun. The mouse is staring at the screens above, his front paws raised, as though surveilling Tarek and Sacha and the whirling carousel. His whiskers quiver. He is otherwise motionless.

"The hell?" Arjun says. "How did it get inside?"

"Why are you doing this, Mr. Mouse?" Reid murmurs. He hears in the distance the breathy notes of the carousel steam organ, the roar of the roller coaster, the ocean, the wind.

Arjun's hand curls into a muscular fist. His gaze is fixed on the mouse, his forearms are taut, his shoulders tensed. Like a demolition crane, he raises his fist above the mouse.

Reid faces his boyfriend. "Please, Arjun," he pleads, unable to steady the trembling in his voice.

"Back down, Airman."

It takes both of Reid's hands to cover Arjun's balled fist.

"Let him live," Reid whispers. ■

FATA MORGANA
Harrison Copp

I once knew a girl who was obsessed with mirages: false horizons, floating boats, inverted coastlines, and other illusions I don't remember. She even kept a journal of all the mirages she'd seen. Each entry had a picture, the date, and a little blurb about the type and location. It had the look of a stamp album or a botanist's notebook. We didn't know each other very well. I always had the sense that I was one of her many acquaintances and that she talked to me simply because I was there to listen. I was never a great listener, though. I don't even remember half our conversations. Her words came in through one ear, pooled in my head, and then evaporated a few weeks later. To be fair, she probably didn't remember our conversations either. That's just the way it was.

Still, our last conversation stuck with me. We were by the bay, squinting through the fog. It was early morning. The sea was icy. It seemed a trying day for seeing mirages.

"Oh, but these are the ideal viewing conditions," she said.

I shivered and tugged at the zipper of my jacket, which was already fully zipped.

"Just what about this situation is ideal?"

"When the ocean is cold but the air is warm," she began, like she was reading from a textbook. "The temperature differential refracts light rays downwards, which produces a superior mirage." She rubbed her hands together, stamped her feet, and pulled her hat farther down over her head. "But I don't see any so far."

"A wild guess, but it might have something to do with the fog."

She laughed. "I have a feeling you're right." She turned back to the impenetrable sea. "But, looking over the ocean, I was hoping to see *it* today." She rested her elbows on the railing for five long seconds. Then she turned back to me. "Aren't you going to ask what *it* is?"

"A white whale?"

"Well—" she interrupted herself with a laugh. "Oh, I see. I should've known. You being a writer. I suppose it is a white whale, in a manner of speaking." She pulled back a strand of hair that had fallen over her face. "But no. It's a bit loftier than a whale. It's of a much grander, much more quixotic scale."

"What could be more quixotic than hunting Moby Dick?"

She smiled like a magician about to unveil a trick.

"A floating city."

For a girl obsessed with levitating boats, God rays, and desert oceans, a floating city should not have shocked anyone. Still, there was something, as she said—loftier—about the whole idea. The city belonged to a different world. Seeing it would be like peering, briefly, through a hole to another universe. One glimpse: you'd never see it again, but your understanding of reality would be forever changed.

"You know that journal I showed you?" she continued. "The city is the last entry. Once I find it, it'll be complete." She shifted her feet and rubbed her hands before turning back to the sea once more.

* * *

A few days later, she simply disappeared. Not a trace. She didn't respond—not to calls, not to emails. She was there one moment and gone the next.

To commemorate our parting, I peeled a yellow Post-it from a stack on my desk. On it, I wrote "mysterious girl obsessed with mirages" and stuck it to the wall, beside a note with the words "woman—can't fall asleep" and another with "man who hates barking dogs." Still staring at the wall, I took a 2H pencil and tried to see how far I could push it before it broke in two. Then I stepped out and watched an airplane crawl across the sky. It left a puffy, ethereal vapor trail in its wake.

* * *

That year, I was working at a stamp shop. It was a new business—stamp collecting was up-and-coming here, after all—and it received a steady stream of customers despite the out-of-the-way location. I didn't know much about stamps, so I mostly worked in the back, organizing new shipments, stacking shelves, and lining albums with thin scraps of paper. It wasn't hard work, and the manager was lenient with my hours. Besides, I didn't mind studying all the stamps. There were enough varieties there to satisfy any collecting impulse. A whole album on stamps from Tannu Tuva. Stamps from the Japanese occupation of Malaysia, with a big "Dainippon" printed over each one. Twenty-nine unique stamps of Holstein cows facing left.

Whenever anyone asked what I did there, I told them I was hunting for inspiration. All sorts of people came into that store.

Many businesslike people with black suits who were there to invest in stamps as seriously as they did stocks. There was the occasional college student who found a few stamps in the attic and wanted them appraised. These were always my favorite: most times, they'd come back with nothing, some worthless stamps, but other times they'd stumble upon a rare type, a misprint or a limited copy, and they'd go home with enough money to feed themselves for the next three weeks. Then there was this one old customer, one of the rare types who'd been collecting since his childhood, and, for all those years, he'd only collected butterfly stamps. He came in with a butterfly shirt, wore butterfly-print shorts, and talked butterflies with the owner. I'm sure if I saw him at the pool, he'd be swimming butterfly, too.

* * *

One morning, a few days after the girl vanished, I was stacking boxes and feeling inspired when the manager came to talk. He said there was a woman outside waiting for me. I craned to look out the store window.

"How'd you find me?" I asked my sister as I stepped out of the shop.

"Are you free?" she said. I looked back inside the shop and saw the manager watching our conversation. He was accustomed to my erratic absences.

She took me out to this café that had just opened across from the station. It had a window—one large sheet of glass—so you could see the tracks, the trains, and every industrial blemish in the station. The patches of dying grass were a particular highlight.

"What's that?" said my sister, looking at my pad of Post-it notes. On the top, I had scribbled "butterfly man, butterfly plan, butterfly stroke."

"It's inspiration."

"And I take it your job at that stamp store is inspiration, too?"

"I'm paid to get inspired. That's any writer's job."

She didn't answer for a while and just stirred her coffee. I didn't like coffee, so I was drinking milk. After a while, she spoke.

"Mom wants you to answer her when she calls."

"This again?"

"She's worried about you."

I leaned back, groaned, and rubbed my forehead. "Nothing to worry about here," I said.

"I should be worried, too. You're stacking boxes at a stamp store.

You haven't written anything for over a year. You live in a dump."

"Many thanks for your understanding."

She turned away to look out the window. In the corner of the café, there was a TV with the news on. The presenter was saying something about typhoons. Bad typhoon season, storms coming from the east, and some meteorologic jargon thrown into the mix.

"By the way, I didn't interrupt your busy work just to discuss Mom or your life."

"That so?"

"One of my friends wanted to meet you. He read your book."

"Oh, *he*?"

"Yes, *he*," she snapped. "Just because you can't find anyone doesn't mean that I can't either."

I leaned back in my chair.

"Well, well," I chuckled. "I have my fans after all."

"Just try to make a good impression."

We sat in silence for the next few minutes. I thought of asking when her friend would come, but she already seemed irritated enough. So I kept quiet and watched the trains pull in at the station.

Eventually, the man arrived. The first thing that struck me— or rather, failed to strike me—was his face. There was something incredibly forgettable about him. Like an extra in a movie. His nose was too large for his head, and he had black, shoulder-length hair, which put him halfway between a hermit and Harry Hosono.

"Hope I'm not intruding," he said, sitting next to my sister.

"Not at all," we both said.

"Solid, solid. I've heard a lot about you," he said, looking at me.

"I've heard heaps about you, too," I lied.

The man ordered himself coffee and a quiche and I finished the rest of my milk. I learned some more about him. He liked going to the gym. He liked solving puzzles in his spare time—crosswords in particular—but the ones in the newspapers were too easy. And he worked in computer science.

"By the way," he said, "loved the book."

"Thanks."

"Solid stuff. I especially loved the relationship between the two mothers."

"You mean the aunt and the mother-in-law?"

"Yeah, of course." He laughed and ran his hand through his hair. "I also liked the cover art. Wherever did you ever come up with the idea of putting a coffee-mark stain on the front? It always throws me off. You see, I drink a lot of coffee. So, you can guess what I thought when I saw your book. I thought, oh no! I stained it already! But it turned out it was just the design. Clever stuff."

Before, the computer scientist had been forgettable. Now he was simply insulting. Whether or not he was my sister's boyfriend was beside the point.

"You know, Abe"—Abe was his name—"they say there's more to a book than its cover. When I look at you, however, I don't get that impression."

"Huh?"

My sister kicked me, hard, underneath the table.

I watched trains for the rest of the conversation. I saw all the people going about their day, funneling themselves out onto the platform, pausing momentarily at the station. All I saw of their lives were these smudges through the windows of the passing trains. From here, their lives almost looked attractive. But see the full thing—the office, the factory, the home—and they'd soon be as mundane as the commute to work and back.

Four trains later, the man left—said he had a team call—and it was just me and my sister again. I stood up to leave. I was anxious to go.

"He may not be articulate, but he at least he's a pragmatist. He's grounded, unlike you," she said as I was walking out.

Back at the store, I spent the rest of the day filing stamps. British sailboats, the safari collection, and the Louis Armstrong thirtieth anniversary set. I didn't feel one drop of inspiration that afternoon.

* * *

Next morning, I was back in the stamp shop, sorting stamps into an album dedicated to French Indochina. I was on my twentieth "*postes indochine*" when my mom called me. I let it ring out. Then I moved on to the animated film stamp collection.

At ten in the morning, the manager came over to where I was working. He was old enough to be my father, wore a leather jacket, and listened to rock and roll. He had a short, square figure with a round face framed by rectangle glasses and a gray beret that never seemed to leave his head, not even when he slept. And he did a lot of sleeping: during lunchtime and late-afternoon lulls between customers, I could hear his snoring from the back room.

"How's your second book?" he said, sitting down next to me. The manager had read my first book—he was one of the first to read it. Like my sister's boyfriend, he could never seem to remember any significant plot details.

"Taxiing to the runway," I responded.

"Oh," he said, drawing in breath. "That's good. What's it about?"

"Can't say yet. Still searching."

"Oh? Well then."

On the radio, Hosono and the Yellow Magic Band were singing along to a rock and roll beat: *Twist, twist, kune kune highway!*

Just then, the bell on the door jingled and in stepped the butterfly man. The manager excused himself and walked to the counter. They were close, those two. Same age, same proclivity for collecting stamps. How they found meaning in those scraps of paper was beyond me.

Everybody had their pursuit, I figured: the butterfly man had his stamps, the manager had his store, and the boyfriend had his puzzles. I guess you could say my pursuit was writing. Still, however many characters or scenes I dreamed up, however aurelian the ideas that appeared in my head, the words seemed flat in comparison.

In the background, the song had ended and the radio announcer began talking about the incoming typhoons. I sat around for a while, listening to the butterfly man and the manager talk, and watched the minute hand move around the clock. I had found that if you looked hard enough at the tip, you could actually see it moving.

The phone rang again. I let it ring out before returning to stamp filing.

* * *

That night, I added two Post-its to the wall. The first was the butterfly note. On the second, I scribbled "computer scientist, long hair, solid."

They say that folding one thousand paper cranes will grant any wish. Would one thousand Post-it notes be enough to write a novel?

I spent the rest of the night counting the Post-it notes and listening to Harry Hosono. When I finished counting the sticky notes on the wall, I began taking stock of my supply. It turned out I would need at least three more pads. *A small price to pay for a novel,* I thought, and then I fell asleep.

* * *

Some dreams float like scraps of imagination. You catch glimpses of them through the air, but you can never be sure what you're seeing—a dream, a long-distant memory, or something entirely made-up. Some people say they long for the dream. But dreams themselves are not at all like dreams of the future. They're messy, confusing, full of strangely familiar people and distorted memories. And once it all whirls by, you're never quite sure if it happened at all.

That night, I dreamed about the floating city. I wasn't one hundred percent confident that it was *the* floating city. But it was a city. And I knew it was floating.

In this city, there were tree-lined boulevards on every major street. The sunlight fell in speckled patches on the ground. There was always a slight breeze, which made the trees hush and the patches of sun dance and scatter. I had a feeling that this was a seaside city, although, with it being a floating city, I guess that would have been impossible. Still, something about the way the air smelled or the lazy peacefulness of the streets reminded me of a city I'd visited long ago. I'd stayed in a room with blue curtains overlooking the sea, and I remembered hearing the low snoring of the ocean waves as sunlight filtered onto the sheets of my bed.

Through an open window, I heard a child playing the piano. No mistakes, just a simple melody.

I continued to walk through the boulevard. In this city, I was ninety percent confident it was summer. Everything was filtered through a bright white, like minimalist watercolor. To avoid the heat, I stayed in the shade. Funny. I didn't see or hear a single car. All I could hear were the cicadas chirping in the trees, the sprinklers in the distance, and that faint piano tune. Come to think of it, I hadn't seen a single person.

I found a deck chair and lay down. Above me, the clouds billowed in the sky. Each cloud drifted across a background of blue, and I studied each puff, shadow, and cumulus ridge. From where I lay, they looked like their own celestial cities. *That's strange*, I thought. Floating cities upon floating cities. Just how far up did it go?

"Are you enjoying the clouds?" said a rooster. "I could lend you a pair of binoculars."

"No thanks," I said.

"Suit yourself," said the rooster. Then it began crowing. Despite my most fierce reprimands, it wouldn't stop.

* * *

Those days, I started seeing floating cities everywhere. I'd see them while filing stamp albums—Laputa in *Gulliver's Travels* from the eighteenth-century literature collection or *Castle in the Sky* from the animated film collection. I'd start hearing the words "floating city" in people's conversations. Excuse me? I would ask. It always turned out that I had misheard.

Throughout all of history, I learned, there was only one photograph of a floating city. "It should be noted," the author of *The Flying Dutchman: Mirages from the Past* made sure to establish, "the number of recorded mirages does not necessarily correspond to the frequency at which such mirages appear. These mirages, after all, manifest suddenly in desolate areas where photographic equipment is often not at hand."

The photo was a grainy monochrome image of what looked like two clouds, one white and the other gray. On closer inspection, however, the tall, geometric edges of the gray cloud were the unmistakable edges of city architecture.

The photo was captured by accident in 1936 in Guangdong Province, China, as part of an agricultural survey. It puzzled locals for years—first becoming a tourist attraction and then, once no more mirages were found, fading to obscurity—until it attracted the attention of a German physicist obsessed with optical illusions. Noting the similarities in shape between a nearby city and the floating skyline in the photograph, he hypothesized that the event was merely a result of a rare type of superior mirage called Fata Morgana. This name, the author made sure to point out, came from the Italian name for Morgan le Fay, the medieval sorceress and sister of King Arthur. Her mirages over the ocean would lure sailors off course and to their deaths.

The floating city, however, was not your typical Fata Morgana. The atmospheric conditions in Guangdong, the German physicist argued, would have needed to be perfect. That's why the floating city was never seen again.

And that was the extent of my research into Fata Morganas. Everywhere else I looked, I turned up empty-handed.

* * *

The days dragged on, and my Post-it mosaic only grew larger and larger. It covered nearly half of the wall. Standing at the edge of my room and looking at the opposite side, all I saw was a swarm of yellow.

That's when I got the message.

"Come meet me at the place we parted," it read. "Tomorrow

morning. Come prepared. You'll see everything."

Come prepared. What did that mean? I could only guess. I lay back on my bed and continued to stare at the wall of sticky notes. One thousand different threads, one thousand different stories. If I wanted, I could write about any one.

Outside, it had started to rain. It was just a soft patter on the roof. The city lights, usually clear through my window, had faded into an iridescent haze.

* * *

The following morning, I awoke to heavy rain. It was running down in sheets over my window.

I put on my windbreaker and drew up the hood. I was about to leave when my phone rang. It was my mom. This was the fourth time in two days. *Nothing to worry about here*, I thought as I tossed the phone on my bed. *I'm almost there. Soon I'll have found what I'm looking for. Then I'll call you back. I'll even swear on it. It'll be the first thing I do.*

I grabbed an umbrella and ducked outside into the rain.

* * *

The train station, predictably, was closed. Over the speakers, a woman's voice repeated the same announcement:

"Due to the approaching typhoon, this station and lines five, six, and thirteen will not be operational for the immediate future. We apologize for the inconvenience."

Some inconvenience. I looked around for another option. The rain poured like panes of glass from the edges of the train shelters. The wind was starting to pick up. I could hear it rush past the crevasses where the train tracks lay.

"Due to the approaching typhoon, this station and lines five, six, and thirteen will not be operational for—"

"I'm well aware!" I shouted and stepped out of the station onto the road. I navigated through the narrow streets, bolting from cover to cover. Water pooled in the blackness of the streets and fell from the tops of square buildings. Not a person in sight. This was exciting. I had this small part of the city to myself, the cafés, the small apartment buildings, the signs, and all the trees hissing in the wind.

There was a taxi farther down the street. The driver was asleep. I banged on the window to get his attention. As I climbed in, collapsing my umbrella, the gray-haired driver watched in muted

horror as water poured from my jacket onto the fabric seats.
"That's going to cost you extra," he grumbled.
"Whatever," I said. "Just take me to the sea." I took out a map
and pointed to the approximate spot where I'd last met the vanishing
girl.
"You're crazy. There's a storm. Waves. Big waves."
"Then take me as far as you can go."
He stared at me for a while. "You're crazy," he said. But the gray-
haired driver started the transmission, and we pulled through the
rain-soaked streets.

* * *

When we approached the ocean, the taxi slid to a stop. The seaside
highway was covered in an inch-deep pool of water, and the driver
was having trouble retaining control. I managed to open the door.
The water and the wind outside was strafing the concrete in angled
streaks.
"Hey!" yelled the driver. "I'll drive you back."
"What?" I screamed back.
"I'll drive you back!"
He looked first at me and then at the sea.
"I'll drive you back! Whatever you're doing here, it's not worth
it!"
I had already shut the door. The driver stayed in the car, waiting
for me for at least a minute before turning the car around and
skidding back towards the city.

* * *

Now I'm walking towards the edge of the road, arms clutched
over my face to shield me from the ocean spray. It's slow work. I'm
tired. I didn't sleep much. But I'm smiling nonetheless. It's not that
I'm happy—I just have to smile. If I don't smile, what's the point of
pushing on?
I'm nearing the place where we last met. I feel close. I'm on the
edge of something, and it's not just the edge of the seawall—it's far
deeper, far more important, like Newton on the edge of infinitesimal,
Einstein on the edge of relativity, Schwarzschild on the edge of the
black hole's singularity.
I'm still thinking black holes when I see it. This roaring, looming
cloud. It's hazy through the rain, shifting and shining, obscured

by ocean spray and crashing waves. But there's that unmistakable geometric majesty. Rectangles on rectangles, floating cities on floating cities, spires and skyscrapers stretching up to the clouds.

Now I'm calm. The wind and rain fade to a faint hum. I'm passing through the event horizon, and I'm changing, really changing. The spray on my face, the water soaking my clothes—this is real. It's as real as the lone figure standing alone before a churning precipice. It's as real as the typhoon waves, crashing and breaking over the seawall. They're crashing and crashing and they don't ever stop. ∎

UNTITLED 8
Paddy McCabe

UNTITLED 22
Paddy McCabe

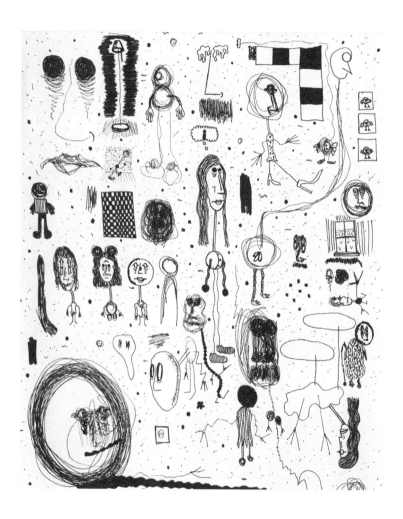

READ NIETZSCHE
Philip Eskenazi

"I t's quiet here," Thomas said.
It's not quiet here, I thought. There are no quiet places left in Holland, even in the forests every last leaf quivers with the noise of the masses, and though it may be true I'm more sensitive to sound than most, a fact Nietzsche says is indicative of a higher nature, to call a café where loud music plays and people talk over the music quiet is idiotic. I said nothing.

It was my own fault. Running into Thomas in the street I should have come up with an excuse rather than going into a café with him to have a beer. I should have just said no. Why did I not say no, I thought, why did I not invent an excuse and say no? It's because I wanted to drink beer. I was hoping for escalation, one beer leading to another, leading to a Belgian beer and so on, until I had escaped myself. No, I thought, it's because I can't take a stand on anything, because I lack the willpower to say no to people. A real Nietzschean would have said no, without justification or invented excuses, would have said no and said goodbye and walked away.

We drank our beer, which was plain, smooth, undemanding, barely noticeable as it slid down your throat. Thomas had invited me to have a beer in Café de Witte Aap, which he believed was the coolest place in town, although in fact it had been a terrible cliché ever since Lonely Planet had named it the best bar in the world in 2009, and on draft they had Heineken, which was the plainest beer in Holland and probably in all of Europe. Heineken became big by standardizing their production process early on, I thought, by mastering the technique to mass-produce beer of uniform quality. Heineken became big through uniformity, I thought in de Witte Aap, which is how Holland became big.

What bothered me most about Thomas was his agreeableness. He got along with everyone, because he had no opinions, no principles and no personality—he was a stainless mirror—and as a result of his complaisance I was now about to have a beer with Giorgio Kaasburg. If Thomas had more sense, he would not want to have beers with people like Giorgio Kaasburg, and even if he did, he would not invite me along, knowing that he was causing me grief. But he had not sensed this, and he had invited me to have a beer in de Witte Aap without mentioning that he was going to meet Giorgio Kaasburg in there. If he had mentioned that, I thought, I would certainly have found the strength to say no.

Giorgio Kaasburg was a man of "modern ideas." I refer here to the term used by Nietzsche, the term used extensively by Nietzsche throughout his works after *Zarathustra*, particularly in *Beyond Good and Evil*, where he uses the term fifteen times, and always between quotation marks, which should prove that the term means something, although the so-called Nietzsche scholars insist on ignoring this term. These Nietzsche scholars had caused me a lot of grief with their insistence to mischaracterize Nietzsche, their determination to misunderstand him, which on the other hand often made me think there was an opportunity there, a market gap, so to say, a thought that always led to despair, because I knew I would let the opportunity go to waste. I was stuck in a PhD at a *business school*, doing research on a topic I found so completely uninteresting that I had no intrinsic motivation at all and depended entirely on my discipline, which had always been faulty ever since my childhood. There were days I barely lifted a finger. There were weeks I barely got out of bed. If I could write a dissertation on Nietzsche, I thought in de Witte Aap, I would be happy. Not happy, because Nietzsche is not supposed to make you happy, he is supposed to cure you of the delusion that happiness exists, but I would be able to work—I would have intrinsic motivation. But this is not true, I thought, because if I wrote a dissertation on Nietzsche I would have to read the Nietzsche scholars, which I knew from experience was much worse than writing a dissertation on a topic I found simply uninteresting.

That two wholly Dutch parents with blond hair and a last name like Kaasburg could give their cheese-head kid the name Giorgio drove me to despair. Giorgio Kaasburg had a degree in sociology. He loved criminals and hated power. Nietzsche coined the term *misarchist*, which he called a bad word for a bad thing, with people like Giorgio Kaasburg in mind.

Thomas finished his beer, and I thought about finishing mine and leaving de Witte Aap before Giorgio Kaasburg arrived. Why couldn't I drink up my beer and say goodbye? Well, Thomas, I could say, this was fun, but I have to leave. Enjoy your evening with Giorgio Kaasburg. But when Thomas asked if I wanted another beer, I said yes.

I always wanted another beer, I was always hoping for escalation, for something to happen, for an event that would change everything. For salvation. I knew salvation would not be found in beer, but I believed that beer could act as a catalyst. I had to meet someone, I thought, a person who would change everything. A mentor. What I lacked more than anything was a mentor. All my life I had lacked a mentor. My father had never been a mentor to me, he only wanted to make me disciplined, he thought I was lazy and wanted to make me disciplined, but he never succeeded, I thought. At least I won that battle, I thought.

Thomas came back with two beers in the vase-shaped glasses with the black Heineken label and the red Heineken star and two fingers of foam on top. The Dutch always want two fingers of foam on top, I thought, and that's good, because beer without foam is no beer, but what these people don't realize is that Heineken makes the beer so that the foam disappears quickly and the beer goes stale in twenty minutes. The faster you drink, the richer the Heinekens become. These are the formulas we teach at the business school. I remember learning, when I was a student at the business school, about mortality salience. According to scientific research, when you remind people of the fact that one day they will die, they spend money more impulsively. At the business school we believe it's important to pass this knowledge on to the next generation of decision makers, I thought, and it filled me with grief.

"How's the research going?" Thomas asked.

His bony face and straw hair made me think of scarecrows. He had a friendly expression but also a guardedness, as if he expected trouble from me. I wondered if Thomas, with his superficial consciousness, had any notion of the depths of my despair, which was, after all, an existential despair and thus a higher form of consciousness, I thought, though I wasn't sure this was correct.

"It's going well," I said. "And yours?"

I had no interest in Thomas's research, which focused on corporate philanthropy, but he did not sense that I had no interest, or perhaps he felt compelled to fill the silence—which I always think is much more pleasing than a bad conversation; a good silence can make my day—and he began to tell me about his latest project in great detail. When he finished, I looked at my watch. "Giorgio Kaasburg is late," I said. "Perhaps he won't come."

Giorgio Kaasburg entered de Witte Aap. At first he didn't see us in our corner on the plateau in the back of de Witte Aap, and Thomas didn't see him, standing in the doorway as he unwrapped a thick scarf from around his big neck. He thinks he's a charismatic man, I thought, because he's tall and plump people look at him when he enters a room, and he thinks it's his charisma that makes them look at him, but it's not, charismatic people are instantly liked, they light up a room, whereas he makes de Witte Aap darker. The barman greeted him and he must have thought that was because of his charisma, but I knew the barman had only greeted him because that was his job, he probably had to greet all the customers per explicit instruction from the manager; he had greeted Thomas and me too when we entered de Witte Aap.

To be a true Nietzschean today is impossible, I thought, because there is no way to escape your contemporaries. We are trapped in this society, molded and oppressed by it. We are inescapably oppressed by this society, because even if you went out into the desert, you would carry your contemporaries with you in the form of your conscience, which, according to Nietzsche, is society internalized. There is no solitude anywhere, I thought in de Witte Aap. Perhaps it's possible in principle to overcome your conscience, but this would take a tremendous strength of spirit, and such strength of spirit is precisely what our civilization destroys in us from the day we are born, so that the type of human being who could redeem us will never arise in this society. Society creates its members, I thought, and it will never create a person that can forge the circumstances in which I could become a Nietzschean. But that I had to be a Nietzschean, that I couldn't live with myself as a non-Nietzschean, this much was clear to me. I repulsed myself with my decadence and sickness, which also fascinated me, as it was a truly great subject for a Nietzschean to study. If I could write about myself, I thought, really write about myself as I am, without deceit or pomp or anything like that, without brushing up the image, as they say, that could be a great study in psychopathology. A truly fascinating work of Nietzschean psychopathology. It would have to be done in complete sincerity, I thought, which is impossible, absolutely impossible and unthinkable, I thought. But perhaps, I thought—No, I thought.

As Giorgio Kaasburg approached, I finished my beer.

"Gentlemen," he said.

"Hello, Giorgio Kaasburg," I said. "I'm going for a smoke."

Outside, I wondered what compelled a person like Thomas to have beers with Giorgio Kaasburg. Here's a guy who is perhaps not particularly bright or sensitive, but not a malevolent type, a more or less sound person, not lacking in social opportunities, who chooses to spend his Wednesday evening in de Witte Aap having beers with Giorgio Kaasburg. Why? I wondered whether he could see what I saw, and I thought that he could not.

People are so estranged from what is good, Nietzsche said, that the Übermensch would appear terrible and evil to them in his greatness.

When I came back inside, the barman greeted me. He doesn't remember me, I thought, he thinks I'm a new customer. I ordered three beers and lifted them with two hands, my middle fingers wrapped around the third glass. That one is for Giorgio Kaasburg, I thought.

"Another beer," Giorgio Kaasburg said, "we just got one."

As long as there have been people, people have lived in communities, Nietzsche said, I thought, which means that those who command have always been outnumbered by those who obey, and as a consequence an inherited instinct for obedience has become dominant in all of us.

"Volmer was teaching behavioral economics today," Giorgio Kaasburg said. "At lunch I said to him, 'The problem with nudging is that it always operates within existing power structures.'"

"I was teaching internationalization strategies," Thomas said. "Greenfields versus brownfields. I'm not sure the students care to know. Maybe one in a thousand will ever face that decision, and I only have five hundred students."

"The sole purpose of education is that 'if you work hard and diligently you should be able to detect when a man is talking rot,' J. A. Smith said," Giorgio Kaasburg said.

Giorgio Kaasburg appeals to a certain folk wisdom, I thought, as if the things he says are obvious. He speaks as though he's obviously right and it's plain for all to see. But then why say it? He believes our mighty oppressors' corruption must be pointed out by heroic leaders of the people who dare speak truth to power. Giorgio Kaasburg is always saying the emperor is naked, I thought, whereas in reality the emperor is dead, and it's his fault.

I finished my beer. "Another round," I said. "More beers."

Thomas finished his beer and went to the bar. Giorgio Kaasburg turned to me. I went to the toilet.

In the toilet it occurred to me that what these people want more than anything is the green meadow, where the herd can rest in comfort and safety and no one has to suffer. They can't stand the thought of suffering, not only with regard to themselves, although that too, but also the suffering of others, which gives them unbearable anguish, whereas the Nietzschean seeks out suffering, schools himself

in suffering, deepens himself through suffering and solitude.
"He wants to be a philosopher," Thomas said, pointing at me. In my mind I wished him an illness. "I think philosophy is dead," Giorgio Kaasburg said. "Philosophy is the ancestor of science, it is what science was before it became scientific. For us there is only the history of philosophy."

What does Giorgio Kaasburg know about philosophy, I thought, if he only knows the philosopher of critical knowledge theory, of fruitless argumentative precision, of semantic analysis to the point of absurdity, the analytical philosopher who lives like any other bloodless bureaucrat and mandarin? What does he know about it if he's never seen a real philosopher, a man who can shape hierarchies, command the spirit of history, create new values? He couldn't possibly know anything about it. I thought about Nietzsche, who said the real philosopher lives unphilosophically and unwisely, more than anything lives foolishly, and feels the heavy duty to undertake many trials and tryouts, and I thought this was true, the real philosopher always risks himself, he plays the dangerous game, Nietzsche said, and he was right, I thought. I do live foolishly, I thought in de Witte Aap, more than anything I live foolishly, but I have no sense of duty, I never risk myself, I don't play any game, because I'm lazy.

"Not all philosophers are useless, of course," Giorgio Kaasburg said. "Peter Singer I respect. I'm now fully vegetarian."

"Good for you," Thomas said. "I'm down to once a week. Argue all you want, but at the end of the day, it's not necessary to eat meat."

I went to the bar and ordered three La Chouffes, which they have on draft in de Witte Aap. The three tulip-shaped glasses were difficult to carry. The beer tasted sharp after the smooth Heinekens. It has a bitter edge, I thought, which is honest and necessary.

"Singer is good in ethics," Giorgio Kaasburg said. "In political philosophy, Rawls solved all the problems long ago. Of course there are still some followers of Nozick, libertarians who think they can just fend for themselves—useless idiots, I call them—but the debate is over."

Giorgio Kaasburg is what Nietzsche called a man of "modern ideas," I thought, who speaks as though he possesses final wisdom concerning good and evil, who lavishes praise and blame and in lavishing praise and blame glorifies himself, who believes himself to be the standard with which good and evil are measured, who believes his morality is the only true morality, not one form among many possible forms, which it is, and a lowly form at that. Giorgio

Kaasburg's morality is the voice of an instinct become dominant, Nietzsche said, I thought in de Witte Aap, the herd instinct, which has broken through the hierarchy and seized power over the other instincts, the herd instinct become sovereign and believing to be morality itself, the actual source of knowledge of good and evil. I drank of my beer.

"Then you have those poor Nietzscheans, lonely souls who cope with their depression by thinking themselves superior, the chosen people, the victims of a wicked slave revolt. Sometimes you feel they just need a good hug," Giorgio Kaasburg said.

Thomas looked at me. Many have turned away from life only in order to turn away from people like Giorgio Kaasburg, who spoil the wells of lust when they speak their unclean dreams and who don't deserve our hatred so much as our disgust, Nietzsche said, I thought.

"What do you think?" Giorgio Kaasburg asked me.

I drank up my beer and thought I should go home. I will go home and read, I thought, and suddenly the thought moved me and I left de Witte Aap. Without saying goodbye to Thomas, without saying a word to Thomas or Giorgio Kaasburg, I left de Witte Aap and walked home, thinking, I will go home and read, telling myself, I will go home and read, saying to myself, out loud, over and over, I will go home and read, right now, read Nietzsche, read Nietzsche, read Nietzsche. ■

ON GOOD TONGUES
Jessica Nirvana Ram

My grandmother tells me *you need a good tongue*
in life, you gotta show love with it, you gotta demand
love with it. In the same breath she reminds me
of the benefits of drinking Ovaltine before bed,
how remembering to heat my milk first is key
& I tell her
     yes, I know. Like a promise,
like a prayer. I do not tell her how often
I hold my tongue, I do not tell her I cannot find Ovaltine
in my local markets. I only tell her yes—
         is that not what it means
to show love with this tongue, to lie for her sake? Her joy
is so dependent on my insistence that I am in the kitchen
every evening dressed in garlic & onion & oil. That I wake
in the mornings to incense smoke & god
         on my tongue &
I do not tell her about the heartbreak until it is over. I tell her
about cut flowers I buy myself from the grocery store,
how they'll sit on my table for weeks, mimicking life
even though they've long died, brittle bones on the brink
of collapse, until I remember to take them out with the trash
& then I do it again.
     I cannot keep plants alive, it is a testimony
to all I did not inherit from my grandmother, her hands so eternally
wed to earth. Her South American soil birthed vegetables, nurtured
a livelihood. I believe her body is bound in Guyana in a way
it could never be bound in the States. I wonder often
if a part of her
     is already buried there & when her legs give out
from a fall I think, yes, it must be. Yes, fragments of her
are scattered about & calling on me. Some days I breathe
her in more than others & when I pray it's her voice,
not mine

that echoes in my apartment.
When I leave my partner of six years, I apologize
for choosing myself over us, but if I am to demand love
with this tongue, I cannot swallow myself
whole for anyone else.
                                        When I visit home,
my grandmother asks me about marriage,
about children, & I tell her *not yet. Remember*
what you told me about getting my education?
How no one can take what's inside of my head?
& she says
                                                        yes, I remember.
But her hands tremble & I know she wants to give me
a wedding before she dies & I know, she will not be able
to give me a wedding before she dies so yes,
                                                        I lie to her.

I lie about Ovaltine & the plants I've killed & the love
I left because
                                        I am too much
like her. A woman so bound by what she believes
she must do that no one but the gardens she's tended
hear her cry & I want to ask my god how much
of that land is salted with her tears but I refrain
because god will not tell me & my grandmother
will not tell me & I cannot show her these hands
I am trying to build a life with, how they are so much
like dried up riverbeds, like barren soil because we
are nothing if not withholders
                                                        of loss.

JACQUES D'AMBOISE, MY INSTANT FRIEND
Orel Protopopescu

Whentacques d'Amboise (born Joseph Jacques Ahearn) died at age eighty-six on May 2, 2021, from complications of a stroke, I felt as if I had lost a friend. Thousands, perhaps millions, must have felt the same way. Few who basked in the warmth of his attention, even for a few minutes, could resist Jacques. His charm came naturally and was as abundant as his energy.

Before Jacques died, I had planned to dedicate my biography of Tanaquil ("Tanny") Le Clercq, *Dancing Past the Light,* solely to my husband. To add a dedication to someone of Jacques's renown seemed presumptuous to me, and although I considered it, I felt shy about doing so. But after hearing of his death, it seemed wrong not to acknowledge what Jacques had meant to me. So I added a dedication, "In memory of the celebrated New York City Ballet principal dancer Jacques d'Amboise (1934–2021), Tanny's dance partner and friend, whose generous, ebullient spirit has guided my work since the day we met at his National Dance Institute in Harlem, NYC, in June 2018." This is no exaggeration. Jacques had played a crucial role in the evolution of my manuscript, originally conceived for young adults. His confidence in me had pointed the way to a new vision of my work. He wrote a beautiful blurb for the book and planned to give copies to people he knew, and he seemed to know everyone.

Jacques and I spent just half a day together on June 14, 2018, but we'd had telephone and email exchanges for a year before we met and impromptu encounters later. Thanks to his personal assistant, Emily Reid, I received missives by mail as well: unpublished memories of Tanny and her husband, George Balanchine, bits of poetry, pen drawings, thank-you notes, and anything else Jacques felt moved to send me, all with his endearing sign-off, *Your Jacques.*

As soon as I arrived at the headquarters of the National Dance Institute (NDI), which he'd founded in 1976 with his wife, Carolyn ("Carrie") George d'Amboise, Jacques made me feel instantly at ease. I relaxed in his presence, as though I had always known him. Dressed in casual slacks and a madras plaid shirt dominated by blues and reds, he gave me a tour of offices and hallways filled with art from his personal collection, which included Carrie's dynamic photographs of dancers. Jacques was no longer the ballet dancer I had seen on film. His hair was white and his gait halting, but I recognized the iconic smile that David Levine had brilliantly caricatured in a 1985 drawing: Jacques's long, lean body in grand jeté is truncated to child-size proportions to make room for a wide, toothy grin doing a grand jeté of its own.

photo by Orel Protopopescu

As we chatted in Jacques's small, book-filled office, I took in the eclectic mix of titles behind him, rows of books on an array of subjects—art, history, literature, science, theater, and, of course, dance. Our conversation flowed with ease, taking its natural course of looping digressions (his and mine) that somehow brought us back to my subject: Tanaquil Le Clercq. Although he'd been a celebrity for most of his life, Jacques didn't have an iota of affectation. He loved people and he loved learning just about anything from anyone, whether they were world-renowned experts or the youngest students at NDI.

In one of the NDI rehearsal/performance studios with sprung wood floors, like those his mentor, Balanchine, had insisted on installing at Lincoln Center, Jacques demonstrated a few dance moves, accompanied by vocalizations, percussive *beeps* and *bops*. His voice was firm, his complex rhythms precise, although he had difficulty standing for long, after multiple foot and knee operations.

Decades of high jumps had taken their toll on this sublimely athletic dancer, known for his ballon. Emily, Jacques, and I then took a cab to a newly renovated Harlem restaurant that he wanted to try, an unpretentious place with delicious salads and sandwiches. A lovely young woman, thin as a Balanchine dancer, Emily accompanied him just about everywhere in his final years, in glasses and no makeup at the office, or dazzling in an evening dress at galas and award ceremonies. It was soon apparent to me, by the way he queried her about plans they had for that evening and whether they could get me a last-minute ticket to join them at the theater, that a certain fuzziness in his short-term memory had made her a necessity. And yet, when I ran into him alone, months later at the Guggenheim, for a fiftieth-anniversary celebration of Tanny's *Ballet Cook Book*, Jacques greeted me by name and introduced me to those with him.

Throughout our lunch, Jacques's long-term memory was excellent. When I brought up Katherine Dunham's influence on the dancers of his youth, he extolled the genius of another influential modern dancer/choreographer of Dunham's era, Jack Cole, also admired by Balanchine. Cole had been inspired by his studies of ancient East Indian Bharatanatyam dance to invent a new style. "Cole dancers," Jacques told me, trained in jazz and modern, called the technique "isolations," that is, keeping the rest of the body still while moving one part at a time.

Seated at the table, he proceeded to demonstrate the movements of what's also called "Hindu swing," gyrating his head, shoulders, and neck in ways that conjured up Bollywood. I had no idea what relevance this style would have on my subject, although I immediately recognized its influence on many Broadway choreographers, especially Bob Fosse. But later I had a eureka moment while viewing a video of the "In the Inn" section of Balanchine's *Ivesiana*. Although Jacques had not directed my attention to this ballet, I saw the Cole influence in a pas de deux performed by Arthur Mitchell and Pat Neary in 1964 that had originally been made in 1954 for Tanny and Todd Bolender. Cole's influence on Balanchine was evident, I wrote in my book, "in the way the female dancer juts her head forward and back or contracts her torso, and when the male dancer wobbles his head from side to side, while his arms assume geometric shapes, like a figure on an ancient stone frieze."

Just before we parted after lunch, Jacques announced his intention to write to the editor of his memoir about my manuscript.

When I wondered aloud why he was sure that she would be interested in a book for teens, Jacques answered, without hesitation, that he knew, from what he'd seen of my work as well as from our interactions, that the finished book would be intelligent and written with a passionate interest in my subject, and that was enough for him.

Although my interactions with his editor did not result in a contract, they convinced me that I had written a book for adults and gave me a blueprint for going forward and securing crucial interviews and permissions. Within a year of my pivotal meeting with Jacques, my book had nearly doubled in size and my first biography had found a perfect home at the University Press of Florida. I was thrilled when, a month before its publication in September 2021, it secured a starred review in *Library Journal*.

I still marvel at Jacques's generosity to a novice in dance writing, as I wrote in a message of condolence to Emily after reading his obituary in the *New York Times*. In her emailed reply, she said that Jacques "believed that if you had an idea, you should explore it to the fullest. To be fearless in the creation of art... And he wanted to help people as much as he could with their endeavors... he felt that same way about you and your book. He was delighted to take part in it."

Above all, Jacques needed to move and to move others. "We meet as strangers, we dance, and we part as friends," he once told a reporter. And indeed, although our dance was verbal, that was exactly my experience with Jacques, my instant friend who listened as well as he spoke.

Well before we met, I had appreciated his striking way with words, as captured in his memoir by his amanuensis, Kay Gayner, whose role Jacques comically acknowledged: "Fingers at a computer, ears to listen, voice to ask questions, patience to make it through my garrulousness."

His portraits of others are equally honest, punctuated with startlingly apt metaphors, sharp but always tempered by compassion. This is a description of a neighborhood gang leader named Farrel who had menaced young Jacques: "He wasn't big or strong. He seemed old, his body hunched into pleats like a cold shrimp."

On the difficult personalities of dancer/choreographer Jerome Robbins and Lincoln Kirstein, the cofounder (with Balanchine) of the New York City Ballet (NYCB) and the School of American Ballet (SAB): "Jerry was tormented, like Lincoln. Each had qualities of brilliance, bordering on genius, and each was gifted with wit— marbled with meanness." And yet Jacques immediately altered these portraits with a memory of a photo of Lincoln marching among protestors in Selma, Alabama, and of Jerry's generosity, how he would take care of "the medical costs for injured dancers, on the condition that the dancers never tell anyone."

Those who never heard Jacques speak might imagine that he was French. But he'd been raised on some of New York City's meaner streets, mostly in Washington Heights, and had never lost the accent. The name d'Amboise came from his mother, Georgette, who decided that it would have more cachet for a ballet dancer. In 1946 she had the whole family, including her Irish American husband, legally take her name. Jacques's parents separated in the 1950s and divorced later, but her last name is on his father's gravestone. No wonder Jacques called his mother "the boss" with amused admiration. She had set him on his path. Georgette, whose brash self-confidence matched Jacques's, found ingenious ways to finance dance and piano lessons for him and his sister with her sartorial and culinary skills. (Her chestnut-stuffed chickens worked magic on the music teacher.)

Behind every great dancer, there is often a ballet mother. Tanny's mother, Edith Le Clercq, a St. Louis debutante, conferred with Georgette, a daughter of the French Canadian working class, as they sat with other members of what Jacques called "the cabal of ballet mothers" in a hallway outside the SAB dance studios. Thanks to Edith, Jacques got a scholarship to join the teenaged Tanny at the elite King-Coit School, which offered after school and weekend theater and art classes. Tanny was a star of the school's professional productions, which attracted glittering patrons of the arts and garnered appreciative reviews in the New York press.

"Ballet is woman," George Balanchine famously said. He claimed that the primary role of the male dancer was to support a ballerina and make her look good. But he was always on the lookout for talented boys to train, because boys attracted to ballet were in short supply when he launched his ballet school and built his company. He made more leading roles for Jacques than any other male dancer and I doubt that there's another one he ever treated as well. Far more bravura stars, like Erik Bruhn, were treated shabbily by Balanchine, whose loyalty to Jacques is unique.

Betty Cage, NYCB's business manager, had once questioned Balanchine about the favored status he accorded Jacques, who could run off to Hollywood to make a film and then come back to reclaim his roles. Balanchine had answered, "Nobody can tell him what to do. He's just like me." That first sentence is an echo, Jacques wrote in his memoir, of words he'd heard from his mother and wife, but perhaps without Balanchine's unabashed admiration. The affinity Balanchine felt for Jacques may be one reason he often cast him in roles that seemed a surrogate for Balanchine himself, the lone male longing for his elusive muse. Being taller and thirty years younger than Balanchine, Jacques was an ideal surrogate who could partner any ballerina in the company, and he was often paired with one favored by Balanchine.

The fact that Betty told Jacques that story, possibly as a consoling gift to him soon after Balanchine's death, indicates that she harbored no resentment of Jacques's privileged status. But others did. Nancy Lassalle, a Sears Roebuck heiress who had studied at SAB in the forties, befriending Tanny for life but never dancing for NYCB, conveyed her displeasure in the back seat of a limousine she'd arranged to take us to the New York City Ballet Archives in New Jersey. When I mentioned my recent meeting with Jacques, saying, "What a charming man!" she gave a haughty sniff, raised her chin, and exclaimed, "Well… *he* certainly thinks so!"

Nancy had most likely read the description of her, in Jacques's 2011 memoir, as a "patron and groupie who dedicated her life to the company and, especially, the school." That "groupie" must have stung, for she was an accomplished photographer, an editor of books about the ballet company, a board member, and an educator close to the erratic Lincoln Kirstein, so close, according to Jacques, that she had absorbed some of his grievances. Jacques could figure out where he stood with Lincoln by reading Nancy's expressions. After a brief absence in 1983, which had coincided with Balanchine's hospitalization with a life-threatening brain disorder, Jacques had returned to rehearse at NYCB. Every time Nancy looked at him, he wrote, she was "wearing the same snarl" as Lincoln.

But to Balanchine, Jacques's endearing warmth and curiosity about everything must have been irresistible from childhood. Jacques loved to learn, and Balanchine loved to teach. Besides, Jacques had married at twenty-two and by age thirty had four children to support, so Balanchine encouraged him to take any lucrative opportunities that came his way. There was a lot more money on Broadway and in Hollywood than in ballet, but Jacques always returned to NYCB. His loyalty to the company and Balanchine was deep and familial. He knew how lucky he was to be, as one company dancer put it, among those who had grabbed hold of "the comet that was Balanchine."

In 1951, Balanchine had revived his 1928 work, *Apollon Musagète* (*Apollo, Leader of the Muses*), his first collaboration with Igor Stravinsky on an original score. André Eglevsky danced the role of Apollo, and his three muses were Diana Adams, Tanny, and Maria Tallchief. In 1957, Balanchine restaged the ballet with Jacques in the titular role. By then, Tanny was no longer dancing. A severe case of polio had tragically ended her career on the company's European tour of 1956. She had just turned twenty-seven.

Apollo was a "quantum leap" for Jacques as a dancer, he wrote in his memoir, just as it had been for Balanchine as a choreographer. Jacques practiced, alone in a studio, for hours, after insufficient private coaching from Balanchine produced what Jacques felt had been a lackluster debut. "I took each step, analyzed it, and practiced," he recalled, "repeating it over and over again at different tempi— slow motion, then fast, faster..." He had "even practiced breathing, where and how I would breathe." For many critics, Jacques's performance is still considered the definitive one that came closest to Balanchine's vision: "A wild, untamed youth learns nobility through art." Balanchine's *Apollo*, Jacques felt, "was my story."

The wild youth had entered SAB at age eight, made his debut in Balanchine and Lincoln Kirstein's Ballet Society at age twelve, and joined the corps de ballet of NYCB, the company that succeeded it, at age fifteen. He was a principal dancer by the time he was seventeen and, being well-trained by superb teachers, in demand as a partner. Balanchine made solos with fast turns and high jumps that highlighted his boyish exuberance.

But Jacques could also exude a slow-burning intensity in dramatic works, as demonstrated by his role in *Apollo*, as well as in Jerome Robbins's *Afternoon of a Faun*, recorded in a Montreal TV studio in 1955, where he dances with Tanny. Jacques told me that when Robbins found out about the recording session, he threatened to sue, since he had not granted the permission that both dancers assumed the producers had secured. But after Tanny's paralysis, Robbins was so grateful to have that grainy video, he desisted.

Jacques had initially rehearsed the role in 1953, he told me, but then refused to do it for two years to protest Jerry's way of lining up and rehearsing multiple casts, so that dancers often didn't know whether they would be performing until the last minute. Someone might think they had landed a part and then Robbins would say, "You lost everything you had. You're falling apart. Get in the back..." So Jacques sat in the back of the studio, ostentatiously reading and ignoring Jerry. He did *Faun* for the first time in 1955 and then regretted his stubborn reluctance. When I told him that I had found a review of his Paris debut, written for *Le Monde* by the novelist Christine de Rivoyre, in which he was described as a "very beautiful dancer, at once virile and sensitive," he expressed pleasure in hearing praise for the dancer he had been, as if speaking of another person, another life.

Faun had been a wedding gift to Tanny from Robbins, who had also wanted to marry her. He was working on the new ballet in early 1953, while she was in Italy on a working honeymoon with Balanchine, shortly after their marriage on New Year's Eve 1952. Four years later, Jacques married Carrie, by then a NYCB soloist, on New Year's Day 1956. The following year, the two couples inaugurated a tradition of annual dinners that began on one wedding anniversary and often ended on the other.

Jacques had been smitten by Carolyn George, nearly seven years his senior, ever since he'd laid eyes on her in dance class. After what he described in his memoir as a long and clumsy courtship that had started, haltingly, when he was nearly eighteen and she was twenty-four, he eventually persuaded her that he was marriage material. Of their four children, two boys and twin girls, two became performers: dancer/choreographer/educator Christopher d'Amboise, a former principal dancer at NYCB, and Charlotte d'Amboise, an award-winning actress and dancer.

Carrie stopped dancing in 1958, apart from the occasional character role, to nurse her firstborn, George, through a bout with a deadly cancer. He thrived. Jacques called him "Miracle" George, and when Jacques was sixty-five, they hiked the Appalachian Trail together, 2,180 miles that Jacques had to complete on all fours, at times, because of his bad knees, a legacy of all his phenomenal jumps. His will was that strong.

That strong will had been evident even at age nine. Wanting to fly, he had believed, as the nuns at his Catholic school assured him, that prayers were granted if one faithfully performed the requisite novena for nine weeks. After dutifully completing this devotion, Jacques jumped off a six-story building in his Three Musketeers costume. Luckily, he landed on the roof of another building, two stories down. Bruised, battered, and disillusioned, but with nothing worse than a sprained ankle, he was later to fly across stages around the world.

Although he had an honorary doctorate and had won a MacArthur Fellowship, Jacques never acquired a college degree, but he had entered "Balanchine University" at age eight and the discipline instilled there had served him well. He discussed a stanza in Pushkin's *Eugene Onegin* with Balanchine after reading three translations: After fatally shooting his friend, Lensky, in a duel, Onegin is full of remorse. He watches the light go out of Lensky's eyes, moving like snow, glittering in the sun, slowly sliding down a mountain slope. Some translators called it a lump of snow, others a sheet of snow, and others a snowball. Jacques wondered, which translation was right?

All were wrong, Balanchine told him. The word did not exist in English. It was a metaphor that encompassed the totality of Lensky's existence, everything he had been and could have been. Jacques summed up this lesson: "A mountain of a life, yet vulnerable to melting." He could have been speaking of himself.

Jacques was intrigued by the sciences as much as literature. Hearing that my husband was an experimental particle physicist, Jacques spoke of the work of his friend Lisa Randall, a theoretical particle physicist and cosmologist at Harvard. He was fascinated by the vastness of the universe, dark matter, string theory, and the possibility of multiple dimensions we could not perceive. Jacques had the rigorous, exacting tenacity of many scientists I've known, and the same lack of vanity. He had a powerful need to know more, do more, but not to stoke his own ego. In that way, he was unlike Balanchine, who "sat on his own throne," as Jacques put it.

That does not mean that Jacques lacked a sense of his own worth. When I offered to pay for our lunch, he refused, saying that he had a generous expense account from NDI. There had been some grumblings in the past, he revealed, about his penchant for inviting people out and exceeding its limits, but he had simply said, "Then double it." No doubt, judging from the generous list of donors to NDI he'd accrued over the years, Jacques was worth every penny. I got a personal thanks from him for my first donation. When I wrote to thank him for lunch and the interview, he replied, "Thank you, Orel! It was a great afternoon with you, listening to wonderful stories."

Despite his insatiable curiosity and passion for educating others, the two years Jacques spent as a full professor and dean of dance at the State University of New York at Purchase did not increase his joy. After many dreary faculty meetings, he decided that academia was not for him. "I'd rather die!" he told his friend Vicki Reiss, executive director of the Shubert Foundation.

* * *

By the time he retired from NYCB, Jacques had partnered at least two generations of the company's ballerinas, from Melissa Hayden (born in 1923) to Merrill Ashley (born in 1950). And in between there were few principal females in the company with whom he hadn't partnered. When Jacques couldn't leap as well anymore, Balanchine found other ways to use his remaining strengths. In 1980 Jacques premiered a role in one of Balanchine's last great ballets, *Robert Schumann's "Davidsbündlertänze,"* paired with Suzanne Farrell in a dreamscape of a ballroom swirling with tempestuous emotions.

But after Balanchine's death in 1983, Carrie, who had successfully transitioned to photography before she'd stopped dancing, persuaded her husband to retire. There were too many roles that he couldn't do as well as before; she had trouble getting a good shot of him in rehearsal.

When Carrie died at age eighty-one in 2009, from complications of primary lateral sclerosis, Jacques fulfilled her wish to have her ashes scattered at the Seventy-Second and Broadway subway stop, close to their home. But she had not said which side of Broadway, uptown or downtown, so he sprinkled some ashes on the tracks on both sides. Knowing full well that this was illegal, he chose a Sunday morning, when there would likely be fewer witnesses. But he had nevertheless recruited some kids "to come in and dance and make a lot of noise," sending Carrie off in style. His own desired resting place, voiced in a 2018 public conversation at NDI, "Balanchine's Guys," is surprising: "Spread me in Times Square or the Belasco Theater." Not City Center or Lincoln Center, where detectives could still find his DNA. I have no idea if anyone heeded his wish, but the northeast corner of Sixty-Fourth and Broadway is now officially named Jacques d'Amboise Place.

The title of Emile Ardolino's Oscar- and Emmy-winning documentary about Jacques's work at NDI, *He Makes Me Feel Like Dancin'*, came from one of Jacques's students. Every year, children from public schools in and around New York City auditioned for NDI. Most had no prior dance experience. The chosen students learned dance routines, more Broadway than ballet, that Jacques often choreographed on the spot. He was "a natural teacher," as Carrie says in the film, who taught kids how to move, count, and wait to move. To encourage them to kick as high as possible, he conjured up the image of an "eight-foot piranha with a thousand teeth." Then he announced, "I'm gonna put my foot right into his mouth."

After watching him demonstrate, the children were eager to try it themselves, over and over.

At first, Jacques taught every class himself. But as thirty students became hundreds, he hired teachers, choreographers, and musicians. His celebrated friends donated music and artwork, and some performed in his shows. Balanchine wrote songs for NDI and came to its annual performances. He let Jacques use the NYCB studios at Lincoln Center, where NDI rehearsed its annual graduation event. Jacques gave a special class there on Saturday mornings for his best students. He wasn't trying to create professional dancers, but he made sure that every child tried. One who didn't might be put on probation, or even dismissed. The children learned that performing required discipline, a lesson that served them well in other areas.

You can get a taste of an NDI number ("Fat City") in Ardolino's excellent film, made shortly before his huge hit *Dirty Dancing*. Narrated by the actor Kevin Kline, "Fat City" was performed at the 6,000-seat Felt Forum in Madison Square Garden, with a huge cast of Prohibition-era gangsters, newsboys, and orphans. Jacques had recruited real policemen from the NYPD, giving them dance classes to prepare for roles as the cops who caught the gangsters. Christopher d'Amboise performed the pivotal role of "Legs" Diamond, giving a literal meaning to the nickname with a mix of ballet and jazz dancing. The audience howled when the character called Fats, perched above the city he'd dominated and corrupted, had his rolls of fat literally unraveled by Legs Diamond. Underneath? A powerless little boy.

There was laughter as well on the evening we all came together to celebrate Jacques d'Amboise's life at New York City Center on June 1, 2022. Videos of Jacques performing signature roles in *Afternoon of a Faun, Apollo,* and other ballets were interspersed with performances by leading NYCB dancers. A live orchestra played a rousing "When the Saints Go Marching In" as about sixty NDI students exuberantly performed. Center stage, in front, was a girl in a motorized wheelchair, using her hands to telling effect, as if sending signals to the stars.

Jacques's children and grandchildren shared memorable stories. Charlotte d'Amboise spoke of how he had enchanted the nurses at the hospital with spontaneously composed poems. Just before they wheeled him out for yet another surgery, Jacques had smiled at his daughter and said, "What an adventure!" Charlotte recalled his characteristic detachment and amusement at the state of his own failing body: "I'm losing bits of myself," he told her. "I don't know why I'm so happy!"

The list of honors Jacques received in his lifetime could fill several pages. President Clinton awarded Jacques a National Medal of Arts in 1998 for his work as a "dancer, choreographer, educator," and he certainly educated me. He was nearly eighty-four when we met, but I felt instantly recharged, as if he had transmitted to me some portion of the exuberance and legendary energy that had kept him dancing solo and principal roles for NYCB from 1953 until his retirement from the company in 1984, just shy of his fiftieth birthday.

Today, Jacques's work of bringing the joy of dance to people of all ages and abilities continues at 219 West 147th Street, NDI's elegant base. Thanks to thousands of donors, including celebrity benefactors, many of them his friends, he was able to seed associate NDI programs nationally and internationally.

* * *

The last time I heard his voice on the phone was in the summer of 2020. He had been recently hospitalized for a condition that the discrete Emily did not name. I guessed that it was serious, since he'd always been quick to respond, by phone or email, but now months had passed without his signature on some crucial permissions. Most pressing was an elegant photo by Carrie that I'd found at the New York Public Library for the Performing Arts, a photo that Jacques had helped me to identify. It features Tanny and Tallchief with other dancers in gorgeous repose at an airport transit point, Labrador, for which I'd found the perfect accompanying quote, words Tallchief had heard from her teacher, Bronislava Nijinska: "When you sleep, you must sleep like a dancer. When you stand and wait for the bus, you must wait for the bus like a dancer."

The New York Public Library could not release the photo without Jacques's signature and out of respect for his privacy, I could not tell the library the reason for the delay. Somehow, Emily pulled off a miracle and I had the signature in the nick of time. But before Jacques would sign a permission form for the use of his unpublished words, he wanted to read all the pages where he was mentioned, with context. I sent him roughly seventy pages and not long afterwards, Emily wrote that he was ready to receive a phone call from me on July 31, 2020.

A caretaker answered and passed the phone to him. Jacques had read my text with great attention and taken copious notes, but

I could tell that there had been some cognitive changes since we'd last spoken. I explained, over and over, that in fact I had not left out the name of a certain ballet or composer, that I'd spared him all that contextual, introductory material. We had this same conversation about every ballet in the book and didn't say goodbye until two hours later. His stamina was still astounding.

There was one genuine omission that bothered him. After Tanny's last performance with him in Cologne, near the end of the disaster-plagued tour of 1956, he had hugged her goodbye onstage before flying home for his first child's birth. "Orel," Jacques complained, "you never mentioned the child's name, George!"

Touched by his fatherly solicitude, I gently explained that the name would not fit in that spot, since my next sentence was about the party Jacques skipped, given by the wife of the American cultural attaché, the reception where, I am almost certain, Tanny was infected with poliomyelitis. Jacques immediately understood that bringing in George's name there would be dramatically off, especially since I wanted to add his funny story about Balanchine's pleasure at the name of the child, thinking that it honored him, when in fact George was Carrie's maiden name. I assured him that I would put that story in an endnote, and I did. We parted "as friends," in Jacques's words.

In the film biography of Tanny by Nancy Buirski, *Afternoon of a Faun*, Jacques asks, "How can you not love the ballerina you dance with? I mean there you are feeling the heft of her and the sweat of her and the taste of her..." It's a question he asked about everything really: How can you not love this miraculous world in which you have the great good fortune to find yourself? Nothing was alien to him. He had the ability, like his friend Tanny, to focus on whatever marvel was right in front of him. I am grateful to have had my own moment in the warm spotlight of his attention. ∎

THE TROOPER
Colton Huelle

They are drowning pickleback shots in the kitchen, and the first thing Damion wants to know about the guy who might start dating his mom—on this point, Kevin feels it is prudent not to correct him—is if he is into metal. Kevin isn't at all into metal, but to soften his answer, he adds that he hasn't really given it much chance.

Kevin wonders at this sudden urge to curry favor with the greasy-haired adolescent son of the woman that he is here to sleep with. He matched with Sheryl on Tinder a few hours ago. Though a quarter century his senior, she was a dead ringer for Reba McEntire, and her pictures showcased a smoldering vitality that Kevin found alluring. The first was an action shot from the Zumba class she teaches. In it, a bright-red, serpentine braid curled around her neck and pointed like an arrow to her metallic-blue sports bra. The second photo was a selfie that made Kevin wonder if she had had work done or if these were old photos. In his mind, he drew crow's feet and marionette lines onto her face. In the last photo, she stood on a boat facing away from the camera, wearing only a yellow bikini bottom.

The pickle juice dribbles off Kevin's chin and dots his white socks green. He thinks about how he has grown closer to his father since he began sharing with him the details of his sexual adventures. "I know it don't seem like it now, but this is a blessing in disguise," his father assured him after Rosalind left him last year. "Go out and put some more mileage on that little pecker of yours." Though it went against his instincts, and though he knew his father was a lecherous old dolt, Kevin took his old man's advice and embarked on a voyage of one-night stands that has done little to alleviate his heartbreak.

"Okay, we'll start you on Iron Maiden," Damion decides. He instructs his phone to play "The Trooper" from the Bluetooth speakers embedded in the door of the refrigerator. He falls to his knees to shred along on air guitar to the song's opening riff, all the while keeping eye contact with Kevin to track his reaction.

When the song ends, Damion wants to know what Kevin thinks. Not his cup of tea, Kevin admits. He is surprised by the richness of the disappointment animating Damion's face.

"So what do _you_ listen to then?"

Kevin likes Father John Misty.

"Who is that, like a priest or something? What's his best song?"

Kevin considers for a minute. His favorite is "Chateau Lobby #4 (in C for Two Virgins)," but that doesn't feel situationally appropriate, so he goes with "Bored in the USA." Damion finds it on Spotify. The slow minor-key piano intro seems to agitate Damion and he turns it off before the first verse is through.

"What is this shit?" he demands. "It makes me want to kill myself."

"It's contemplative," Kevin says, feeling a bit more defensive than he might have expected.

Nothing about this night has turned out to be what Kevin might have expected. In Kevin's experience, when summoned to a woman's apartment at ten on Friday night, it is generally the woman who answers the door, and not, say, her cherub-faced son, who looks thirteen but stands at least four inches taller than you, who, quite tall yourself, are unaccustomed to being towered over. Nor is it common to then be introduced to the woman's sister, Maggie, a plump blonde with big beaver teeth and trucker humor, who, when introduced to you, cackles and says, "That's right! We're sisters, so don't go thinking that you've stumbled upon a two-for-one deal. We don't do *everything* together."

Kevin's instincts urged him to flee. But there was something perversely seductive about the absurdity of his position. And not even cackling Maggie could spoil the sight of Sheryl adjusting her unruly black tube top. So the four of them got roaring drunk and exchanged small talk as though it were a group date, a committee gathering to decide whether this young man and this not-so-young woman should sleep together.

Currently, Sheryl and Maggie are across the hall, getting high with some neighbor who always has excellent weed. They wanted Kevin to join them, but he hasn't been high since college. Rosalind smoked weed, a lot of it, and had for as long as Kevin had known her. When they first started dating, she thought it was cute that he mostly got scared when he was high. She liked to pull his head into her chest and say, "Momma's got you." But shortly after they moved to New York, she started complaining that he was a bummer to get high with and a waste of weed at that.

Before she left, Sheryl promised that they'd only be fifteen or twenty minutes. "It gets her in the mood," Maggie loud-whispered to Kevin. Sheryl rolled her eyes at her sister's crude remark but confirmed it with a wink before she walked out the door. That was thirty-five minutes ago.

* * *

Kevin follows Damion back into the living room and watches him collapse sideways over the arm of the white leather couch. For about a minute, he lies still and stares vacantly at the ceiling. Kevin starts to worry about alcohol poisoning and wonders if he should roll Damion over onto his stomach. But then Damion starts laughing and kicking his dangling feet as if treading water. Kevin yawns and takes a seat in the white leather armchair opposite the couch.

Earlier, it occurred to him that Sheryl's living room bore an uncanny resemblance to the one that he and Rosalind had fantasized about when they were at UConn and dreamt of moving to the city: abstract paintings hanging on exposed-brick walls, bright wood floors, picture window framing a Manhattan skyline across the river. He was not surprised to find a claw-foot tub in the bathroom. This too had been a staple of Rosalind's dream apartment, and the sight of it, like so many things, made Kevin nostalgic for the future she had once planned for them.

"Ever done acid?" Damion asks Kevin.

"Can't say I have."

"That song you played reminded me of when I dropped acid on the Appalachian Trail with my cousins last year. We were sitting around a fire in camp chairs, and I looked at them, and suddenly I was sure that I had never seen them in my life, that I didn't know any of them from Adam, and none of them knew me, like maybe I was just a stranger who had walked up and asked to join them."

"Some of his songs are happier."

"But the really fucked up thing was that somehow, I had forgotten that I had taken acid, and so I didn't think that I was having a bad trip or anything, and I got to thinking that maybe I had always felt this way, like a stranger, I mean, only I never realized it."

"I'm sure that's not true."

"It comes back to me sometimes. Earlier tonight, I had the thought that I didn't know my own mom or my aunt any better than I knew you. And I just kept having this thought over and over, like: *Nobody knows you.*"

Kevin gets up for another pickleback, and Damion follows. "Have you seen, like, a therapist or something?" Kevin asks.

"Shrinks don't know shit."

"I don't know, man," Kevin says with a shrug. He wants to insinuate that he sees a therapist himself. He doesn't. He almost did, after Rosalind left. But the one he called said she wasn't taking new clients at the moment, and Kevin took this to be a sign that another answer was on the horizon.

"I'm just saying," Kevin continues, "what you're describing sounds pretty awful. I'm sure you've got it under control, but maybe a therapist might be able to help you find a way out of it."

"I don't have it under control," Damion says. There is a crack in his voice that wasn't there before. "I think I really am a nutcase. I'd been trying to pretend I wasn't, but I think I knew it even before the acid, and then suddenly I couldn't ignore it anymore." Now, he is crying, and trying unsuccessfully to hide it. Some alien reflex lifts Kevin's hand awkwardly to Damion's shoulder. On contact, Damion shrinks away, but smiles too. "You're real as shit, man," he says. "I hope you date my mom." Just then, they hear the front door open, and by the time Sheryl appears in the living room, Damion has disappeared.

"Sorry," Sheryl says, keeled over laughing. "We got caught up watching a nature documentary, and then I noticed Maggie getting handsy with my neighbor under the blanket."

* * *

One night, when Kevin was in eighth grade, his mother asked him to join her and his father on the couch to talk about sex. She did the whole condom-and-banana trick, while he and his father stared at the peach-and-blue checkered rug. His parents were nineteen and twenty when they had Kevin. His father's only contribution to the conversation was to stress that having a kid at nineteen was the greatest mistake of his life. It was a familiar refrain, one that marred Kevin's childhood with guilt.

From the time he was old enough to think of such things, Kevin knew that he wanted to have kids, and he knew that his own kids would be raised on a refrain that gave voice to how wholly they were wanted.

He and Rosalind had talked about having kids almost from the onset of their relationship, but less so as it neared its end. New York had changed her from the doting partner she had been at UConn. Back then, she pinned herself to his arm at parties, tagged along with him to run errands, and spent the night in his dorm room more often than she didn't. But shortly after they moved to Brooklyn, she became flighty and agitated. It annoyed her when he tried to invite himself to parties with her coworkers at Intimax, a startup company about whose mission she was oddly evasive. She started spending whole weekends in Manhattan and acted like he was interrogating her if he asked what she and her friends had gotten up to.

It's been over a year since Rosalind left him in search of "a more freewheeling life." They are both accountants, so he wondered at the time how freewheeling either of their lives could really be. And then, a month ago, on the subway, he saw her making out with a man in a cowboy hat and skintight green pleather pants. *Touché*, Kevin thought.

* * *

Soon, they are in the bedroom. Sheryl pushes Kevin up against the wall and begins kissing his neck. Her hand has found its way under his shirt and busies itself with his chest hair. Between half-hearted moans, Kevin asks, "Is Damion, like, okay?"

Sheryl extracts her hand and takes a step away from the wall. She shakes her head, mystified. "Why exactly are we talking about Damion?" she snaps. Kevin can see from Sheryl's arched brow that if he continues this line of conversation, he risks being thrown out.

"I don't know, he just seems kind of troubled and not very open to getting help."

Sheryl cocks her head and steps forward. "Did you come here to fuck me or give me parenting advice?"

"Yeah, no. The first one. Definitely."

"Good," Sheryl says, taking him by the wrists and spinning him towards the brass bed.

Over the past year, Kevin has come to understand sex primarily as a celebration of the body, from which he has learned to divorce emotion. What happens in the brass bed does not feel like a celebration of anything. The force that compels his hips seems to Kevin not of his body. Or is he himself no longer of his body?

That he is thus preoccupied escapes Sheryl, or seems to. She is howling for him. Or not him precisely. He feels more like a voyeur than a participant as he counts the smudges on her headboard, perhaps left by former lovers. Sheryl's phone chirps on the nightstand, and her cries and commands grow louder in Kevin's ear. Another chirp. He steals a glance at her phone and sees that the text previews are from Damion, in font large enough for Kevin to read with ease: *JFC keep it down* and *he cant be THAT good*. Kevin returns his attention to the seven amorous finger smudges.

And then a sound louder than Sheryl's moaning calls Kevin back to his body. A heavy metal riff that he can now identify as "The Trooper" bleeds through the walls and through the crack beneath the bedroom door. It seeps beneath the hardwood floor and shakes the bed from below.

"Ignore it," Sheryl commands him.

But this proves impossible, especially when Damion begins to sing. Sheryl taps Kevin's shoulder three times, and when he rolls off her, she springs to her feet, drapes herself in a navy-blue bathrobe, and sticks her head out into the living room. Kevin tries not to find words in the screaming match that follows. When Sheryl returns to bed, she crawls under the covers and a moment later asks, "Where did he go?" They try and try, but he cannot be found again.

* * *

Three days later, Kevin receives a text message from a number he does not recognize: *hey sorry the other night was weird what r u doing today? (BTW this is Damion).* Kevin's first instinct is to ignore the message. Something spooked him that night, and every night since, his racing heart has plucked him out of bad dreams he wakes from without remembering.

What bothers him most is that he knew right away that something was off, and instead of leaving, he drank himself out of feeling uncomfortable. Moving forward, he resolves to honor his instincts. Another lesson from that night: his hookup phase is over. Perhaps the bizarre dissociative episode he experienced during the lovemaking was his higher self calling him back. From now on, Tinder is for finding love. Someone to start a family with.

Kevin does not know this, but across the East River, in a hotel room in Chelsea, Rosalind is attempting to extricate herself from the bear grasp of a snoring comedian, glimpsing through sheer blue curtains the first light of a similar epiphany.

* * *

Kevin is at lunch with a coworker when Damion's second text arrives. *plz I rly need to talk to u?* Kevin huffs through his nose and shakes his head. He hopes his coworker will ask him, "What is it?" But they're not close like that.

what about? Kevin types, but when he reads the words on the screen, they strike him as far too curt. Before he can craft a gentler rebuff, a third message appears beneath the last.

i jus feel like u get me?

After work, instead of going home, Kevin takes the train to the botanical garden, where he finds Damion sitting on a bench beneath a cherry blossom. The Japanese Hill-and-Pond Garden was one of the first Japanese gardens cultivated in the United States. On their first weekend in Brooklyn, Kevin thought to surprise Rosalind with a walking tour of Prospect Park. But Rosalind only had eyes for the bright lights beckoning to her from across the river. The tour started at the botanical garden, and that was the only stop they caught before Rosalind told him that if they left right then, they could catch the next ferry to Manhattan. And didn't that sound romantic?

"I like that red thing," Damion says when Kevin joins him on the bench. He points to a vermillion structure on the far side of the pond: two posts sticking out of the water, joined by two crossbeams.

"It's called a torii," Kevin recalls from the tour. "It's a gate for the shrine on the top of that hill. It's supposed to symbolize a passageway between the worlds of the profane and the sacred."

"I'm sorry for cockblocking you," Damion says.

Kevin suggests they check out the rest of the garden. As they walk, the conversation begins in fits and starts, then winds its way into a fragmented monologue that Kevin struggles to follow beyond the broad strokes:

Damion studied computer science at Brooklyn College for a semester before dropping out to mine cryptocurrency.

His father is rich—Wall Street rich. He doesn't have any other kids, and the younger woman he left Sheryl for cheated on him, so it's all going to Damion when he croaks. Between that and the crypto, he's gonna be set.

He has a vintage Members Only jacket that he uses to pick up ladies. He generally does okay for himself in that department, but he's hit a bit of a cold spell lately.

The reason that his mom is so loud in bed is because she wants him to move out.

"Don't you want to move out?" Kevin asks.

"I mean, sure, eventually." Damion kicks up a small cloud of gravel. "But right now, I just——" His voice cracks, as it did the other night. "I don't know how to be around people who don't know me."

"What do you mean?" Kevin asks. "You were around me the other night. I don't really know you."

Damion retreats into another disjointed monologue, and Kevin lets him. In the rose garden, Damion is carrying on about some girl in one of his CS classes whom he was kinda crazy for but who stopped talking to him after he dropped out. Kevin nods and periodically emits a sympathetic hum. He wonders if this is what it means to "get" somebody. As they leave the garden, Damion asks Kevin if he's going to be seeing his mom again. He nods when Kevin says, "No, probably not." "You deserve better," Damion says. "She's not very emotionally available. Anyways, thanks for showing up."

"You got it," Kevin says, cognizant of a new warmth in his gut. "You can hit me up again, man. If you need to talk or whatever."

Damion opens his mouth to speak but produces only a mucous rattle. Instead, he just smiles and grazes Kevin's shoulder with a playful little punch before turning to descend the subway stairs.

* * *

On their next walk, Damion returns to the subject of moving out. "I'm afraid that I can't hack it on my own," he says. "And it's like, if I move out and get a job and roommates and all that, and if I have a breakdown out there in the real world, then everyone will see it and it'll be real, and I'll know forever that I'm really, truly crazy." All of this comes in one strangled breath, and Damion now seems on the verge of hyperventilating. Kevin guides him to the nearest park bench, and Damion breaks. He makes no effort to hide his tears and pays no mind to the rubberneckers who pass by with strollers or Pomeranians or canes, some of whom look embarrassed and others who disapprovingly at Kevin. Is he doing enough to console his weeping companion, he wonders. Tentatively, he pats Damion three times on the back of his neck.

"You're a lot stronger than you realize," Kevin says. He wonders if this is true, and then immediately feels bad for wondering, as though his lack of conviction could end up being a major determiner of Damion's fate, vis-à-vis his perception of his own strength as gleaned from Kevin's tone. "You're a trooper," he adds.

Damion dabs at his eyes with his knuckles and then offers Kevin his fist. Kevin bumps it with his own, and they both laugh. Without deciding to, he begins telling Damion about Rosalind. "I just keep thinking that she's going to walk through the door again, only it'll be the old Rosalind."

But *which* old Rosalind? For the first time since she left him, it occurs to Kevin that Rosalind was always changing on a dime. New hair, new clothes, new affectations. One summer she got six facial piercings and by the end of the year, all the holes had closed.

The only difference was that her most recent metamorphosis left no room for him. He doesn't say any of this to Damion. It's too fresh a consideration for words.

It is Kevin who initiates the third walk, and the fourth. Their walks continue through the summer and into the fall. Some days, Damion is raw and vulnerable. His voice cracks around attempts to articulate his fragility. On others, he dons an ill-fitting bravado and walks with a borrowed swagger. Kevin soon becomes accustomed to the fluidity with which Damion moves between these two states.

And then, one day in October, Rosalind calls. Father John Misty is playing at the Rainbow Room, and she can get free tickets from one of her coworkers, whose fiancé works there. She's been thinking of him lately, and this felt like a sign that maybe it was time they found their way back to each other.

* * *

The post-concert lovemaking is momentarily interrupted by the sound of one of Rosalind's roommates peeing in their Jack-and-Jill bathroom. But, unlike following Damion's blaring of "The Trooper," Kevin has no trouble recovering from this distraction. Afterwards, Rosalind says, "Next time we'll go to your place." It is strange for Kevin to hear her refer to the apartment as *his* place. Here she is beside him again, blowing her bangs out of her eyes, preening for him like she did when it was *their* place.

"You know how Amish kids, when they come of age or whatever, go out into the world and party and stuff just so they know for sure that they really wanna be Amish for the rest of their lives?" she asks Kevin. "I think it was like that for us. We both needed to see what else was out there, but now we have. And it's like, now we can come home."

"Do you still want kids?" Kevin asks.

Rosalind boops Kevin's nose with the pad of her index finger. "Of course I do. We'll take them out on those little paddleboats in Central Park. My boss just posted a picture of her and her son doing that and I was like, *I want that.*"

Kevin draws her close and kisses the top of her head. Briefly, he considers telling her about Damion, about the strange new tenderness he feels for him. He wants her to see in this tenderness something profound and elemental and necessary for this next chapter they're starting. But his instincts counsel patience. She might not understand just yet. It could muddy things.

* * *

It is the middle of March—those fragile weeks, the threshold of spring. Kevin and Rosalind clink margaritas across a sidewalk table in Greenwich Village. When they arrived at the restaurant, it was sixty-two degrees without a cloud in the sky. Now a raindrop blurs the text on the paper menu that Kevin is studying.

They retreat indoors just before the sky opens up. They take a seat at the window, and Kevin looks out onto the street through a curtain of rainfall. He recalls a hiking trip he took with his roommate the summer after his freshman year of college. Part of the trail led behind a waterfall. Where was that? Upstate somewhere. When it gets warmer, he'll bring Damion somewhere like that. It'll be good for him to get out of the city before he goes back to school in the fall.

When the weather got too cold for walks in the park, Kevin began teaching Damion to cook. He is not much of a chef himself, but he knows how to chop an onion and can follow a recipe, which was more than could be said for Damion. It was slow going at first, but the kid can make a pretty decent chicken parm now. Kevin is on good terms with Sheryl, who appreciates what he is doing for her son.

Keeping true to his resolution to honor his instincts, he still has not told Rosalind about Damion. But lately, his instincts are telling him that it's time. Soon, he tells them. He just needs more time.

"I have a confession to make," Rosalind says, squeezing Kevin's knee beneath the table. "I may have had an ulterior motive for dragging you to the Village."

"Oh?"

"There's an apartment on Jones Street, right around the corner. It's one bedroom, $4,200 a month, which I know sounds steep, but I am *so* over having roommates, and you must be tired of Brooklyn by now. And besides, we're ready for this. It's everything we've always wanted."

Kevin smiles and places his hand on Rosalind's. He is a little buzzed from the two margs and a little gassy from the tacos. After this, they will go see the apartment. It will have an exposed-brick wall and a claw-foot bathtub. He will take the realtor's card, and as they walk down Jones Street, she will pin herself to his arm. They'll take the train back up to her apartment in Harlem. They will make love without trying to be quiet for her roommates. Then, in the morning, he will tell her about Damion. She will think it's sweet. She will ask when she can meet him. Of course, they'll have to get a sleeper sofa in the living room, so he'll be comfortable when he stays over. He'll have his own key. She *will* say this, he tells his instincts. ∎

MONSOON SEASON IN CHIMAYÓ
Justin Groppuso-Cook

for Toni Bowden

She places sweetgrass
on the dash with orange peels, unfolds

my fist along its crease. We light
hickory & piñon, leaving

the casita as morning peeks
through cracks in the door

& hail sweeps the cliffs in polyrhythms.
At the gorge, she floats

in a bed of quartz & I
stand still within the rapids; she lays

me across the current & we become
rain steaming iridescent

the instant it touches stone,
hot springs melting snow. We collect

raw flint to spark on empty roads,
sip thickening clouds among

the peaks where she gives
me back my breath, lips cracked

like the earth—trading language
in the sanctuary of our bodies. We hold

this holy dirt as it coagulates
within the coming mist.

EMILE
Andrew Porter

I n the months before Emile died, we used to go over to his house on the weekends to swim. This was about eight or nine years ago, when my wife and I were still in our early thirties, still childless. Back then, Emile used to throw these elaborate parties in the evenings, on Friday and Saturday nights, parties that would often go until the early hours of the morning, but Angela and I always liked to stop by earlier in the day, before it got too crowded, when it was usually just Emile and us, the three of us just floating there on rafts in the middle of his pool, sipping on margaritas or frozen daiquiris or those special pineapple cocktails he used to make with triple sec and mezcal. At the time, he had just broken up with his partner of many years, David, and he was often in a funk about this, always wondering if he had made a mistake, if he should call David up or invite him over, try to reconcile, but eventually his thoughts would move on to something else, to another topic, and his spirits would brighten again.

Over on the other side of the pool, near his house, Emile had a beautiful Spanish-style terrace, a sort of shaded patio area made of terra-cotta tiles with flowering agave and bougainvillea and golden trumpet surrounding it and these elegant Mexican lanterns and iron sconces on the walls. There was a lone freestanding fountain to the side of the outdoor bar and on the other side several smaller wall fountains and a large garden filled with various succulents and cacti, blue agave and prickly pears.

Whenever Emile was feeling happy, he'd walk over there and put on music—usually one of his favorites, Nina Simone, or Count Basie, or Ella Fitzgerald—and then he'd slide back into the pool with fresh drinks for all of us, or a bottle of champagne, holding the bottle high above his head as he moved around the shallow end, the sunlight shimmering on the water.

In a few months from then, Emile would learn that he had osteosarcoma, a severe type of bone cancer, and by the time it was diagnosed, or discovered, it had already spread to his lungs and his lymph nodes and eventually would spread to his brain. But for the months of that summer, and it felt like a long summer, maybe our longest, Emile was oblivious to this, and so were we, and in our innocence, our unknowing, we enjoyed every weekend with him, the free-flowing alcohol, the vertiginous jazz music, the laughter, the sun, all of us sweating in the midafternoon heat of a San Antonio summer, telling stories about our younger years, those years before we knew each other, talking passionately about books that we loved, movies we hated, arguing, laughing, often falling into hysterics when we'd had too much to drink, the three of us just floating there in our own private world, a world that felt removed from time, a world that seemed to have nothing at all to do with anyone else, those long, lazy hours before his other guests arrived, before the younger and more raucous crowd appeared, his wealthy neighbors, his architect friends, all of those beautiful men, in that small window of time before they all arrived, it was just the three of us, and I can still remember it now, Emile lying there supine on one of his rafts, a cocktail balanced on his belly, the cancer already inside him, already filling his bones, just floating there on his back in the midafternoon heat, saying, *I'm plastered, I'm hammered, I'm gone.* ∎

TEARS OF A CLOWN
Stephen Earley Jordan II

An 8-track plays number 1
on the stereo while I laugh
because I'd never seen tears of a clown—
I walk around, smiling, pretending to cry,
entertaining the adults until they get annoyed.
The house fills with Smokey's smooth voice
knocking down the walls, finding its way
into the ears and souls
of those long gone. The adults play cards
and drink drinks while I sit in my room
on the burgundy comforter lightly coated
with coal dust atop white sheets
with Black feet stains.
Mama always said to bathe before I go to bed—
but my feet always get dirty.
She dances, telling me to spin her.
I'm half her height and she ends up turning me
so the room spins and I'm drunk
on her giddiness. Her kisses smell
like stale Jim Beam
and menthol cigarettes.
I turn away and she kisses me again, laughing.
She puts me to bed, turns out the light,
and closes the door.

BAD, BAD CALVIN TRIMBLE, DDS
Greg Ames

Forget what you've heard about the South Side of Chicago. We had florists and pharmacies, a Frank Lloyd Wright house, many antique shops, and some really good open-air markets along the lakefront. It was very peaceful. And for about eighteen months, from 1961 until 1963—yes, I admit it—I was the baddest man in the whole damn town. Everybody said so.

How bad was I? People still want to know the answer to this question. They write me emails from as far away as Fairbanks, Alaska; they invite me to bare-knuckled brawls in Kansas City and Albuquerque. There is no way to answer these men satisfactorily. How can one quantify badness?

Frankly, I thought I had finally put this business to rest decades ago. As a dentist with a private practice in Oak Park, Illinois, I find all this recent media coverage a terrible distraction. My patients are being accosted in front of my office. "Did Doctor Trimble ever hit you?" the reporters ask. "Is he still bad?"

A recent Jim Croce revival in New York City brought on this hullabaloo. Now all the daytime talk shows want me to appear. Teenage boys are challenging me to fistfights in the street. Just yesterday a lady in the Jewel rammed her shopping cart into my ankles. It's starting all over again.

Maybe I shouldn't say this, but I despise Jim Croce's music and always have. It is discordant and harmonically unresolved, and I wish he'd never written that song about Leroy Brown. Personally, I think it's in poor taste to rank men by how *bad* or *mean* they are. We are all God's children, after all.

Am I bitter? Heck no. Just tired of all the controversy. What people don't understand is that I didn't mind being the second-baddest man in the whole damn town after Leroy Brown took my title. Shoot, that was okay with me. If anything, it took some of the pressure off. I welcomed Leroy with open arms. Serving as his understudy was a treat. Leroy never took days off. If he had a sprained ankle or a court appearance, I could step in for a day or two. But that rarely happened. Thanks to Leroy's almost religious devotion to badness, I had enough free time to attend dental school at Northwestern.

* * *

How did I fall? Simple. Leroy Brown took my title without a fight, without a harsh word spoken. I just woke up one Saturday morning, took my pug for a stroll down South Shields Avenue, and saw all six-foot-four of Bad, Bad Leroy Brown coming my way, and it was pretty clear to all concerned that I had become the *second*-baddest man in the whole damn town right on the spot! Everybody knew it, even Pugsie knew it, and he couldn't see too well.

My reign was short but sweet. It wasn't like they put it right on my driver's license or anything. Baddest Man in the Whole Damn Town. It was just one of those things that I kind of liked. It was neat. I would walk around town chuckling to myself about my badness.

Every now and then, of course, I'd have to throw a cinder block through a funeral home window to keep up appearances. I had to. I kicked a foot-patrol policeman down a flight of stairs while he arbitrated a domestic disturbance. I ignited an inferno in an abandoned paint factory, but I made sure beforehand that no children or unhoused people were trapped inside. And in one of my worst acts of badness, when I was in a bourbon-induced blackout, I shattered a man's first and second bicuspids with the butt end of a Louisville Slugger. It happened during a pickup softball game in Armour Square Park. I now give one free crown a year to a surprised patient as a private form of atonement for that savage act. Is it a mitzvah? Not anymore. I just spilled the beans. And I won't sit here and attempt to whitewash all the little daily bad actions, the ones that solidified my place as the Baddest Man in the Whole Damn Town. Every month I stole a pack of Juicy Fruit from the corner store in my neighborhood, telling the aggravated clerk to spread the word that Chicago's baddest man just came through. He didn't dare to stop me. He just sighed, and said, "Why, Calvin?"

There is no official ceremony. The true Bad Man wouldn't show up to something like that. No, the citizens of Chicago simply nominated me with their eyes. Their eyes said: *You're bad.* And my eyes replied: *Yes, I know. This is how I like it.* They said: *We are scared of you.* I nodded and said: *You should be.* They said: *But it's strangely alluring, your badness.* I said: *You ain't seen nothing yet. I'm on a rampage, baby.*

But after Leroy's appearance, I had to ask myself who I really was. I wasn't the Baddest or the Saddest or the Maddest Man anymore, nor was I the Richest or even the Most Hygienic Man in town. I was just Calvin Trimble, thirty-four years old, the only son of

Bev and Clarence Trimble, a nobody, a loser. I trudged around with my head down. Now their eyes said: *Move it, buster.* My eyes said: *I'm doing my best.* But we all knew I wasn't. I was in the dumps. For months after losing my title, and before I hit upon the idea of going to dental school, I just didn't want to get out of bed in the morning. Things got ugly. I couldn't afford payments on my Pontiac. My wife, Lily, could no longer abide my lethargy or my confusion. She said, "You're a stranger to me, Calvin. Honestly. What is happening to you?" You see, Lily never believed that I was that bad in the first place. Unaware of the true badness in my soul, she thought I was just "confused" and "aimless." When I told her that I was still one of the three baddest men in the whole damn town, she laughed and told me to get cracking on that classified section. But now she wasn't so sure about me, she said. Maybe I was bad, she said. Maybe she had misjudged me all along. Even Pugsie regarded me with distrust.

The darkest year of my life was 1973. Jim Croce was world famous. Every time his hit song came on the radio, it felt like a dagger in my gut. Lily said, "Calvin, what's the matter? It's just a song." But I understood the deeper implications. Croce was thumbing his nose at me through the FM dial. At first, I tried to drink the pain away. I guzzled Rheingold beer in bed, getting up only to relieve myself and/or to vomit. After Lily moved out to her sister's place in Indianapolis, I had the whole place to myself. Afternoons I stomped down to Lew's Tavern. I was still the baddest damn man in Lew's, most of the fellows made a point of saying so, but it wasn't the same. I think they just felt sorry for me. Leroy Brown had knocked me down for a ten-count and everybody knew I wasn't getting up. Or so we all thought.

* * *

Let's face it: The bad man is really only a frightened child who is scared of rejection and abandonment. His badness is a preemptive strike against an anticipated rejection. The best thing one can do for the bad man is to offer him a hug and a platonic kiss on the cheek. I invite everyone reading this to follow my suggestion. The next time you see an aggressive young man acting the thug on your street corner—he is often recognizable by the amount of tattoos (fear armor) he wears—approach him from the front so as not to startle him. He may be a bit jumpy, of course; it's a rough business being so bad all the time. Show him that your hands are empty. Be sure to make copious eye contact. Smile. Say, "I am armed today only with hugs." Remember you are merely a vessel for peace. Take this young man into your arms and give him all the hugs and kisses he's been denied. Hold on tight. He might, at first, struggle. He will most definitely squirm. This is to be expected. Be gentle but persistent. Grab hold of his wrist and whisper into his ear: "Stop fighting the world. Stop punching me in the neck and ear. I accept your badness but I choose to cherish the virtuous in you."

This is what most people don't understand. The Baddest Man finds himself a citizen in a world of one. If you have never been there, then you can't comprehend the pain of that isolation. The Baddest Man is not the zookeeper or the spectator; he's the animal in the cage. Others have put him there, and he has agreed to it on account of his low self-esteem. The community wants him to stay there. It is a sick, dysfunctional relationship. If we declare that Leroy or some other young man is "bad," then some of these so-called "good men"—you know who they are—can more easily get away with their crimes. Some good men "misdirect funds" at work or visit a "massage therapist" on their lunch breaks. Some destroy the planet for their own profit. This behavior gnaws at them in mysterious ways, and they consider getting help for behavior they know is hurtful to themselves and others, but then they hear about a bad, bad man like Leroy Brown, or they hear about a Calvin Trimble, DDS, and, well, they don't feel like changing anymore. *At least I'm not something like that*, they think. *Look at that Calvin Trimble. He's on an epic rampage.* That may be true. But they are lying to themselves. These hypocrites—the men who loudly promote their own goodness—are the most dangerous ones of all.

* * *

Old age dulls a man's appetite for transgression. Badness is a younger man's game. The allure of self-destruction continues to entice me, of course, but in my semiretirement from dentistry, I find that I have mellowed considerably. Now I prefer to sit on the back porch, enjoying the company of my wife, Lily (we divorced and remarried), and Pugsie II. I read a lot of Greek and Roman history. If a blue heron lands by my pond and just stands there looking stupid, I'll take a shot at him with my Crosman pellet gun—who wouldn't?—but for the most part, I'm just grateful to be alive.

We all grow old and die. Every middle-aged man, no matter who he is or where he has come from, will eventually learn the same lesson, which is this: there will always be someone badder than you, someone tougher and meaner than you, and he's going to step up and take your place soon. Here's my advice: Don't fight it. Better to surrender peaceably. It might just be the blessing you have always sought. Hold out your hand to that eager young mischief-maker and say: "Welcome to the neighborhood, my friend." In all likelihood he will flex and posture; he might strut around in concentric circles, bobbing his head; he'll certainly bathe you in a spray of up-to-date obscenities. Don't be alarmed. Try to remember that he is as frightened by the world's chaos as you are. Look that loveable scamp square in the eye and say: "Your badness is certainly impressive, sonny, and we all honor its presence, but one day it will no longer sustain you. And when that day comes, and it certainly will, we, who have gone before you, will still be here, waiting, with open arms, to welcome you to our growing ranks." ■

UNTITLED 39
Paddy McCabe

UNTITLED 13
Paddy McCabe

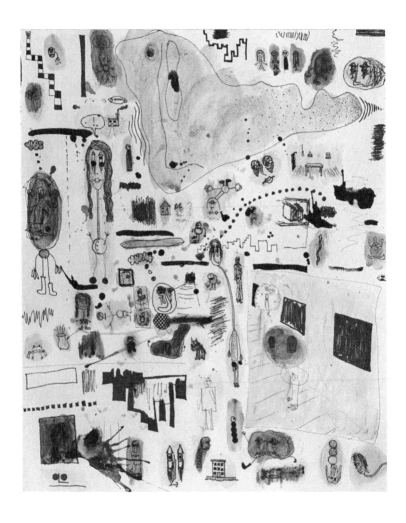

MRS. FISHER
Jessie Ren Marshall

She did not love him in the beginning. Saw him as just another body at another desk. Another name printed on her roster. *Stephen.*

In the books she assigned, characters were brought low by love because love was a crucible. It came. It tested you. It left.

Stephen did not want to be called Steve or Stevie or Phen. Marion drew an X beside his name because he'd been there. And beside the X she'd written *SEVEN.*

* * *

"I solved the mystery of the smell," Marion said to Dolly. "There's a dead mouse in the camping stove."

The mouse had been an orphan, Marion decided, and hungry. This was its backstory. Next, rising action, in which the mouse had gotten stuck in the vent at the base of the stove and could not extricate itself. Could not go forward or back. Then, a climax: one of the women in the house—Ma, Dolly, or Marion—had turned on the flame and the mouse had been transformed.

Dolly didn't look up. She was scrolling her phone with one hand and palming a lukewarm Starbucks with the other. She must have stolen it when her boyfriend Eddie brought her home from the nightshift at Pearl's Grocery. *I walk right in and take it off the counter,* Marion had heard her telling Ma.

"Can you remove the mouse?" she asked Dolly. Staying strong, making eye contact. "I can't. I'll be late to school."

Dolly crunched her nose in disgust. It had been a mistake to mention *school.* A place Dolly had never liked. Without looking up, Dolly told her sister to go fuck herself, slowly, with an ice pick.

Dolly reached for her soggy cereal. Marion glanced at her watch. 7:19.

"Dolly," she said, "it would be nice if you helped with the mouse. But no matter what, you are my sister and I am grateful you're in my life."

Marion delivered this speech in the detached and loving language she'd been practicing at STAND UP FOR YOURSELF

NOW! Marion believed STAND UP FOR YOURSELF NOW! might one day turn into a viable business opportunity. Like, maybe she would give speeches to women who wanted to be brave? But so far no one had joined the group she'd formed on Meetup.com, so at the appointed time Marion went to the pavilion in the dog park and practiced speaking in the firm, slightly lyrical voice of the TED Talk women.

I am enough.

You are enough.

What makes you think you aren't enough?

...STAND UP FOR YOURSELF NOW!

Dolly dropped her Grape Nuts in an aggravated way and pointed her spoon at Marion. This was a little threatening because the spoon had been mangled in the trash compactor back when they had a trash compactor and its edges were now jagged. Dolly called Marion a snot-nosed snob who thought she was SO GREAT because the state paid her to make grammatical slideshows. But who cared about gerunds? Nobody!

Marion didn't argue. Instead, she left the house and walked to her car and reminded herself of the truth.

1. They were not slideshows. They were interactive PowerPoints displayed on a SMART board.

2. Someone must care about gerunds, because Marion was required to teach them.

3. Although she had worked for the state before, this was her second year at Holy Cross. A private school.

When she took the job it sounded so exclusive—a *private* school! Like a *private* club or a *private* jet! In reality, the kids at Holy Cross were problematic. She'd heard about attempted kidnappings, suicide pacts, eating disorders, multiple personality disorders—all the standard *Gossip Girl* plots. Now it was her second year and as far as she could tell, the only difference between public and private school was that at Holy Cross, Marion could get fired for anything. Anything at all.

* * *

She arrived so late that the 7:45 clusterfuck of cars, kids, parents, and buses was nearing peak cluster, peak fuck. At the crosswalk she avoided looking directly at Emilio Powers, the school's athletic director and crossing guard. Emilio liked to flirt with her aggressively and then raise both palms in the air to say, *you know I'm kiddin', right?*

She brushed past his neon green vest but Emilio held her elbow and said, "Marion! I was starting to think you'd quit."

"Ha," she said. "Ha, ha."

"Must be nice to be a regular teacher. I know I'd like to show up to work at Screw It o'clock."

She escaped through a side door of Ogdenfry Annex, a locker-filled hall named for a dead lumber baron. Marion had the same classroom this year, 707-B. At first she'd thought the sevens on either side were lucky. But seven turned out to be her unlucky number. She'd needed seven stitches after a branch fell on her tent during the annual fall campout. Seven parents had called to complain when a hidden user on her class blog had posted comments like TONI MORRISON IS A SLUT. And it was on the seventh day of the seventh month of the year that her husband Alec had asked her to leave.

Marion glanced at a laminated sign on the wall beside her door. The sign hadn't been there before. The sign said *MRS. FISHER*.

No one else would care about the Mrs. / Ms. / Miss distinction. Sometimes her favorite students just said *Fisher*, like they were on a basketball team together and they wanted her to pass them the ball. But this was not really an apt comparison, because her favorite students did not play sports. Her favorite students took anti-depressants in the middle of class and wrote bad poetry on her whiteboard during lunch.

She stuck her brass key into the lock, jiggling the knob the way it liked to be jiggled, and realized something awful: if she relinquished Alec's surname, she'd have to go back to being a Kleggsman. Ugh, Kleggsman! The sound of it was like being hit over the head with a log. Ma was a Kleggsman. Dolly was a Kleggsman. It was a fate Marion thought she'd escaped.

She entered her classroom, retrieved a bottle of white-out from her desk, and returned to the hallway. But the sign did not look right after she'd done it. The white-out's white was not the same white as the paper. In the end she'd only highlighted the change, not hidden it. Well. So what? Maybe this was better. She took a blue pen and under the

MRS. FISHER

she scrawled, *cuz i'm single and ready to mingle.*

There. She felt better about the sign now. And no one would ever suspect Marion of generating such lewd, ungrammatical graffiti. After all, she was a teacher.

* * *

Alec was a doctor and came from money. Ma and Dolly hated him. They called him uppity, two-faced, superior, annoying, boring, cold. Marion understood why. Alec had been the boss. He planned good things for Marion. Mitigated her flaws before she fell prey to them.

For instance: before he requested her departure from their marriage, Alec called Ma to make sure Marion would have a place to go. He'd already arranged for a van man to collect the furniture Marion had bought with her own money. The papers were ready to be signed. Alec had thought of everything! What could she say? The future was decided. Impermeable.

Marion was given two days and two nights alone in the house to clear out her things. Then Alec would live there with his emotional-affair partner. After he was gone, Marion sat on the bed and stared at the wrinkles she'd just noticed on the backs of her hands. When she looked out the window she saw the afternoon sun reflected in Mr. Holland's windows, so she went outside to sit with the boulder. The boulder made her feel calm. The boulder was not moved by love or loss. It gathered the heat of the day in its tightly woven cells and held that warmth for as long as it could.

After the sun set she went back inside to open the cabinets and drink whatever alcohols she could find. She'd looked at the microwave clock and it said 7:07. Weird.

* * *

They came in simultaneously, a herd of buffalo responding to the electric prod of the bell. Marion crossed to the front of her desk and leaned against it with her arms folded. This was her most teacherly pose. She also imagined it was kind of sexy. Would there be a last-minute hire this year, perhaps a Bradley Cooper type from the parts of *The Hangover* in which Bradley Cooper's character is teaching middle school? If The Universe provided her with a Bradley Cooper type as a new hire or even a long-term sub, Marion might start to believe that the current awfulness of her life—being a Kleggsman, living at Ma's—was merely the set-up for a dramatic reversal of fortune.

The second bell rang and Marion turned to her audience.

"Hello, tenth graders!"

The students had clapped when she said this last year. Such was their elation at no longer being freshmen. But these sophomores did not clap.

"I'm Mrs. Fisher." She paused. Frowned. "But in a few months I might be something else."

They stared at her blankly.

"I'm like you," she continued. "Sophomore year is full of changes. Who knows how you and I will transform? We might find new names for ourselves under the Christmas tree."

Oops. She should have said "Winter Break tree."

One student, a boy, raised his hand—but then, she shouldn't make gender assumptions! Even English teachers had to pluralize arguably singular subjects. Such were the times.

"Yes?" She referred to the seating chart. "Stephen?"

"Actually," he/she/they said, "I have a nickname. Call me Seven."

Marion noted the coincidence. 707. 7:07. "And what pronouns do you use, Seven?"

Seven scrunched his/her/their nose in thought.

"Objective pronouns, I guess. Because you can use them for both direct and indirect objects."

The class laughed. Marion could tell they really liked Seven.

"I appreciate your humor," she said. "But which gender pronouns do you use?"

"Oh." Seven made an embarrassed face, and the class laughed again. "He."

Marion wrote the word *SEVEN* on her roster.

"And what pronouns do *you* use, Mrs. Fisher?"

She looked up and met Seven's gaze. It was shocking, really. They never thought of her as a person, so why would she need a personal pronoun?

"I like possessive pronouns, Seven. I feel immensely gratified when a student uses the correct spelling of 'its' in an essay."

She expected laughter. After all, she'd just employed *a callback*, a popular comedic trope. But the class just stared at her.

"Regarding personal pronouns," she continued, "I use *she*. And my surname will be changing soon, so if you want, you can call me M."

M? What did that mean?

The bovine quality of her students' faces made Marion want to jump out of her skin. She had been like that once. As a child, she'd felt sad in her soul—unloved, unpaired, unknown—but had felt comforted by the belief she would eventually grow up to be loved and paired and known. But she had been wrong. Marion was invisible;

she was not even seen by the two dozen faces gazing up at her.

"M is short for Marion," she said softly. She picked up and put down a pile of handouts. "Marion is my name."

It was awful, awful. A teacher hoping for a nickname was too intimate. The kids would call her "thirsty."

"You don't *have* to," she added hastily. "Mrs. Fisher is fine. It is— whatever." Rolling her eyes now. Imitating them. Going for the cheap laugh.

Seven raised his hand. Marion pointed at him and he smiled at her. Flicked the smile on like a lightbulb.

"Hello, M!" he said.

Marion stared at the boy in wonder. It filled her heart full, to hear those words again.

* * *

Before she became a teacher, Marion was a waitress at Antony's Pizza. At that time she lived with three other women in a house twenty minutes from Ma's. Ma told her to go to the E.R. one evening because Dolly was having her stomach pumped. She'd taken too many pills or maybe her boyfriend had put the pills her drink? Either way, it was totally Dolly.

Marion spent her mornings studying for the Praxis so she could be a high school teacher instead of a waitress. She hated Dolly. Hated Ma too. Marion had come from nothing and still was nothing—at least, this is what she believed back then, before she'd learned to hold space for others people's journeys like she did in STAND UP FOR YOURSELF NOW.

At the hospital, Dolly was acting loopy. She found it hilarious that Marion felt shy in front of the medical team and, in a little mouse voice, would imitate her hesitant questions whenever they entered the room: "Em, excuse me?" "Em, can I please get more drugs?" And when a nurse told Marion they couldn't release Dolly until she ate a full meal, Dolly giggled and said, "Tell that to my eating disorder."

Marion returned to the hospital the next morning. Alec pulled her aside. He showed her a picture of a liger on his phone and kept talking about it until she laughed. When he asked her to dinner, she looked at his nametag. *Dr. Fisher.* She thought it sounded like a good, normal name.

He took her to a "real" pizza place, more upscale than Antony's, where they dined on dainty pies with paper-thin crusts. During the meal he called Marion *Em* because he thought it was her name—

short for Emma, perhaps—and Marion thought it was terribly sweet and intimate that he'd chosen her nickname so quickly: *M*. Two weeks passed like that. Then Marion introduced herself to one of his colleagues and they realized he'd misinterpreted Dolly's shenanigans. Marion felt horribly embarrassed. But it turned out alright, because for twelve years, the letter became a shorthand for their quiet affection.

Alec was not an objectively handsome man. He didn't have much hair and his eyes were goggly like a frog's. But he was decent. Clever. And inherently different from the Kleggsmans. He said things like, "I know you'll pass the Praxis, honey." And when Marion did, he said he was proud and brought home a bottle of champagne.

But his family hadn't liked her. His brothers made fun of Marion for pronouncing "Seychelles" as "Say Chili's." And it had been the venomous disdain of Alec's mother that inspired STAND UP FOR YOURSELF NOW. After years of enduring Hannah Fisher's polite-yet-scathing insults—so much harder to evade than Ma and Dolly's direct blows—Marion started keeping a notebook of positive thoughts, and before visiting her mother-in-law she would flip through the pages to buoy her spirits. Still, she would never forget the Christmas dinner when Hannah turned to her with a cruel smile and said, *Teaching is a noble profession, but the people hired for the role are rarely exceptional.* Alec had said nothing and buried his face in wine.

But if love is measured by action, if love's sole proof is time, Alec loved her. He took care of Marion in small ways. Bought her clothes in neutral colors. Bought her foreign foods. Taught her what "off-piste" and "coup d'etat" meant. She felt he'd enjoyed her lack of pretension at first. Saw her ignorance as innocence. But in the end, she'd held him back. Marion could see that now.

* * *

September, October, November. Fall left its mark on her classroom in the form of pin-sized holes. Her wall had hosted sign-up sheets for the fall play and student council announcements and posters for SAT registration and join-our-club exhortations printed on pastel paper. She made it through Homecoming week and Parent-Teacher conferences. She saw the armory pond freeze over and then go all pondy again. She bought a new stove, a full-sized one, for Ma's house. Dolly broke up with her boyfriend and found a new boyfriend who also worked at Pearl's Grocery and who also had a truck. Marion didn't hear from Alec.

After the leaves dropped, Marion stopped scheduling meetings of STAND UP FOR YOURSELF NOW! and took up smoking cigarettes instead. Marion had been a smoker from age fifteen to eighteen. As an adolescent she'd only pretended to inhale, but now she went full smoke. The taste of tar made her feel nostalgic and young.

Like a flare cutting through the dark, Marion sometimes had a profound moment with Seven. There was the day Seven came to school very early and told her about his older brother's brain injury from football. Seven said his parents were struggling. They forgot to buy cereal. Forgot even his birthday. That morning, Marion gave Seven her lunch, an egg-salad sandwich and sour cream chips. As she sat behind her desk wishing she knew what to say, Seven sat at his desk and ate everything she gave him. When he was done he grinned at her and kissed his fingertips. How lovely to be Seven, she thought. Seven, who could take everything from her and not feel weird about it. How lovely to be a boy.

There was also the time Marion snuck into the fall play auditions and sat in the dark auditorium to watch Seven onstage. Script in hand, hair askew. The drama teacher asked him to read John Proctor's monologue about sleeping with young Abigail, and a delicious chill ran through Marion as Seven wiped away false tears and said, "For I thought of her softly. God help me, I lusted."

Then there was the winter formal. The gym had been transformed, or at least nudged toward transformation via blinking lights and tinsel. Seven was on the decorations committee and Marion had been assigned to oversee the preparations. She sat on the lowest bleacher and graded Robert Frost essays and secretly watched Seven. She liked the way he made the other kids laugh but never made fun of anyone but himself. She liked that he admitted he'd forgotten to buy more Christmas lights and the way he problem-solved the lack of space on the refreshments table by adjusting the plastic wreaths. Seven was going to be a really good grown-up. Probably handsome, too. Marion hoped being handsome and popular wouldn't ruin him.

Another teacher showed up for chaperone duty and told Marion to go home, so she drove to Ma's for dinner. When she arrived, Dolly was at the kitchen table painting her nails green and chewing out Ma. *Why didn't you call the septic man?* Ma was cooking fried eggs on the new stove. *It's embarrassing to have men over,* Ma said. She banged the pan down to unstick the stuck eggs. *We live like pigs,* Ma said. *Duh,* said

Dolly. *That's why I go to Lowell's.*

Lowell was Dolly's new boyfriend. He wasn't an addict and only did oxy on special occasions.

Ma opened the fridge and took out the Velveeta and hot sauce and put them on the table beside the piles of newspapers and unopened correspondence. "I don't want a septic man crawling around," she said. "Who knows what he'll find in there?"

Marion put the newspaper in the bin and put the bills in her purse. On Monday at lunch she'd write out the checks.

Ma dropped the pan of eggs onto the space Marion had cleared and said "Bon Appetite" before she turned to light a cigarette. Dolly closed her nail polish and lit one too. Oh what the hell, Marion thought, and lit one herself.

"So look, I can call the plumber," Marion said between puffs. "Just tell me what's broken?"

"The whole damn toilet is broken," Dolly said. "Ma keeps flushing shit down it."

"I do not," said Ma. "It's you and your maxi pads."

"Ew, Ma! That trash is Marion's."

"Speaking of trash," Ma said, and threw something at her oldest daughter. A thick envelope. Not like the others.

"Divorce papers," Ma said triumphantly.

"I thought someone had to serve her those," Dolly protested.

"Shit," Marion said. Was she having a panic attack? She breathed in the velvety charcoal of smoke.

"There are different kinds of papers," Ma explained. "Mar signed the first ones already. Didn't even hire a lawyer."

"You're so dumb," Dolly said to her sister.

Marion put the thick envelope in her purse with the others. "I'll call a plumber tomorrow," she said quietly.

"Don't even," Dolly snorted. "We need a septic man. A full-on *man*. This goes way beyond the toilet."

* * *

Alec didn't want a baby. He wanted to go to Turkey and learn to brine olives. Wanted to bike through South Korea and eat thousand-dollar sushi in Japan. But Marion wanted to stay home. So instead of a baby or a trip, they had a boulder.

To be precise, Alec had the boulder. He explained it away as an impulse purchase. One day he'd seen a billboard for boulders on the drive to his brother's house, and he kept thinking about how funny it would be to order one, and the next thing he knew, he was on the phone with the boulder people. He had it dropped into the backyard because technically you weren't allowed to have a boulder in the suburbs.

The boulder was mostly blue, but at certain times of day it looked violet or pink or elephant gray. It was exceptionally heavy. Marion hated it. She was an English teacher and could not view a large rock as anything other than a harbinger of doom. The boulder was a Trojan horse. Chekhov's gun. The white whale. Mount Kilimanjaro. Gatsby's green light. There were simply too many examples in literature for her to allow the object to exist unmetaphorically.

But in the weeks of rising spring that followed, her feelings began to change. She visited the boulder after work. Graded papers beside it at the end of the semester, during those final aching weeks of teaching summer-sick kids. There had been so many essays to read then. A towering stack that filled her with both pride and dread, and there was a heatwave that made May feel like August. But the dark side of the boulder stayed cool. One afternoon she fell asleep in its smooth shade, and after she woke, she understood that if the boulder represented something, it lay within her own interior world and not her husband's.

But surprise! He was having a mid-life crisis after all. Back in February he'd started having an emotional affair with a woman at work. An emotional affair? Marion Googled it. Apparently emotional affairs were common now? Apparently they were worse than physical affairs in some ways? Marion tried to stay positive. She threw herself into STAND UP FOR YOURSELF NOW! and made plans to repair her relationships with Ma and Dolly.

But at night she dreamed of the boulder. The boulder in moonlight. The boulder dressed as a soldier, guarding against the inexorable passage of time. The boulder as a Buddha, telling her to stay present with her loss. Marion woke from these dreams feeling betrayed. What a comforting friend the boulder had been, and what a liar it was. The Greeks were slaughtering the citizens of Troy. Chekhov's gun had gone off. She must be in the middle of Act III, waiting for the end.

* * *

Marion wasn't supposed to go to the Winter Formal, but she wanted to see the girls in their pretty dresses and pretty earrings. See the boys in clean shirts with clean faces. In the school parking lot, under the stark light above her driver's seat, she covered her mouth in a bright shade of lipstick.

The dance was almost over. She looked at her watch: eight thirty-seven. Funny. Marion was thirty-seven years old. In the lobby she caught a glimpse of her reflection in the dark glass of a trophy case. She looked old and used up. Not like her students! Flouncing, flirting, sweating. Equal parts misery and daring. She waved at a pair of girls sitting outside the gym, two student council officers who were counting up the cash and tucking it in their lockbox. She knew they'd be alright, these girls. They were very good at counting; they would find someone to love them.

Marion stepped into the gym and blinked against the dimness. She hadn't been looking for him, but there he was. Blue button-down shirt, black Chinos, spiked hair. Nothing special about him. A boy in a sea of boys.

"Hello, M!" he said.

"I'm going outside," she replied.

She squeezed past the children and went out to a loading dock area where her bare legs puckered in the cold night air. She was alone. No one vaping or drinking. Weird. The music in the gym stopped, and the silence filled with a muffled cheer. Snow Prince and Princess were about to be crowned.

She dug into her purse. Hands shaking. Odd. But managed to light a cigarette. Breathed in, and then. Oh, then. Seven appeared beside her.

"Whoops!" She dropped the cigarette to the ground and Seven picked it up. Brushed off the wet gravel. Handed it to her, still lit.

"You didn't see this," Marion said.

She sucked on the dirty filter. When Seven held out his hand for a drag, Marion hesitated, then passed it over. Letting a student watch her smoke a cigarette was just as bad as giving him one. Both would get her fired.

"Thanks," Seven said. "You're cool for a teacher."

"I'm divorced," Marion said. "I'm not cool. You're cool. You're Seven."

Was he laughing at her? No, he never laughed at anybody. Spying on him had taught her that.

"Actually," he said, "I might want to be Stephen again. What do you think?" He smiled, but Marion did not.

"I think you should stay the same," she said.

He took another suckless puff. Seven wasn't really smoking the cigarette. Just like her. Like she'd been before.

"I don't have a choice," Seven said cheerfully. "Life is change. Isn't it, M?" She couldn't tell if he was being quasi-Buddhist or was making fun of quasi-Buddhists or was just trying to sound smarter than he was. But she liked the way he said *M*. The cold sizzle rushed through her again. She'd lived more life than him, sure. But she used to be fifteen. That heart was in her still.

She reached for the cigarette and that's when it happened. Seven met her hand with his own and let his fingertips caress down her palm. It was done in an instant. The cigarette was back with her, and his cold hand had slipped into his pocket. Maybe Seven didn't think of this moment, not before, not after. But it had happened. This connection. This touch.

Seven's smile flickered and went out. "Mrs. Fisher? You okay?"

"Oh, Seven," she murmured. "I could really use a friend."

It was awful. Awful. She didn't deserve a Bradley Cooper type. Or Alec. Or anyone.

Seven felt the change immediately. Bad air all around them. He stepped back and tugged at the elbow of his shirt, mumbled "Snow Prince," and left.

Marion startled awake as if from a dream. Said, "Oh my god," and dropped the cigarette.

What the fuck was she doing?

* * *

Twenty minutes later, Marion crouched behind Mr. Holland's hedge to spy on her old house. It was 10:07 P.M. Not a good hour for an accurate assessment. The replacement could be asleep in Alec's bed. They could be out to dinner. They could be in Turkey squeezing olives for all Marion knew.

Crouching, shuffling, she veered through the side gate into the backyard. Her purse caught on the chipped wood of the fence. Her toes were numb. Was it going to snow? No, it didn't smell wet. She tugged the purse free. Felt her hands shake again. Thought: maybe I should invest in some gloves. Thought: my problem is not a lack of gloves.

She began to suspect he'd removed it. Then saw its shape in the dark. Familiar. She had to restrain herself from running to it. Her old friend. Marion's feet caught against the hard dirt in the raised beds of her frozen garden. She reached out a cold hand to meet its shoulder. Put her cheek upon it. Dragged her numb mouth across the stone face and let her bare knees drop onto the grass.

She laid her neck against the boulder and tried to ignore the twinge of pain in her back. When the moon finally appeared, Marion made a wish on it, that she could take the boulder with her. Magically fit it into her purse next to the envelopes. Drop it on top of Ma's table and eat eggs with it every day.

But the boulder was what it was. Superbly indifferent. Her ridiculous attempts at love would never disturb it.

* * *

"Hello, M."

"Hello, Boulder."

The ground was cold, but the boulder didn't mind. It was accustomed to a frigid and unyielding earth.

"Boulder," she said, curling into its curves, "nobody loves me."

"What is love?" asked the Boulder.

Marion thought before answering. "It's letting someone see you. The good parts and the bad."

"What is bad?" asked the Boulder.

"Oh, it's stuff you'd like to change about yourself."

"What is change?" asked the Boulder.

"You know, you're getting kind of annoying," said Marion. "And here I was, thinking I needed you."

"I don't need anything," the Boulder said. "Or anyone."

It said this kind of haughtily in her opinion. But she forgave it quickly and said, "I know, Boulder. I wish I were more like you."

"You will be someday," the Boulder said. "When you're dead."

Marion knew what the Boulder said was true, but still, it wasn't very nice. The Boulder didn't have good manners, but that didn't stop her from sobbing on its shoulder.

When she'd finished she said to her friend, "Goodbye, my Boulder. I'll miss you."

The Boulder didn't offer Marion any sentiment in return. But that was all right, because what else could you expect from a boulder? *Stand up for yourself now,* she told herself. *What makes you think you aren't enough?*

The boulder couldn't stand up, but Marion could. She got to her feet and slammed her palms together and headed for the gate. If she escaped without getting caught, she'd try to be grateful. Like, for her job. For all the things she hadn't fucked up yet, even though she'd arrived at Screw It o'clock.

She drove back to Ma's slowly, snaking through the dark streets with the radio on and the heat blasting. Love would leave her quickly now. It had done what it needed to do. Came. Tested her. Left. And what happened next? She didn't know. The books she assigned always ended there, in the aftermath of loss.

No wonder her students disliked them. ■

TEMPLE OF HOPE
Varun U. Shetty

I lay my hands on a cold desk—
every grain quivers with a prayer,
a wish, a regret.

The computer is a lamp at night.
I stare into it like a moth. I find a story
of disease, and only disease.

ICU monitors sing like cicadas, songs
that may or may not mean something,
a metronome I hold on to.

The whiteboards tell you what to aim for every day, reminding you
that getting your blood pressure up is a worthy goal,

and so is being pain-free,

and so is getting up out of bed.

The stark white hospital light floods every corner like hope,

but the news, with its numbers and words, is now meaningless
because all they can hear are the sounds of their hearts
sinking.

Hope built this room that the janitors now clean,
removing every residue of loss.

People smile a lot no matter what.

People say thank you no matter what.

I look out the window of a room. I see the great lake.
The sailboats drift away from a melting sun.

This room isn't lit with the white light yet.

The sheets are clean,

the whiteboard, empty.

THE DESIDERATIVE INFIX
Mark Crimmins

1

I listened carefully to every word that proceeded forth from the cakehole of Dobson and regurgitated as much as I could on the in-class tests. The guy was easy enough to figure out. What he wanted to hear was what he had a tendency to say. If you confined yourself exclusively to writing transcripts of the particular brand of bullshit he spewed forth on Mondays, Wednesdays, and Fridays between eleven and twelve, he had this remarkable ability to consider you a genius. In his bourbon-beruffled brain, all the voices he heard were his own.

But I had a problem. I shelled out a hundred bucks a pop to the essay-writing service on Knowles Street above Little Lebanon, rewarding myself with a shish kebab dinner for my enterprise when I picked the papers up the day before the due dates. I always ate my celebratory meal at the little window table across from the tourist poster of Beirut that hung on the wall. My man Marco, my "tutor" at Re:Write, did a good job with the papers. Marco being a grad student in philosophy didn't hurt—I pulled As on all the assignments he wrote. Dobson seemed to think Marco was the shit and I got all the credit. It was nice. The comments on my *Beloved* paper were typical.

Excellent stuff: you do a fine job of highlighting the distinctions between the Morrisonian and Faulknerian perspectival shifts; your comparison of Beloved's arrival in the narrative to the birth of Venus is quite percipient; and your phenomenological analysis of Beloved's monologue demonstrates a high level of critical acumen.

So obviously I wasn't concerned about the papers, and I got the hang of the tests pretty quick. My problem was with the participation mark. Dobson wanted "active participation" and there were a number of clever sods in the class who grabbed the lion's share of the allotted space. Moreover, by dint of the fact that they were clever sods, they tended to get big-time brownie points with the Dob by saying stuff that was pretty impressive in class, even if it made you want to stab them in the neck with your cool orthopedic pen. Needless to say, I wasn't subsidizing Marco's master's degree in continental thought in order to get a B out of the class. Nuh. And I could see it coming: Dobson was gonna shaft me on participation and render the fact that I was now poor even more noxious by ensuring that the 20 percent "discretionary mark," as he called it, came whistling down onto the vulnerable throat of my inability to think of slick things to say in class, neatly lopping off the head of the possibility that at the end of the term I would be rewarded with my hard-earned (and expensive) A and thus maintain the average I needed to continue my career as a James Tipton Memorial Scholar. I needed some swanky stuff to say in class and I needed it fast. I was going to get into Harvard grad school and fatso at the blackboard there wasn't going to stop me with his little leather elbow patches, his gargantuan tum, and that tuft of hair stranded at the front of his bald patch like a tumbleweed without moment.

2

Fate intervenes in the form of an email from the Wabi crew. They're throwing a party in the dance studio above the Elmo on the first Friday in November, and I'm *there*. Task's spinning this set of funky-ass minimal tech house, and I'm a lawng way from twelve hours before, when I was listening to some poorly remixed Pomumbo Mojumbo take on Shirley Jackson's "The Lottery" from His Royal Highness Dobcat the Dob. Task is just laying down those sweet trax and taking me places I ain't never been in class, but in the middle of his set, he chills things in a big way so I go to the bar at the back for a beer.

I'm just chugging this Heineken, talking to the coat check girl about what the scoop is with those windows behind the bar—every time I look back there it's like I'm hallucinating—and Max appears at my side. I haven't seen him since Speedy J gave the Labor Day revelers a religious experience at Element, so we've got some catching up to do. We talk about all kinds of shit but eventually I get onto the subject of school and—because it's Freytag I guess—I end up telling him about Dob the Dob and my diminutive dilemma. Task's still up there on the Technics, locked into some super low-vibe groove, and Max starts telling me about Hiphelp.

"It's this cool site outta the Bay Area. Totally legit. You just log on, register, select a discipline, get in the chat room for your topic, pick an interlocutor, pay, like, a few bucks, and you've got ten minutes of conversation about your subject. They post some old transcripts online, so you can see what it's like for free. It's a great site. Really easy to navigate. Well worth the money. I heard a lot of their staff are moonlighting lit profs. They really know their stuff. I think it was a couple of Stanford brats that started it. Anyway, you should check it out. Those guys'll give you plenty to say in class, no problem."

Not long after this, Task starts winding it up to peak out his set and we head back towards the dance floor. It's only when I'm walking home across campus around six with a thirty-two-ounce sorbet Slurpee that I remember the conversation with Max, and when I reach home, I get on the Net, type in the address, and there it is: Hiphelp.com.

3

All you had to do was select Litchats, click on a subject heading, get into a chat room, and there was the discussion of the book you were interested in. I decided I'd know what was up better if I already knew the book in question. I'd read *White Noise* five times, so I decided to give that a go. I clicked on the title and entered the space. There was a dialogue going on between badstude and sprechtmaestro.

b: Okay, so where do I begin with this novel?

s: Start at the beginning: with the narration itself.

b: Okay.

s: The novel is what Gladney says, so you have to analyze what he says to figure out who he is. It's a classic case of first-person singularity.

b: Um, meaning?

s: Meaning it'll cost you two five-dollar credits to get a more in-depth answer.

b: Shit! I only have one credit left!

s: Rules is rules, baby. That's all I can give ya.

b: Can you at least talk for just a bit about Babette?

s: She's a slut.

b: No she isn't—she's forced into it.

s: Whatever.

b: My prof's a poststructuralist.

s: Okay—it's a bit foggy up here on Nob Hill—let's say Babette is an agent of the proactive impulse.

b: That's the stuff.

s: She wiggles and squirms in the panopticon of the male gaze.

b: Nice!

s: Mink figuratively bludgeons her to orgasmic death with his transcendental signifier.

b: Now we're talking.

s: Within the oppressive construct of an *écriture masculin,* she has no other option but to become a devotee of Dylar.

b: Just sec. I'm gonna use my roommate's Visa to buy some more credits. Back in five.

s: Ciao.

I figured I could slip into this gap while badstude was away. Dobson had put *Infinite Jest* on the syllabus, and it looked like it was gonna be a nightmare coming up with the right stuff to say about it in class. I decided to give old sprechtmaestro a try. I hitched myself up in my chair and reached for the keyboard.

n: Any chance of a powwow about David Foster Wallace?

s: He's kinda hot right now. Got any credits?

n: No, but I've got my card right here.

s: Select Restricted from the Main Menu and click on Private Consult. Four credits gets you five minutes.

n: Whoa.

s: Wallace is the man baby. I mean the man, baby. It's gotta be what it's gotta be.

n: Okay. Gimme a minute.

I selected a twenty-credits package, followed the instructions, and paid. Five minutes didn't seem like a long time to discuss a novel over a thousand pages long, but hey—I was jigged from the Wabi party and just wanted to get a grip. Now I had sprechtmaestro all to myself. I guess badstude was just SOL. Or maybe sprechtmaestro was ambidextrous and would jiz her with his left hand while he jazzed me with his right.

n: Okay, so what do I say about this book in class?

s: Tell me about the prof.

n: He's a tight-ass who thinks he's hip.

s: Age?

n: Fifty-sixtyish. A lifetime no lifer. Mister likes it both ways. Loves his po-mo schlock and at the same time he's totally old-school. He even talks about grammar.

s: Talk about the man who wrote the book's penchant for group genitives.

n: It's got group sex in it?

s: I'm talking about syntax.

n: Okay.

s: Talk about stylistic features that subvert linguistic and cultural norms.

n: What the hell's a group genitive?

s: Look it up in Brown's *Grammar of English Grammars* later.

n: Okay, what else?

s: Suggest the periphery of the text is the center: get into the footnotes.

n: Just a second…

I was reaching for a pen and a piece of paper to scribble some of this stuff down, but sprechtmaestro was ahead of me.

s: You can print off a transcript of this conversation for one credit when we're through.

n: Thanx. Tell me more about the footnotes.

s: Ask him about 2CB. It's mentioned in the eighth footnote, FN 8. Let him demonstrate the fact that he's chemical savvy.

n: Okidoki.

s: Even if he doesn't know what it is, he'll like the fact that you haven't heard of it—it'll make him feel less out of touch.

n: OK.

s: Point out that you seem to have found an error in the subfootnotes to FN 110. Check out subfootnote *d* on page 1,006, cross-ref it with the list on page 1,021, and suggest that the little *d* should actually follow the date of the Filbert letter.

n: Done.

s: Use FN 77 to argue that the novel itself is a massive parodic exercise in narratorial attention surfeit.

n: Nice. How about another stylistic feature?

s: Get into the compound adjective clusters.

n: How?

s: First circle them all as you read them. Then go online and buy the definitive article on compound adjectives. It's in HighBeam's database. It's easy to find. Pavel Denisovic, "THE WINE-DARK, GONG-TORMENTED, SCROTUM-TIGHTENING SEA."

n: Got it. How about the big picture?

s: Talk about the temporal schema as a critique of commodity culture. Get the chronological sequence from the list on 223. Read and quote Walter Benjamin's article "The Work of Art in the Age of Mechanical Reproduction." You might also want to read Dieter Hogan's "The Work of Art in the Age of Mechanical Reproduction in the Age of Digital Reproduction." That's in the same database.

n: How do I get a handle on the style?

s: Take the fifth paragraph of the forty-ninth section as a touchstone. Talk about the DFW sentence. Especially the long sentence. The longest one's 734 words long. It's on pages 431–433. Contrast it with the 623-worder on 487–489. Then unpack the paragraph on 581–587.

n: I'm almost outta time. Can you say something about the cultural stuff? The prof is big on culture.

s: Look into the Canadian connection. Go to HighBeam again. Buy Joseph Dearborn's "A Tremendous Canada of Light: Representations of Canada in the Contemporary American Novel." It's in *Modern Fiction Studies.* Summer 2002. Time's up. Ciao.

I printed off the transcript and saw that sprechtmaestro was back in the chat room haggling with badstude over credits. It'd been worth checking out. I logged out, showered, and read over the transcript before I fell asleep.

4

I'm in class the next week, struggling not to strangle Clever Sod Exhibit A: Angela Leigh. Dobson's been rabbiting on about the issue of naming in *The Crying of Lot 49*, and Angela puts her hand up to interrupt him so they can bond over the mythopoetic resonance of Oedipa Maas. She's wearing super-funky Swear shoes, white-and-gray camouflage pants, a Luscious sweatshirt, and a black Bebe baseball hat with a red logo.

"I just want to say that I agree with you. I think it's amazing the extent to which Pynchon creates a cultural palimpsest with this novel. There's so much inscription and reinscription, so much layering of historical strata that it's almost impossible to feel like you're actually tuned into anything except the wealth of allusion."

Neither of them know it, but I'm actually recording everything they're saying with a little gizmo I bought from I-Spy at the beginning of the term. Dobson comes right back at Angela, who's emerging as the Queen of the Clever Sods.

"I know what you mean, Angela. It takes a considerable amount of concentration to keep up with Pynchon, and you're never quite sure you're getting it all."

"Peter Pinguid and Stanley Koteks are pretty easy to peg, but I was wondering if you thought the protagonist is a sort of Freudian red herring?"

"Good question. What we need to remember, Angela, is that Pynchon is playing with us here. He's practicing the art of fiction within certain ludic parameters, but we can't ever locate their precise boundaries."

"So what you're saying is that there's an uncertainty principle at work in the associative chain?"

"Yes. Very well put, Angela. The postmodern is characterized by instability in the relation between signifier and signified, and Pynchon is a good—perhaps the best—example."

"Do you think Pynchon is returning here, in a way, to the kind of narrative praxis he employed in the early stories? 'Under the Rose,' for example?"

"Well, you're right to suggest that we should keep an eye on Pynchon's developmental trajectory. While the two texts are only five years apart, I think we can safely say that Pynchon evolved from the sort of data density that was in danger of reaching saturation point in the story you mentioned, which I nevertheless credit Bellow for publishing in *The Noble Savage*. In 'Under the Rose' the action remains clogged, whereas *Crying* gives a swift centrifugal movement to the sequence of event."

"Don't you think the action is centrifugal in 'Rose,' though?"

"Perhaps, Angela, perhaps, but I think we need to maintain an important distinction between the precise qualitative nature of these disparate centrifugalities."

"Could you, um, tell us a bit more about this distinction?"

"Well, why don't you come to my office after class, and maybe we can continue this discussion there."

"Okay."

Needless to say, I'm not the only one in the class who finds these periodic verbal copulations a bit on the hard side to take. Ginny Lopez is rolling her eyes at me across the room and shuffling in her seat with irritation. The other clever sods in class are sitting up, necks forward, waiting for a chance to upstage Angela in the broad minefield of minutes ahead of us, but as it turns out, no one gets a chance to wag a tongue. It's only as I'm having a smoke after class that I remember sprechtmaestro had used that word *praxis* in his chat about DeLillo with badstude. I don't have the luxury of not knowing Angela's voiceprint well enough to know right off that she's a different verbal animal from badstude, but it's well within her abilities to adopt a rhetorical disguise. I might not be the only person in the class who takes advantage of Hiphelp's services. That's the difficult thing about college these days—there's no keeping up with the inventive cheating of the keeners. But it wouldn't really help me if Angela Leigh was getting the dope on the texts from Hiphelp or not. If she was, I couldn't assassinate her without assassinating myself. If she wasn't, that still didn't help me with my participation mark snag. She was so getting an A for participation she already had a pointy head.

5

I got a copy of *Infinite Jest* and started underlining the bits that sprechtmaestro thought were important. We were only spending a week on *The Crying of Lot 49*, after which we were going to read two collections of short stories, *Will You Please Be Quiet, Please?* and *Song of the Silent Snow*, the Carver for our seventies selection, the Selby for our eighties gig. Say what he might about historical discontinuity, Dobson was a sucka for chronology. That left us three weeks to finish up with the wily practitioner of the group genitive. But before we got to Wallace, we had to turn in a paper on one of the collections, and, of course, I needed to start making my presence felt in class. It was getting late in the term and I hadn't said enough.

Marco at Re:Write did a bang-up job of putting Carver in his place on my first paper to pull an A+. When I got the paper back, I took Marco to the Squire and Squirrel and plied him with Guinness. Dobson was elated with my work:

Andy,

This is so good a paper that I could write a paper on it! (Actually, I was wondering if you'd mind me using some of your comments, including your wonderful title, "A Fusion of Minimalist Horizons: The Diurnality of Aufhebung in Carver's Dawning Ensemble," as part of my upcoming paper for the Carver panel at the Modern Language Association Convention in San Diego?) This was a wonderful piece of writing, one that convinces me your graduate school aspirations are not entirely unfounded. I have made a photocopy of your essay and will consult it in the research for my appendix to the Dublinday edition of Carver's complete works, forthcoming from Princeton University Press. It is a pleasure to read papers such as yours, which make teaching worthwhile and fulfill one of the highest mandates of tertiary learning—to ensure that the education process is a two-way street. This paper places you near the top of the class. I look forward to your end-of-term comments and your summations on the final. Best of luck, and congratulations on an outstanding paper!

So Marco had earned his Guinness. Moreover, he gave me a hot tip on a *Concise Encyclopedia of Western Philosophy* that was on sale for five bucks at ABC Books. He said it would be all I needed to be able to back up the philosophical claims he had made in my papers, if it came to that. For the Carver discussions, I just barfed up little chunks of the paper Marco had obliged me by writing. I picked it up a week before the due date so it could seem like the culmination of my reflections in class. Selby I got right into. Everybody knows targeted readings of some texts are crucial to maintaining the appearance that you're deeply involved in a course. I had a few discussions with sprechtmaestro about *Song of the Silent Snow*, and Dobson clearly thought what I had to say was au courant. He went apeshit over the erased contraction stuff, preferring the more Derridean *contraction under erasure*. He thought my reading of the fortune cookie as an objective correlative with inscape was just the bomb.

And whatever happened to Angela Leigh? Once I started making slick comments, she was on me like a swarm of bees after class. Which way was I walking? Where did I study? Which grad schools was I thinking of applying to? Did I think the Princeton prep course for the Graduate Reading Exam was worth the money? Had I taken any practice tests at the testing center? She even started running a few paper ideas by me before she started to write. By the time we'd finished the Carver and the Selby, Angela and I had emerged as the prime combatants in the verbal arena. The last three weeks of class were going to be a war for oral supremacy on the battlefield of *Infinite Jest*.

6

I decide I'll supplement my in-class sycophancy with a few visits to Dobson's office hours. We chew it a bit about Carver and Selby. When I stop by a third time, his office door is closed. He's inside and he's not alone. I wait a few minutes and knock. I hear paper shuffling and whispering. The door opens and Angela emerges. Her hair's a bit ruffled. She's escorted out with a friendly pat on the shoulder from TopDob, who tells me he just needs to make a quick phone call and then he'll be right with me. He closes the door, leaving me alone with my Nemesis. She immediately asks me how far along I am with the Wallace readings. I lie, telling her I haven't even bought the novel yet. She says she's only got as far as the microwave suicide scene and that she was kind of traumatized by it. That's what she came to discuss with Dobbie. There was some personal stuff she needed to talk about that related to this, which was why the door was closed. After she's pumped me for what she can, she says she's gotta run and *fwap fwap fwap* she disappears down the stairs.

When she's gone, I notice the drop box attached to Dobson's door isn't empty. I pull an unsealed manila envelope out of the box and check the name on the front: Angela Leigh. So eager to get through Dobson's door she forgot to pick it up on her way in. So intent on getting what she could out of me that she left it behind on her way out. I stick my ear to Dobson's door. He's following through on his promise, talking to the departmental secretary about his flight arrangements for the MLA convention. It sounds like I have a few minutes. I don't waste any time. I pull Angela's paper out of the envelope and have a quick sken at the typed comments beneath the large A+.

Angela,

You seem very comfortable wrapping your mind around issues of sex and subservience in Carver. I think you capture the main thrust of what he attempts to do with his tales of banal existences lived out in the corral of marital doom. I really liked what you had to say about the transcendental potential of ecstatic submission. I think you're right—Carver emphasizes the mundane in order to highlight the manner in which transgression can also function as a saving device, an upward fall. Your prose is very nicely shaped, and the disparate elements of your thesis come together nicely in the satisfying climax of your conclusion. Bravo!

I've barely stuffed the paper back in its sheath after copying this down when I hear Dobson bang down the phone and stride over to the door. He thanks me again for my paper on Carver and tells me how excited he is to present "more polished" versions of a few of my ideas at the upcoming conference. While he's talking, I notice Angela's Bebe cap on the rug behind his desk.

7

Five days before the final rounds of class discussions were to begin, I still hadn't started the novel, and I was getting a bit concerned. But sprechtmaestro had been earning his keep of late, and I had a plan. The Hiphelp guru had given me notice. I had to read *Jest*, he said, and absorb all of it. This was the text that would wear out the other keeners. I just had to put in an insane amount of work in a short time. I'd established that badstude was none other than Angela herself in a discussion I'd had on Hiphelp a week before. A disembodied voice emerging from the mists of San Francisco a continent away, sprechtmaestro had proved a bit more difficult to diddle out of his professional integrity than Angela had thought. Tired of badstude's finagling, sprechtmaestro struck back at her by letting me know— for only ten credits—that she was constantly on the site and failing miserably in her efforts to scam the service.

Sprechtmaestro convinced me I could absorb *Infinite Jest* in fifty hours, and while I was giving this proposition the old bake test in the brainbox, I received a bit of good news in the form of a check. My winnings for coming fifth in the World Rubik's Cube Speedsolving Championships at the Science Center the preceding August finally came in the mail. The $500 replaced the $200—plus Guinnesses— that I'd shelled out to Marco for my papers, leaving 260 bones I'd forgotten were mine. I rented a PT Cruiser and made a reservation at the Sheraton on the lake up in Thorndale. It was the off-season, so I had no problem wangling an early check-in and a late checkout for the Friday night and the Sunday afternoon before the Monday class when we'd start on Wallace. Sandwiched between two two-hour buffers were fifty hours in which I could sequester myself with the novel and upload it into my head using mnemonic techniques I'd learned from a little book Marco had given me.

I spent all my time at the Sheraton reading the novel, nourished by four large pepperoni pizzas I'd ordered from 2-4-1 and jacked up on Sudafeds and a two-four of Classic Coke. I worked to the clock, reading packets of twenty pages every forty-five minutes and then taking a break to do five minutes of mnemonics and five speedsolves of the Rubik's cube by the window to keep my mental agility in high gear. After the speedsolves, I'd stare at the lake for five minutes and just try to clear my mind and tune into the view. Back at home, I had twelve hours to review my color-coded markings in the text and to shift every facet of textual detail from my hippocampus into my cortex. There were nine class slots to work with, so I did some planning. By Monday I was ready.

8

Diary of a Prospective Harvard Grad Student: Monday 17 November 2003

Angela snarfs the chance to get the first word in when Dobbie asks us for our first impressions, speaking right into the mini-mike I have rigged up in the hood of my Lithium sweatshirt. *I'm really interested in these symbols that take the place of chapter numbers. I think it's clear that Wallace is invoking the lunar here, and this seems to tie in with the theme of madness in the novel and negative luminescence in the Incandenza family.* Dobcat, of course, thinks this is *merveilleuse*. Ginny Lopez says she thinks the book is too long. Colby Williams deems it pretentious. Bart in the back corner, the processing power of a Cray supercomputer between his ears, goes into overdrive talking about the novel's allusive density. He's actually invented a formula to chart the ratio of allusive density in texts, and he assures us all that Wallace is way off the charts. I play dumb with my stuff about the significance of the group genitive, which Dobbie has noticed but nobody has scrutinized closely. I turn a few heads when I tell the class there are 919 group genitives in the text. Who's going to check that number? From there I move into saying that the prominence of this grammatical anomaly suggests an inquiry into the idea of possession as such, and—rejecting the tyranny of stylistic convention—reinforces the novel's status as a work that subverts traditional fictional form. Dobson finishes up by reminding us that the text is complex and admonishing us to read all the footnotes.

Diary of a Prospective Harvard Grad Student: Wednesday 19 November 2003

Angela looks exhausted when I walk into the classroom and take my customary place in front of her, my faithful hoodie falling open behind me like a feed sack she can nibble from if she gets peckish during class. The sweet little nozzle of the I-Spy mini-mike is pointed right at her tonsils. She seizes the initiative fast with some fancy mouthwork about digressivity in Hal's brother's first monologue. Following sprechtmaestro's advice, I ask about the issue of drugs in the novel, a tactic worthy of Tostão: Dobson talks for half an hour about the novel as a pharmacopoeia. But Angela's back just before the bell with some super politically savvy remarks about the FLQ crisis.

Diary of a Prospective Harvard Grad Student: Friday 21 November 2003

Ginny Lopez steals Angela's fire with a slick job of getting her hand up first when Dobson asks about the suicide scene. Catrina Jones and Candace Zhao spark up a marathon discussion about tennis in the novel, and the rest of us are pummeled into silence. Bart manages to jump in to confirm that Wallace's mathematical analyses of tennis can only be appreciated with a sound knowledge of higher mathematics. Dobson tells us to be ready to discuss the middle of the novel next week.

Diary of a Prospective Harvard Grad Student: Monday 24 November 2003

Angela looks like she's read the novel four times since last Friday. Her eyes are two little light-emitting diodes of determination. Zack

Bingham praises the six blank pages at the end of the hardcover edition, arguing that they are an integral part of the novel. Angela holds that the novel deconstructs itself. I jump in to say that if that were the case, Papa Incandenza's least favorite word probably wouldn't be *deconstructed*. I add that the transcript of the phone conversation betrays no disagreement on this matter between the Incandenza brothers and then dribble into how this relates to Wallace's use of the desiderative infix, which even Dobcat needs defined. The infix stuff proves well worth the coin I've slung sprechtmaestro's way to find out about it. Angela snaps back that she's not sure all this otiose grammatical stuff is that relevant. She says it smacks of outmoded New Critical formalism. I say if that's the case, then Derrida's paper on Lévi-Strauss at Johns Hopkins in 1967 must have been completely irrelevant. Dobson interjects by saying he doesn't want this discussion "to disappear *derrière* the *rideau* of purely academic *disputatio*."

Diary of a Prospective Harvard Grad Student: Wednesday 26 November 2003

Angela's back today with her respect for the novel's social concern, which is clearly a stab at my esoteric bullshit. She's all over the Boston halfway house stuff as a critique of the welfare system. She lauds Wallace for his grounding in the concrete and particular. In addition to this, she simply *has* to say something about the suicide scene. She's been so deeply moved by Wallace's portrait of death by microwave that she's been having nightmares of finding her roommates splattered all over their kitchen in rez. A rare personal reference from Exhibit A. Could it be she's cracking? I follow up with a statement about the counternarrative of espionage. Dobson ain't gettin' no affective fallacies outta *moi*.

Diary of a Prospective Harvard Grad Student: Friday 28 November 2003

Angela's so exhausted today that I have no problem beating her out of the blocks with my stuff about the compound adjective. My comment draws from her a sigh of annoyance so full of frustration that I'm stumped for how to spell it when I type up the transcript later. Still, I manage to link compound adjectivity with the infix stuff to forge a point about Wallace's grammatical peculiarities and their relation to the Wallace sentence in general. Angela counters with more social commentary. She's concerned about the references to

Nucks and the generally prejudicial portrait of Canadians in the text. I reply that Wallace's incorporation of Canadian material into the text strikes a new and cosmopolitan note in contemporary American fiction—a transcendence of borders. But then Angela gets in the last word with a long eulogy to Wallace's use of street language. Could badstude be taking a few cues from me?

Diary of a Prospective Harvard Grad Student: Monday 1 December 2003

I've gotta get all this stuff in about the long sentences in the book before Angela has a chance to shape the direction of discussion, so I set Dobbie's tumbleweedy dome in a lather with my observations about the Wallace sentence. I've typed up and printed off copies of the three longest sentences in the novel and distributed them to my sickened classmates on crisp ("For Quality Documents!") Weyerhaeuser sheets. I have the sentences divided into categories and even bust a bit of Chomsky when Dobson asks me if I can diagram one of the sentences. Dobcat's head bobs approvingly as I stand beneath the syntax tree I've drawn on the board and suggest that Wallace writes in transformational grammar.

Diary of a Prospective Harvard Grad Student: Wednesday 3 December 2003

It's no great surprise when I walk into the room that Angela is already distributing her graph depicting the functions of the footnotes in the novel. I have to hand it to her—it's pretty impressive stuff. The only problem is that Dobson looks at her slightly more sidewise than usual while she's doing this. When your opponent's imitating your moves, you know you're winning the contest. It takes her twenty minutes or so to explain her graph and read the relevant passages, niftily tying her arguments together by returning to her point about the rootedness of the novel in the real. But then she undermines herself by actually trying to argue that the footnotes are the roots (as in, tree roots) of the text. This gives me a chance to cross-examine her. I ask about her method of reading the footnotes, and she lets go the fact that she read the entire novel first, then read all the footnotes. Dobson pulls a face as she says this. He then asks me about my method of reading the novel. I say I think it's best to read the novel using Murray Petrovich's method for reading complex texts, called integrated positional analysis and based on a nodal model of narrative architecture. Fortunately for me, time's up when Bart says he has a few questions about my terminology.

Diary of a Prospective Harvard Grad Student: Friday 5 December 2003

Dobson follows his own convention of asking us to give our impressions and analysis of the novel as a whole for the final class period. He asks us to keep our comments to a few sentences, and he specifically wants to hear first from people who've been quiet in class. For once, Angela Leigh aspires to be the last to speak. When Dobson gets to her, she puts her tongue to work.

"I just want to say that this novel is a work of genius and I absolutely can't believe the audacity with which Wallace has done this—this is better than *Gravity's Rainbow*, *JR*, and *Underworld* combined. I just think it's kind of a shame that so much of the class discussion has been mired down in considerations of Wallace's syntax and punctuation. This takes us away from the novel's best features: its cosmic design, its sense of tragedy, and its refusal to forego meaningful social commentary in favor of purely aesthetic concerns."

I haven't spoken by this point, and Dobson is the one who asked for Angela's opinion before mine. Now he turns his tufty head towards me and—with a glance at his Gianfranco Ferré watch— says that I'll have the last word. I deliver my little memorized speech without a hitch.

"I agree that the novel is a work of genius—a vicocyclometer, as Joyce called *Finnegans Wake*, with which the parallels are obvious. By the same token, I think we could call *Infinite Jest* a proteiform graph, even a chaosmos. I also think Wallace's commodified fictional history is a creative coup, and I'm sure my classmates will agree with me that—in honor of the author—2003 should henceforth be known as the Year of the John Bonham Cadillac Ad. The only thing more impressive than the novel itself is the organic nature of Wallace's oeuvre as a whole, with *Brief Interviews* and the math book growing out of *Infinite Jest* and *Girl with Curious Hair*, *Broom of the System*, and *Supposedly Fun Thing* functioning as a foundation for the pyramid of *Jest*."

Dobson thanks me for my eloquent and concise summary. He says a few things about the final and we're through. While I'm lingering after class, Angela storms by me without a word into the winter sunshine.

9

The day of the final we had our first snow of the year, and I walked across campus as the sun was setting. I looked past the dome of the library at the Monet panorama taking shape in the air, billions of crystals refracting the rage of the sun, each flake like ash descending. Over on the dim horizon, a whole diapason of oranges and pinks took shape and then—as I watched from the silent center of the quad—all other colors slowly bled into crimson. ∎

FOUND
Kirk Glaser

hands dig   ash under nails
marble shards   mark the spot

a jewelry box   *did he steal?*
sun beats   hours to nothing

found beyond   fire-pooled metal
a few beads   sweat pocking ash

a spark glints   not to be
confounded   with mere glitter

of broken glass   carbon-scorched
facets unscathed   the diamond

leaping to hand   grandmother's ring
shank and shoulder   melted to

rusting nails   the brilliant
home in her   cinder-creased palm

she never saw   the house burn
but keeps hearing   glass crack

in dreams   she drew
the woman   skin shattering

her hands   cups of flame
a diamond   falling into

her palm   like a hope
too adamant   to burn

THE OLIVE TREE
William V. Roebuck

We have a goldendoodle named Charlee. She has the size of a young dog but with a huge residue of playful romp and what-the-heckness of a puppy. We'd been having a brutal winter, overall, with several January snows that had pushed the Washington, DC, area to the extremes of the area's meteorological variations. Plants in the yard were toughing it out like the rest of us. At one point, I saw a couple of young saplings I'd planted the previous year, bowed over under the weight of ice and snow, as if stapled to the ground. Trees don't shiver and their leaves don't chatter, but the fragile olive tree and pomegranate looked like they felt the urge. Charlee did not know all this. She had a thick, warm coat and seemed to enjoy playing or resting in the yard, even on the most frigid days.

Between winter storms one week in early February, I headed off to the Outer Banks, about a five-hour drive south. I was planning to work remotely for the week, taking along our other dog while my wife kept Charlee. It was blustery and cold at the beach, unseasonably so for North Carolina. After three or four days of Zoom meetings, editing articles, and addressing various personnel issues for a foreign policy institute ("think tank" in Washington parlance) focused on the Middle East, I got the call from my wife.

She eased into it, casually making sure I had a glass of wine in hand, and then plowed ahead, with care: Charlee had had "an accident" with one of our young trees. My wife feigned anger, with a mild exclamation directed the lovely creature's way, and it became clear to me: first, that something had gone terribly wrong with my little tree, and second, Charlee would be well protected from bearing any of the consequences (a bit of scolding) for her depredations.

What exactly had she done and what difference did it make? To make it clear, let me back up some twenty months. I had returned in the summer of 2020 from service in northeastern Syria, where I had been embedded as a diplomat with elite US Special Forces elements. We lived on the ramshackle compound of an abandoned cement factory in the remote Syrian countryside; the makeshift military base was reinforced with concertina wire and Kurdish guards. The Special Forces were fighting the remnants of ISIS and I was manning the diplomatic ramparts, so to speak, maintaining informal but critical relations with our local partner in the fight against ISIS, the Kurdish-led Syrian Democratic Forces, or SDF. I had spent the previous two years, from early 2018, either on the ground in Syria or doing the diplomatic circuit in Washington and Europe, helping hold together the global coalition organized for the fight against ISIS.

It was time for me to wrap up my service in Syria, which ended up being one of the great adventures in my twenty-eight-year diplomatic career, and head back to Washington. To help an old diplomat out, these Special Forces operators, as they call themselves, offered me a seat on their C-130 military cargo aircraft that was ferrying a bunch of them back to Fort Bragg, in coastal North Carolina. I made my way from northeastern Syria to neighboring northern Iraq for this flight home. We took off from a military airbase in Erbil, the capital of the Kurdistan Regional Government.

To make me feel welcome—and ensure I didn't get lost, I imagine—the US military assigned a couple of "control officers" to loosely escort me home. One of them, a particularly engaging guy named Josh, described for me in general terms, as we awaited the plane to fill, his service in Iraq and his excitement at seeing his family again. He noted he was bringing a few very young-growth olive trees and pomegranates to plant on his property. I saluted his good fortune, communicating how exciting that was. To feed the conversation a bit, I mentioned how I felt a strong attachment to olive trees after so many years of seeing beautiful fields of them in various Middle East climes. Despite my initial protestations, he ended up bequeathing me one young olive tree plant and one pomegranate plant, each with about two feet of growth, and both with origins in the fertile hills of northern Iraq. Olive trees, I learned subsequently, do not grow from seeds but rather from cut roots or branches buried in the soil and allowed to root. *Olea europaea*, in botanical lingo, has been cultivated in the Mediterranean for the past six thousand years. The Bible, particularly the Old Testament, is littered with references to the olive tree (and significant references to the pomegranate as well, including the lovely Song of Solomon reference to "thy temples are like a piece of pomegranate within thy locks"). When we eventually touched down in Fayetteville a couple of days later, after overnighting at the large US Air Force base in Ramstein, Germany, Josh delivered the small, fragile plants to my hotel room.

I planted them in Arlington that summer of 2020, first in large pots we kept in the house that first winter, and then eventually in the soil of our front yard. A drupe, or stone fruit, like cherries or peaches, in which a fleshy outer covering surrounds a hard, seeded pit, the olive has been prized for centuries, as even culinary novices might surmise, for the high concentration of oil (nearly 30 percent) in its outer flesh. Olive trees' tolerance for cold weather, I read, had its limits: while most of the significant cultivation in the US is in warm, relatively dry California, they grow well in the southern third of the country, an area in my mind I optimistically stretched to include northern Virginia. With the summer 2021 replanting in the yard, both young trees had a good running start on that tough winter weather I mentioned earlier, which struck in January 2022. Unfortunately for the olive tree, it did not take into account the havoc a goldendoodle pup could wreak.

On that phone call to the Outer Banks, my wife downplayed the extent of the damage and highlighted action she was taking to reverse the mugging my doodle had administered. The reality sunk in when I returned from the beach. Back in a pot in our kitchen, a stumpy remnant of the young olive tree sapling sat, looking forlorn and beat up. Its once three-foot little trunk was now barely a foot tall, with a couple of misaligned, partially amputated branches giving it a stick-figure look. The distinct olive leaves, already beat up by the rough cold, were nowhere to be seen.

My wife spoke very positively about the beat-up sapling's prospects but let drop that the tree doctor at the nursery where she had rushed the tree, post assault, had expressed concern the young olive tree had been left outdoors during the frigid winter weather. It amounted to marital hint dropping that there could be an arboreal death in the extended family. It was the type of typically complex message my wife had the habit of sending: think positive but in the event of a plant tragedy, blame lay with the extremes of climate change, and certainly not with Charlee.

One couldn't be mad at the beautiful doodle. But I did love that little olive tree. I had spent much of my career in the Middle East, and olive trees had been a feature in most of the (more fertile) places I worked in, including even parts of Saudi Arabia I traveled through as a young man—while teaching at a military school in Taif—as well as in Tunisia, Jordan, Syria, and Israel, including territories it then controlled, the West Bank and Gaza. I had once made a trek to one olive tree farm in the West Bank where the farmer also operated a rudimentary olive press, with a blindfolded donkey walking in a slow circle to propel the grinding action that crushed the olives for the precious oil. The technology, as well as the inches-thick olive-peelgunked sides of the press, seemed to date back to the Middle Ages. The motley collection of jars and metal containers in which the olive oil had been collected for sale appeared more of British Mandate era.

Perhaps a product, I like to think, of the tough, rocky soil in which the olive tree thrives in the Middle East, untreated olives carry an intense bitterness, which requires a sustained curing process—soaking in lye and then brine is one favored method—to leach out the compound oleuropein. The Romans were thought to have developed an early, expedited version of this process to render the olives edible. I had often eaten the meaty, firm, dark-green (and well cured!) little olives typically served in Palestinian and Israeli Arab restaurants when I served in Jerusalem as a young American diplomat in the late 1990s—and later when I was posted to Tel Aviv to cover political developments in nearby Gaza. From Tel Aviv, I would sometimes meet up with other American Foreign Service Officers serving in Jerusalem at an Israeli Arab restaurant along the highway between the two cities. We drank cold Israeli (Maccabee) or Palestinian (Taybeh) beer, and over olives, hummus (a moist paste of crushed chickpeas, usually puddled with a dollop of olive oil), and other typically Middle Eastern appetizers like falafel fritters and a lovely eggplant-based dip of baba ghanoush, we would swap stories and apologize to each other for various shouting and shrieking we had been guilty of due to the previous week's pressure-filled work of shepherding congressional visitors, reporting on charged political and economic developments in Israel and the territories (West Bank and Gaza), and maneuvering between—at that time—fiercely competitive, turf-conscious leadership in our respective US missions at the embassy (then in Tel Aviv) and the US consulate, in Jerusalem. (The Trump administration moved the US embassy to Jerusalem in 2018.)

In my initial Israel assignment—in Jerusalem—my job was to monitor Israeli settlements' growth in the West Bank and areas of East Jerusalem and cover Palestinian political developments. And here is where my olive tree connection took root, so to speak, most tenaciously with me. On numerous occasions, these two elements of my job description collided over olive trees. Palestinian land on the outskirts of Jerusalem or Bethlehem, or farther inside the West Bank, on rolling hills around Palestinian villages, located near originally small but often rapidly expanding Israeli settlements, was sometimes transferred or confiscated to absorb settlement growth or to build bypass roads to allow Israeli settler families to be able to travel freely and safely in the West Bank without having to traverse Palestinian villages. The mechanisms for these transfers and confiscations represented an overlapping, complex mash-up of traditional land ownership records (and sales transactions, including to Israeli buyers); Israeli military regulations then governing aspects of land registration, use, and construction in the West Bank; and the political—and security—nomenclature of the 1993–95 Oslo Accords, which divided the West Bank into zones A, B, and C. Ownership and use of Palestinian land were hotly contested, as was every provision of this welter of laws and security regulations that governed this contestation.

One of my first assignments as an inexperienced political officer at the consulate in Jerusalem was to go out to a Palestinian village that lay between Jerusalem and Bethlehem, just inside the territory of the West Bank, and report on a seizure of Palestinian land and the small protest it had provoked. Driven by a consulate driver out to the site, I dutifully talked to the parties. Distraught Palestinian family members wept and raged as Israeli Defense Force (IDF) bulldozers plowed up old-growth olive trees, planted decades earlier, to make way for a settler bypass road. The IDF insisted the land was located in a zone that gave them the right to build the road for transporting nearby settlers. The uprooted olive trees were pushed off to the side, in piles, in essence destroying most of the grove of trees over whose fate I had been summoned.

In the course of my one-year assignment in Jerusalem, I moved all over the West Bank, reporting on similar episodes, often alerted by involved parties, media reports, or Jerusalem-based attorneys assisting in these land cases. Left-wing Israeli activists and politicians affiliated with Peace Now raised similar cases in the media. In another incident, Israeli settlers set fire to an olive tree orchard to protest an incident of Palestinian violence. In a third incident, aspects of which remain etched in memory, a Palestinian farmer brought out on his simple patio yellowed land documents with the markings of what appeared to be the British Mandate authorities, who ruled in what was then referred to as Palestine, before the creation of the state of Israel in 1948. The landowner insisted the paper represented proof that his threatened olive trees were on land to which he had clear title. I remember him asking me to communicate this to my government, which in general terms, I did.

Much of this was a long time ago—in the late 1990s and early 2000s. The specific events have blurred over time and it is no disservice to these memories to acknowledge my recognition and welcoming of Israel's strong alliance with the United States and, more recently, with key Arab allies, through the Abraham Accords: objectives for which I and my fellow diplomats exerted concerted efforts over the past decades. But international relations and regional partnerships aside, I have retained a deep affection for olive trees, which, along with their sister arbors, the pomegranate, are reminders of a traditional agriculture-based life that I witnessed and experienced in different parts of the Middle East over the course of a career flung over four decades.

My shorn, well-surgered olive tree sits in a pot in our kitchen; with its bare, stumpy trunk and few limbs, its life seems to hang in the balance—its olive-producing days well, perhaps hopelessly forever, in front of it. Meanwhile, my lovely goldendoodle pup sits in my lap. I can feel her little heart beat against me: young fauna and flora summoning up another long-passed contestation for land and space primacy. As I sit with my young dog, gazing at my fragile olive tree, a shard of memory, a once-treasured, long-forgotten phrase, flashes by, too quickly for judgment about proportion in human emotion to shunt it aside: "It is a fearful thing to love what death can touch." A nice, but perhaps overly hefty thought for the slender occasion. I find myself wondering whether one can feel affection for a tree. I am not sure. But the feeling I have, looking at the pitiful remnant in the pot, and shaped so powerfully by memory and experience, sure feels like a premonition of mourning.

I eventually track the phrase to a notebook of quotations I kept for a few years after college. Not seeing any attribution, I google the phrase, discovering its author to be Yehuda Halevi, a twelfth-century Spanish Jewish doctor who wrote philosophy in Arabic and poetry in Hebrew and is considered one of the greatest Hebrew poets. He died shortly after making his way to Jerusalem in 1141, his life and work part of the ebb and flow that give history, including its modern iterations, the force of echo and tenacious relevance.

I would like to write that a couple of months later, as long-delayed spring finally began to emerge, the battered young tree showed signs of life in its limbs. But that is not the case. It remains a stick figure, awkwardly upright in a pot of dirt. Only at its base, seemingly separate from the tiny trunk, one sole green shoot has tentatively eased out from the soil. My wife and I try not to focus on the shoot too much or overanalyze the extent to which it may indicate the tree's root system has survived.

My goldendoodle, on the other hand, continues to grow, romp, and climb in my lap to hang out, as oblivious of the girth she is beginning to display as she is of the history of her conflict with the olive tree. In the yard, planted beside the site of the uprooted olive tree, the pomegranate has survived the cold winter. The bare spot on the ground beside it is the only sign of once and hopefully future coexistence with the young olive tree.

Survival, contestation, love, prospect of death—all the basic elements required to plant a tree, keep a goldendoodle, or live a life. My wife insists the olive tree will survive, an insistence that carries with it the implied judgment: "You aren't being positive enough." So I assert that optimism is a choice and insist that I too believe—choose to believe—that my little olive tree will survive. Who knows, perhaps I have made the right choice. ■

MIDNIGHT IN OSLO
Drew Calvert

I t was early April, and Quinn Weldt was bungling his taxes. He bungled his taxes every year, but this was a special season indeed: penalties owed in two states, missed payments, fiscal slaughter up and down the balance sheet. For a while, he'd worked as a ghostwriter for business professors, helping them publish book chapters and articles in "venues" such as *Forbes* or *Harvard Business Review,* but recently, for reasons having to do with spiritual health, he had made the decision not to offer his services anymore, which meant the revenue stream had ceased to flow. It was, in part, a matter of pride. While doing his taxes, he'd tallied payments received for drafting two-thirds of a business book, *The Trust Paradox,* and seen that he was owed an extra five thousand dollars—money he hadn't received despite contributing his labor, money that would have been useful for reducing his student loan balance and then, theoretically, pursuing the life of a novelist. The professor whose book he'd written disagreed about the payment and the two of them had exchanged increasingly legalistic emails before Quinn had finally given up. Still, he sensed there might be a way to reduce the amount of tax he owed for the previous year. He needed help.

And so, in early March, he'd made an appointment with H&R Block in Sycamore Mall, in Iowa City, and met with Sharon, a tax analyst, who, after a brief review of his 1040s and 1099s, as well as his self-employment receipts, mileage log, and list of deductions, made an ominous whistling sound and said that it was a good thing he had come to see her. At first, he worried she might overcharge, but after ten minutes or so he knew that he could trust her, or felt that he could trust her, or simply *chose* to trust her as a token of his abiding faith in the nation's social fabric. (It was 2017.) It helped that she had trophies, photos, and stuffed animals on her desk, which signaled competence and warmth, and it helped that when she reached into her desk drawer for a stick of gum, she offered him a fresh piece. In fact, this simple act of kindness may have won him over. It put him enough at ease to make a joke about the IRS and the irony that President Trump appeared not to have paid any tax, despite his very obscene wealth, and Sharon had laughed appreciatively in a way that didn't necessarily prove her affiliation but that left him with the sense that she was sane and reasonable. He gave his folder of documents to her to study in more detail, made an appointment for April 5 to file his tax return, and went back to writing his novel.

Quinn still hadn't finished his novel, his first, despite having mentioned it to friends, colleagues, his younger sister, his seatmate on a domestic fight, an Uber driver, a bookish uncle, a handful of Airbnb hosts, and, of course, the literati, the gatekeepers of fellowships and grant money and summer retreats. In fact, he knew his novel was dead. It was set—unconvincingly—in 1890s Chicago, which allowed the author to satirize the America of the 2010s. Fictional gurus delivered crazed speeches from their platforms at the 1893 World's Fair; fictional entrepreneurs invented comically useless products; a fictional William Jennings Bryan traveled around the country with his fictional jaded speechwriter, a stand-in for the novelist. Wall Street panics, corporate titans, socialists, novel spiritual cures—the book was about the "New Gilded Age" set in the Gilded Age. It didn't make a lot of sense. He'd written mostly out of spite, and now he could see that his spitefulness had overshadowed the book's humor and even its moral conviction. It was a record of despair. He tried to explain the nature of the problem to Maja, his ex-girlfriend, who now worked as a nurse in LA. Although she was sympathetic, he could hear the familiar note of exasperation in her voice, which inspired the realization that to tell a former girlfriend about an unfinished novel is to orchestrate a meaningless collision of dark matter. The more he described his satirical book, the more clearly he could see that he had written a failure. It wasn't even an interesting failure, like Samuel Butler's *Erewhon* or Herman Melville's *Pierre*. It was an unredeemable failure, like his last romantic relationship. When, in a fit of childish pique, he said he thought it might be time to burn the entire manuscript, Maja calmly suggested he recycle it instead, so as not to cause even more damage. In any case, it was on the cloud.

Quinn had decided that April 5 would be a day of errands. He didn't work on his novel at all; he left it in the cardboard box beside the other cardboard box in which he'd kept his tax forms before surrendering them to Sharon. Instead he went to the grocery store, and the hardware store, and the post office. He even got a haircut. Perched aloft in the wide leather swivel chair at Great Clips, he listened to the hairdresser tell a story about her son, who had served five years in the military but hadn't received the benefits he was promised by the VA. Her son was a disciplined man, she said, but he could also be playful. Whenever he took her to dinner, he would offer the crook of his elbow in a gesture of mock gallantry and refer to their handicapped parking spot as "the VIP section." Oh, but that was long ago, she said. He hadn't done that in years. Quinn watched in the mirror as the hairdresser paused, scissors in hand, to remember how it felt to link elbows with her son. He tried to think of something to say, something kind yet unsentimental. But he was at a loss, and he sensed the hairdresser drifting back to her own sphere of melancholy. Finally, he said he hoped the VA got its act together. The hairdresser nodded and asked if she should use the number five clipper guard. The rest of the haircut proceeded in silence. Afterwards he walked across the mall to H&R Block and rang the little bell.

The woman at the front desk looked under-slept and overwhelmed, her mottled skin and frizzy hair exposed to the harsh fluorescent light. She greeted Quinn with a yawn and asked for a confirmation number, which she typed incorrectly several times before getting it right. He had been through the same tedious process during his last visit and had found it no less depressing. But Sharon had been a pleasant surprise; he'd been happy to work with her. Her smile and reassuring tone reminded him of an organized and kindhearted aunt—approachable, a problem solver. She was the only person alive who knew how thoroughly he had failed to become a solvent adult. When he'd shown her the letters from the Illinois and Iowa Departments of Revenue, she'd told him not to worry so much, that money was "pictures of dead people." And then she'd explained some subtle tricks for gaming the federal tax code. She had made him feel, if not relaxed, then at least not fatalistic.

The receptionist was frowning at her screen. She clicked, scrolled, and clicked again, but the frown only intensified. She asked if he had come to file his tax return with Sharon. He had, of course, and he told her so. He showed her the email and text message confirming the appointment. The receptionist frowned again and said that Sharon was out of the office that week on "personal emergency leave." She was in Norway—or maybe Denmark. The receptionist couldn't remember which. The upshot was that Quinn would need to make another appointment with a different tax analyst. Alternatively, he could schedule another filing appointment with Sharon, though he'd have to wait until she returned from her personal emergency leave.

Quinn was determined to stay calm, despite his strong conviction that the receptionist was mistaken. After more clicking and scrolling, he learned that Sharon's next available slot was April 21, three days after the national deadline to file his tax return. This was extremely discouraging. The receptionist urged him to speak with one of their other veteran analysts, Bill, but Quinn was not convinced that Bill was anywhere near as adept as Sharon at calculating quarterly payments, maximizing deductions, or even making sense of what he called his "terrible algebra," a private joke alluding to a line from a Henry James letter nobody gave a shit about. Also, whatever his qualifications, there was a more enduring problem: it was Sharon, not Bill, to whom he had entrusted his tax documents; it was she with whom he'd consulted about his grim filing status. He made this point as cogently as possible to the receptionist, whose demeanor and body language was by now fairly rigid. She explained again, slower this time, that Sharon was dealing with personal issues, and not on US soil. Quinn began to lose his patience. He asked if they could search for his file. The receptionist said she felt uneasy snooping around a colleague's desk. She raised the prospect of Bill again. Quinn was staunchly anti-Bill. He tried to explain that he had made an appointment with *Sharon*, not with Bill. The receptionist, now ice-cold, apologized for the inconvenience.

Standing at the receptionist's desk, Quinn tried to appreciate the absurdity of a tax analyst fleeing to Scandinavia during the one month of the year when she was most urgently in demand. He decided almost instantly that she was in Norway, not Denmark, and that she was merely vacationing. He needed this poetic license to focus his mounting rage. He pictured Sharon in Norway, reading guidebooks, tasting the local cuisine, fishing for bills in her fanny pack, her conscience totally clear. He imagined her going in search of her "roots"—a large, chatty woman in her forties with an abstract claim to European pedigree, snapping tasteless selfies next to ancient churches and pristine fjords. He tried counting backwards from ten. Then he made a final attempt to explain the severity of his case, pointing out that he now had his own "personal emergency."

The receptionist sighed the way one does when forced to explain a complicated story to a child. She said that Sharon's fiancé had left her three weeks ago and that Sharon had booked a one-way ticket to Norway—or Denmark—on a whim. The truth was that nobody knew when or if she would return. They hoped to get a message soon.

Quinn felt a sudden rush of tenderness for Sharon. Despite himself, he made further inquiries into her situation. He learned that Sharon's fiancé was an unbelievable asshole. The fiancé had moved to a suburb of Des Moines with Sharon's best friend, who was pregnant with their child. The receptionist said she'd always known the fiancé was an asshole. She enumerated his many faults while Quinn made audible tutting sounds to signal his disgust. As if in conclusion, he said that men were not a very kind species. The woman agreed wholeheartedly.

Quinn lingered and chatted for another five minutes or so, mostly about the special kind of pain that results from betrayal, but soon there was nothing more to say, and he had other errands to run. He needed to contact his landlord with an update on the lease. He needed to buy a gift for a friend who had recently given birth. And he needed to do his annual sweep of Facebook to ensure he hadn't missed other births or deaths. He took a seat on the wooden bench outside H&R Block, logged in to his Facebook account, and scrolled through his friend requests. Many were several months old. His younger sister's boyfriend, who was a nice guy, and good for her, had sent a request back in September. Now they were friends, seven months late. The process had taken less than a minute. But where did it end? Where? There were hundreds of emails he could be writing to friends and family around the world, emails that would likely do more good than any novel of his, emails he could not write on a chipped bench in Sycamore Mall with his two idiot thumbs. He decided he would finish his errands and then bike to Prairie Lights to draft his belated emails.

Quinn checked the to-do list in the Notes app on his iPhone. He called Wells Fargo and disputed a purchase he hadn't made. He called his landlord and left a message. He walked to another part of the mall and bought a pink onesie. He was accomplishing many things, but not the main thing. The day of errands had been built around the filing of his tax return much as a great basketball team is built around a towering center. But he would need to put his financial situation out of mind, or nothing else would get done.

As he biked along Summit Street, heading towards the café, he tried to remember which writers had bungled their taxes extravagantly, and what their fates had been. Edmund Wilson came to mind, but there were probably others. David Foster Wallace had written a whole novel, or most of one, about the IRS before he'd hanged himself in his garage. It wasn't a great precedent. Still, Quinn could appreciate the link between taxes and literature: both were abstractions of civic engagement.

Biking north on Gilbert Street, Quinn tried to convince himself that it wasn't exactly a *moral* failure to fail at writing a novel. It was actually very common—but then so was moral failure. Maybe he had saved himself from a terrible profanity. Was that it? Was he too profane? Or was he not profane enough? He was very conflicted about the sacred and the profane, about whether a novel should "vex the world," as Jonathan Swift had once written, or whether it should make a single reader's heart go pit-a-pat. Recently, he had read a book called *The Preparation of the Novel*, which wasn't really a book at all but a series of lectures Roland Barthes had written *instead* of a novel. He thought the lectures were wonderful, but he couldn't say why. Surprisingly, it almost made him want to become a Catholic again, which certainly wasn't Barthes's intention. The night he finished reading the book, he called Maja, who, like him, had once belonged to the Catholic Church, and asked if she thought they'd turned their backs on God prematurely. She said she didn't think so and reminded him that the Christian vote had swayed the recent election. Then she told him a story about a woman who'd broken both arms in a fall and cried in her hospital bed because she couldn't scratch her nose. Maja scratched it for her, but the woman still cried. *It's not being scratched*, the woman said, and this became a catchphrase for their post-relationship. *It's not being scratched*, Maja would say, as she went through her depression. *It's not being scratched*, he would say, on the days he failed to write. For a while he stopped writing altogether and spent his days reading Loyola's *Spiritual Exercises*, which recommended similar feats of imaginative empathy but had a more splendid goal: to make the spiritual exerciser a better human being.

By the time he reached Prairie Lights, it was late in the afternoon. He found an empty table, took out his laptop, and made a list of all the people he needed to email. The list became rather daunting, so he ordered a large coffee, and while waiting for his coffee he remembered the book of poems he'd been carrying in his backpack, so he took it out and began to read. As he read, he felt a familiar cold flame near the top of his spine. The poems were gorgeous—and funny, too, his favorite combination. The poet was coming to Iowa City, so he'd have a chance to hear her read. Too often, though, he skipped the readings. He'd never mastered the art of being a literary person, despite his love for literature. Possibly he was an asshole—it was something he'd need to think about. The poems were outrageously good. He couldn't believe how good they were. He wanted to call the poet and tell her, but that would only ruin the magic. He'd learned this through experience: the week before, at an after-party, he'd heaped drunken praise on one of his literary heroes, a novelist in her sixties with electric prose and acid wit. Nothing terrible happened, but the shame felt like a blight on his soul, and he made a secret vow not to rant about his sordid love for an author ever again. So, no, he wouldn't call the poet. Besides, he had emails to write. Maybe he could write just one and send it to the entire list? Then he could wander the earth, reading poems.

But first, the professor. Quinn was eager to have the final word. The market-based "principal-agent" relationship they'd affected over the past few years was nonsense, and he felt the need to explain why. *Principal-agent* was *master-slave* laundered through economics departments, a cute name for a shabby arrangement: psychologists working for business schools and writers—even failed writers— working for psychologists. There had to be a better way for the culture to self-reflect. As he typed out the subject line, he recalled a conversation they'd had the year before in Chicago. The professor had recommended a book, a treacly collection of personal essays, and Quinn had made the mistake of being honest about his preferences. The professor scoffed at his highbrow taste. People either want to be entertained, he said, or they want to be helped. Most novels he read were neither entertaining nor helpful. Besides, they were living in the golden age of television!

Quinn had no rebuttal at the time—the professor had a point. He himself had worried about the nature of his vocation, which involved transmuting emotions into narratives for "greater truth." He often tried to persuade himself that the process was a natural one, like the second law of thermodynamics or photosynthesis. But what if it were natural in the way theft was natural, or the way murder was natural? He'd gazed onto the unrelenting beauty of Lake Michigan, with its tidy armada of yachts by the pier, and felt himself admit defeat.

But now, ensconced in his favorite café, Quinn was determined to make his case in writing, where he had the advantage. He tried to summarize Adam Smith's theory of moral sentiments. For Adam Smith, Quinn wrote, the irreducible human trait wasn't reason, or speech, or labor, or the impulse to build trade networks or joint-stock companies or design communication devices. Instead, it was our ability to respond to "sentiments," or the passions and feelings of others, which is what the novel curates in its own messy way. He explained that all of his favorite novels were basically un-filmable, that film is certainly more efficient for representing life in action— not to mention settings—but that fiction is better at offering access to other people's minds. Factoring in production costs, it was no contest, really.

But this was a pointless exercise, as so much of his life had been. He deleted the email and started over, this time writing a terse reply announcing he'd be moving on. He wished the professor all the best, gallantly resisting the urge to advise self-sodomy, and told him he could keep the cash. When he clicked Send, he felt buoyant and fearful at the same time. He looked outside and saw the day's light had begun to fade.

He had hoped to end the day awash in virtue, errands complete, but he didn't feel that way at all. Everything was out of place. Maja was off in California, no doubt having athletic sex with solvent vegan entrepreneurs. He was freshly unemployed. Soon enough, he would be in prison, tallying days on the cell's brick wall above his bunk. And Sharon was in exile! She was probably in Oslo, he thought—walking the streets of Oslo with her fanny pack and broken heart, caught in her own terrible web. Deciding the rest of her life.

He tried to picture Sharon's life. She was a fairly heavyset woman—could that be why her fiancé had cheated? People actually did such things. People were mostly not very nice. But Sharon was nice, he knew that much. When she'd offered him the stick of gum, she'd said: *For the boredom.* A beautiful line. Now *that* was literature.

Quinn had never been to Norway—everything he knew about the country he'd learned from the autofiction of Karl Ove Knausgaard, a man who'd achieved celebrity by violating the trust encoded in personal relationships—so he couldn't picture exactly what someone like Sharon might be doing. Whatever it was, he hoped that she would find solace on her trip—that she would encounter something on the streets of Oslo to cheer her up. He suddenly had a crazy desire to pray for Sharon's happiness, to make something manifest, to cause through sheer concentration of mind a person to sidle up to her on the streets of Oslo and say something kind, maybe even a little strange, the sort of thing Peter Walsh might say to Clarissa Dalloway, the sort of thing Sharon the tax analyst might say to Quinn.

The café was starting to clear out; it was around dinnertime. Oslo was what, six or seven hours ahead of central time? It would be around midnight there. What might she be doing? He imagined Sharon, sleepless, bereft, roaming the streets of Oslo at midnight, even though he knew she might as easily be in Copenhagen. He couldn't picture Oslo at all, except for the fjords. He knew there were fjords. What about the city itself? He pictured the tastefully floodlit columns of banks and government buildings, of which there must be one or two. Ancient churches. Cobblestones. He pictured a town square of sorts, with a high clock tower, also lit, and Sharon crossing beneath it. Soon there were others filling the square, versions of people he'd known and loved, people he should have been kinder to, people who might have been kinder to him, some of them living and some of them dead, some clearly there to haunt and some to keep him company. He needed this scene, just for the moment, just as others needed the scene of Jesus turning water to wine. He watched these kindred apparitions mingle and stroll through Oslo's streets, admiring its cleanliness, exalting in its alien fjords. He wanted to cry out to them, embrace them, kiss them, apologize. He wanted to say he was sorry for having summoned them so pointlessly. He wanted to give them a better scene. Something dramatic, something true. At the very least, he could fill in the details, add a bit of color and light—the violet iridescence on the surface of an Oslo fjord, or, to keep things simple, stars. Stars were dramatic enough, he thought. A blizzard of stars, a spackle of pearl—even the merest glimmer would do. Surely there would be stars overhead in Oslo on a night like this. ■

ODE TO THE PLATE
Pablo Neruda

Plate,
center disc
of the world,
planet and planetarium:
at noon, when
the sun, plate of fire,
crowns
the
high
day,
plate,
on the tables of the world
your stars
appear,
enormous
constellations,
and the earth is filled
with soup
and the universe
with fragrances,
until the jobs
call the workers
and again
the dining room is an empty wagon,
while the plates are returned
to the depths of the kitchens.
Affable, clarified vessel,
you invented the spring in a stone
then the human hand
repeated
the refined hole
and the potter copied its freshness
so that
time with its thread
would put it
definitively

between man and life:
the plate, the plate, the plate,
ceramic hope,
holy bowl,
exacting lunar light in its halo,
beautiful rounded diadem.

-translated from the Spanish by Wally Swist

ODA AL PLATO
Pablo Neruda

Plato,
disco central
del mundo,
planeta y planetario:
a mediodia, cuando
el sol, plato de fuego,
corona
el alto
dia,
plato, aparecen
sobre
las mesas en el mundo
tus estrellas,
las pletoricas
constelacinones,
y se llena de sopa
la tierra, de fragrancia
el universo,
hasta que los trabajos
llaman de nuevo
a los trabajadoras
y otra vez
el comedor es un vagon vacio,

mientras vuelvan los platos
a la profundidad de las cocinas.
Suave, pura vasija,
te invento el manatial en una piedra
luego la mano humana
repitio
el hueco pura
y copio el alfarero su frescura
para
que el tiempo con su hijo
lo pusiera definitivamente
entre el hombre y la vida:
el plato, el plato, el plato,
ceramica esperanza,
cuenco santo,
exacta luz lunar en su aureola,
hermosura redonda de diadema.

ODE TO THE SMELL OF FIREWOOD
Pablo Neruda

Late, with the stars
out in the cold.
I opened the door.

The sea

galloped
into the night.

Like a hand
from the dark house,
the intense aroma
of the stored firewood
emerged.

The odor was visible
as if the tree
were still alive.
As if it still throbbed.

Visible
as a garment.

Visible
as a broken branch.

I walked
inside
the house
surrounded
by that balsamic
darkness.
Outside
the points
of the sky sparkled
like magnetic stones
and the smell of firewood

touched
my heart
like fingers,
like jasmine,
like some memories.

It was not the sharp
smell of the pines,
no,
it was not
the break in the skin
of the eucalyptus,
neither was it
the green perfume
of the vineyard,
but
something more secret,
because that fragrance
existed
only once,
only once,
and there, of everything in the world,
in my own
house, at night, by the winter sea,
there was waiting for me
the smell
of the deepest rose,
the heart cut from the earth,
something
that invaded me like a wave
detached from time
and became lost in myself
when I opened the door
of the night.

-translated from the Spanish by Wally Swist

ODA AL OLOR DE LA LENA
Pablo Neruda

Tarde, con las estrellas
abiertas en el fria
abri la puerta.

         El mar
galopaba
en la noche.

Como una mano
de la casa oscura
salio el aroma
intenso
de la lena guardada.

Visible era el aroma
como
si el arbol
estuviera vivo.
Como si todavia palpitara.

Visible
como una vestidura.

Visible
como una rama rota.

Anduve
adentro
de la casa
rodeado
por aquella balsamica
oscuridad.
Afuera
las puntas
del cielo cintilaban
como piedras magneticas
y el olor de la lena

me tocaba
el corazon
como unos dedos,
como un jazmin,
como algunos recuerdos.

No era el olor agudo
de los pinos,
no,
no era
la rupture en la piel
del eucaliptus,
no eran
tampoco
los perfumes verdes
de la vina,
sino
algo, mas secreto,
porque aquella fragrancia
una sola,
una sola
vez existia,
y alli, de todo lo aque vi em el mundo,
en mi propia
casa, de noche, junto al mar de invierno,
alli estaba esperandome
el olor
de la rosa mas profunda,
el corazon cortado de la tierra,
algo
que me invadio como una ola
desprendida
del tiempo
y se perdio en mi mismo
cuando yo abri la puerta
de la noche.

HARPOONED
Richard Jacobs

One evening this past May, I read *Billy Budd, Sailor* and knew instinctively that I should teach it to my eleventh-grade English classes during the next school term. I anticipated problems, some with the students, some with our district's creed-bound school board. Would any member of that august assembly have read it or read of it, and would an objection to the necessity of addressing the tale's homoerotic sensibility be raised? All that could wait—I felt invigorated at the notion of bringing something I hadn't taught before into my classroom, especially a richly suggestive story about innocence and evil. Poor Billy. Poor Captain Vere. Despite its sometimes paralytic diction, *Billy Budd*, I believed, would lead my better students to the kinds of impassioned philosophical discussions that lift the profession of high school teaching toward its highest-minded ideals. With luck, even the most doggedly unread kids would pitch in. These thoughts stirred my memories of reading *Moby-Dick*. I hauled myself out of my easy chair, refilled my tumbler with Scotch, and climbed the stairs to the room Irene, my longtime part-time love, still referred to as my study. I rummaged through a dusty bookcase and found the trade paperback I'd last read a dozen years before. This mammoth edition came packed with a learned introduction, diagrams of ships' decks, explanatory footnotes, and a glossary of nautical terms. No reader employing it would have to match wits with Herman Melville unaided, a bracing prospect even for a degree-bearing, highly trained American teacher of English like me.

I blew the lint off the head of the book and flicked through its body, marking the folded-over page corners and the notes my younger, more ambitious self had scribbled in the margins to prove that he knew his way around a text as heretical and yet as sacred as any ever written. My fingers vibrated with excitement, for I remembered the book as a moil of lamentation and jubilance, of elegy and inquest—a harpoon hurled upward into the bowels of heaven. I wanted to begin reading it right away. A snapshot fell out of the pages, a 35 mm refugee from the past, for I had not opened the book since the summer I'd read it. The snapshot flipped to the floor, facedown.

Transfixed, I stared at its square backside. Instinct forbade me from picking it up, and I searched my mind for the reason. When it surfaced, I set *Moby-Dick* atop another abandoned paperback tome on the crown of the bookcase and took a long sip of my Scotch. I bent low, plucked the photograph from the rug, and gave myself a last moment of asylum. Then I turned it over and set my eyes for the first time in a dozen years, give or take fugitive appearances in dreams, on the image of Carrie Rankin.

The sight of her long-limbed beauty, even in the miniaturized field of the photograph, awakened in me an anguished wonder. Her eyes, a vibrant umber in color, beseeched me anew. Her mouth, wide as opposing petals in the corolla of a lily, proffered a demurring smile. And though sheathed in jeans, her legs blazed like two flares from the sun. She stood alone in a cleared space, a magnolia tree behind her. Carrie's guarded expression and stance bespoke mild reproof, for she had begged me not to take her photograph. It would be my first betrayal of her. This vision of her—of her billowy black hair, her slender form, her unrelenting gaze—took up a terrible residence within me. For I had loved Carrie Rankin one golden year in my youth, loved her though pledged to another, and had made her love me. Thirty-one to my twenty-seven, married to a brute, mother of a twelve-year-old son; when she needed me most, I vanished. In the time that followed, I banked my memories of our romance in a cellar of my mind like a pile of embers and skulked away to let them cool down to ashes.

I stood in my study feeling Carrie's presence—not in the room haunting me but in the world, doing good. Who was she now? What did she cherish? What did she fear? I longed to know. Her image wrested from me an awe for the backward reach of time, a reach that had deigned to sweep me so near to what had once been in my power to hold but which now locked me in a groundswell of regret. I shook my head at my younger self as at a student who had purposely not done his homework.

* * *

Shutter your inward eye. Pretend to virtue, if you dare. Allow years, even decades, to elapse, peaceful as a string of warm days spent by a lake. It will not matter. Your past will catch up to you. It will tap you on your shoulder like a stranger in need of directions. You'll turn round to a mirror held up to your face. Then you'll know yourself for what you are. ∎

GHOSTS ARE AS REAL AS DREAMS
Malcolm Rothman

I

The Big Mistake

I can't begin to tell about the weirdest thing that happened to me during my four years in the Navy without mentioning another young hospital corpsman, my friend Claude Gregoire. Smart, bighearted, well-read, and funny, he was an overeducated stranger in the strange land of the Second Battalion, Second Marines, and was, like me, a college dropout. Besides being a decent tennis player, he was an able conversationalist, a winsome young southern gentleman, and the embodiment of New Orleans's motto, *Laissez les bons temps rouler!*

One morning not long ago, while holding on to a waking dream, I pictured Claude and I saying goodbye in the diesel funk of the Jacksonville, North Carolina Trailways station. We promised we'd stay in touch, get together a year after we got out of the navy and party ourselves stupid at Mardi Gras. And we would have done, except he was on his way to Vietnam to a Marine Civic Action Platoon. Eight weeks later he was shot by a sniper while giving vaccinations in some obscure hamlet a few kilometers outside of Quang Tri. When I read in the *Navy Times'* obits that he'd been killed in action, I knew I'd have to get away from Lejeune and the military for a few days. I decided to visit the least military people I knew, civilian friends Jim and Bronwyn in Manhattan. He was a psych grad student at the New School for Social Research, and she was studying dance at Juilliard. You don't get any more un-military than that.

I arrived at the Port Authority Bus Terminal late the next Friday afternoon. When I had called my friends to ask if I could visit, they told me I could, but that they wouldn't be at their rent-controlled apartment in the West Village until after ten. Which meant I had several hours to kill. That was no problem. The Times Square area, specifically Forty-Second Street between Seventh and Eighth (known to us locals as the Deuce), was my old stomping grounds. A short walk would take me to where I had misspent much of my spare time in high school watching double and triple features at the decrepit movie houses, gobbling two-for-a-quarter, bone-studded hamburgers at the

Papaya King, watching the rubbernecking out-of-towners, haunting the seedy penny arcade that housed Hubert's Flea Circus and giving a hard time to the Bible-thumpers on the corner of Forty-Second and Eighth. After checking my AWOL bag in a locker, I headed for the door. But before I reached it, I was accosted by a "clippy," that is, a hippy with a clipboard. He asked me if I was a GI. My short hair, shiny Oxfords and government-issue glasses being a dead giveaway, it was pointless to lie. He said he was with the Columbia University chapter of SDS and that they were holding a teach-in that night in the Low Library auditorium. The event would include an open mic for active-duty GIs, and would I be interested in attending and speaking. I thought to myself, *Hell yeah, I'd be REAL interested.* My anger and grief over Claude's being killed and the senseless war that took him had been building inside me all week. I agreed and followed him onto Eighth Avenue, where a windowless van was idling. When he opened the side door, I saw two guys in civvies sitting on the floor who were obviously military and an unsmiling young woman behind the wheel. I got in and tried to make myself comfortable. (Looking back, I find it incredible that there was once a time when I would fearlessly hop into a windowless van with complete strangers. In Manhattan yet.) After a while we took off for Morningside Heights. The clippy was pleasant enough but not very forthcoming about what we could expect when we got to Columbia.

When we got there, we walked up the steps of the Low Library. This, too, was a familiar place; I'd spent many an afternoon during high school and on vacation from college sitting on those steps reading, taking in the sun and pretending I belonged there. Entering the building, we crossed the rotunda to a lecture hall. When we were seated up front, I looked around the house. It was almost full and was buzzing with conversation. There was tension in the room; earlier in 1968, there had been an extremely violent protest in this building that ended up being dispersed in an extremely violent fashion by the NYPD. There was no guarantee how this evening would end.

The scheduled speakers were called and thus began an avalanche of anti–Vietnam War rhetoric. Ossie Davis and Mark Rudd were among the speakers. A scruffy guy named Andy Stapp came up to the podium. He had organized something called the American Servicemen's Union and had been booted out of the Army with a dishonorable discharge. I was in dangerous company. But as the teach-in continued, I became more and more infuriated. Everything

I believed that was criminally wrong with the war and the people who had caused it was iterated and reiterated. At last, the scheduled speakers were finished. A revivalist energy crackled in the air. It came time for the servicemen's open mic. One by one we were ushered up to the stage, accompanied by the applause of the audience. My turn to speak came. I delivered a couple of minutes of incoherent babbling, topped off by an equally incoherent eulogizing of my friend Claude. When I had run out of steam, I raised a fist and staggered off the stage with tears in my eyes. I got down to the foot of the stairs and was approached by an older fellow who asked me if I wouldn't mind giving him my name and address so he could send me some of their literature. Buzzing on adrenaline, I thought, *Well, he's got a beard. I guess he's all right.* It was at that moment I did something that would later come back to haunt me: I gave him my information. But by now I had had enough of this circus. I ran out of the building, found the 116th Street IRT station and got my ass back to the Port Authority and then to Jim and Bronwyn's.

The next two days with them were heaven. They couldn't have approved more of my attending the teach-in. For the rest of the weekend, they treated me like a brother. We drank, smoked dope, ate at restaurants and saw a movie at the Beekman. The night before I was to leave, their cat nestling between my legs, I fell asleep on their sofa as happy as I had been in a long time. Then, I got my first visit from Claude. In my dream, I was in the Vietnam of everyone's nightmares, desperately struggling through a twisted, steaming jungle. I came out onto a clearing, and there before me stood my buddy Claude looking confused, tired, sweaty and dirty. Our eyes met and I couldn't turn away. Smiling, he raised his right hand and wiggled his fingers to say hello. Then, he took his index finger and slowly brought it across his throat. And then, as if his finger had been a straight razor, blood spurted from the gaping wound he'd made. I woke up with a start. The cat hadn't moved. After breakfast the next day I was off to Camp Lejeune to serve my time and to wait for what would come next.

II

GUANTANAMO! The Musical

Fast-forward three months. What came next was assignment to another battalion. I was on an Air Force C130 cargo plane on my way to the navy's second-worst duty station, the US naval base at Guantanamo Bay, Cuba, aka Gitmo. Suspended in the uncomfortable webbed seating that lined the bulkhead, I wondered if Gitmo was as bad as people said. The thing that made being stationed there so undesirable was that being surrounded by miles of barbed wire and a hostile Cuba, there was no off-base liberty; what happened at Gitmo stayed at Gitmo—and so did you. The "brothers" used to say, "You don't git none at Git-mo!" There were off-duty activities on base, but not many. And those infrequently used. Unlike today, with the internet, Blu-ray movies and satellite phones and TV available anywhere in the world, at that time there was no real-time communication with the mainland or home. There was FM radio, but all you could get was Armed Forces Radio, shit-kicker music from Florida and 24/7 salsa music from the local station in Guantánamo City. So if you weren't into getting drunk on twenty-five-cent beers or fifty-cent Bacardi and Cokes during your off-hours (and make no mistake about it, many were), you had to be creative to keep from going insane.

One morning, I read in the base newspaper that there would be an audition for a production of the musical *110 in the Shade* at the base's Little Theater. It seemed too good to be true; as a disgraced, flunk-out music major, I was red-hot and ready to do something, anything, that took me out of the soul-sucking, day-to-day boredom of life at Gitmo. As for singing and dancing in a musical? Holy shit! I'm your man! If you want, I'll even sweep the place up after rehearsal! Two days later, I auditioned for and won the lead role of Starbuck. Now, you might recall that this musical is based on the play *The Rainmaker*, and the movie version starred Burt Lancaster as Starbuck. Well, let me state the obvious: I'm no Burt Lancaster. As a short, stocky Jewish kid from Brooklyn, it was going to be something of a stretch for me to bring this off. But I was the only guy on a base of sixteen thousand sailors and marines who had the chops to handle the role. And as I came to learn years later as a professional actor, if the person casting you thinks you're right for the part, don't argue— just do it. We rehearsed for weeks and weeks like most community theaters do. The company was made up of officers, enlisted men, officers' wives and a couple of Jamaican civilian workers. Best of all, the atmosphere was surprisingly relaxed with no attention being paid to rank; everyone was on a first-name basis. The director, a naval supply officer, had been a speech communications major in college and was more than competent. My Lizzie (the female lead), Betsy Allen, though not an exceptional singer, was game, energetic and completely believable in the role. She happened to be the wife of the top counterintelligence officer on the base—the guy who briefed the admiral every day—and he himself was in the ensemble. Bob Allen was an approachable, unaffected guy and the son of a retired Air Force general. And as it came to pass, he was also the man who saved my bacon.

The week before the show opened, the thing I had been dreading for more than two and a half years happened: my orders to Vietnam were delivered to battalion HQ. I was to report the next week to the naval hospital in Bethesda, Maryland, in preparation to join a MILPHAP team headed to Vietnam. What's a MILPHAP team, you may ask? I didn't know either, nor did anyone else I spoke to. I told the director what had happened, and in a panic I told Bob. I asked him if there was anybody at base headquarters he could talk to in order to get my posting pushed back a couple of weeks. He said he'd take it to the Marine CO and make the case that my quitting the show would mean it would have to be canceled. He told me to not worry. He would take care of everything.

That night, I had another dream of Claude. I dreamed that a MILPHAP team was a graves registration unit. Those are the guys who collect dead bodies and prepare them to be shipped home. (One of the worst jobs you could possibly have that doesn't involve getting shot at.) As some body bags were being off-loaded from choppers, someone tapped me on the shoulder. I looked around and it was a Claude. He looked squeaky-clean and healthy. Looking around, he said, "Hi, Bubba. You're in graves registration?! Who the hell did you piss off? Hey, you wanna see something cool, check this out." He led me to the closest body bag and unzipped it. It was me inside.

The next rehearsal was two days later. I arrived early to see if Bob had found out what was going to happen. He had already gotten there and was looking grim. He said, "Colonel Naas is furious. He's screaming about having stuck his neck out asking division for a postponement of your orders, and he found out that you're being investigated for sedition. Sedition! They're getting ready to court-martial you, my friend. They're sending down a CID man tomorrow to investigate you and some other guy. The colonel is taking this personally. He thinks this is some kind of hippie scheme to make him look bad! What I need you to do is come home with me and Betsy tonight after rehearsal. We'll have a couple of drinks, and you can tell me what exactly you believe in and what you plan to do about it." After rehearsal we drove to the married officers' quarters. After a vodka tonic, we got down to business. What did I believe in? "I don't know," I said. "Peace, justice and equal rights for all Americans?" I admitted that I had spoken at the teach-in at Columbia and was shocked to hear that he knew all about it, and how apparently unable I'd been in the past few months to not shoot my mouth off about my anti-war sentiments. He had my file inside a cover marked SECRET on his lap. He opened it and read the most damaging parts to me. I was aghast. I told him that the people who had taken my name and address at the teach-in kept sending me pamphlets and broadsides, but I kept throwing them away. He asked what I actually planned to do about all this. That was easy. With one more year to go on my enlistment, I had every intention of going wherever the Navy sent me and, should I be lucky enough to survive, getting the hell out with honor, going back to college and never looking back. He looked me in the eye for a long minute, saw that I really meant it, and said, "Okay, fine. Maybe this isn't as bad as I thought. I'll pass this on to the CID guy tomorrow and make your case again with the colonel. I'll tell them that I know you and downplay the notion that you're disloyal or any danger to the war effort. I honestly don't think you've got much to worry about… other than getting your ass shot off in Vietnam, of course. And just in case you're wondering, your opinions about the war and civil rights are not very different from mine or Betsy's. But there's just one thing I want you to do in return for all my trouble."

"What?" I said. "Anything!"

"You'd damn well better hit it outta the park as Starbuck next week."

Two days later, the battalion XO came to my sick bay and sourly told me that my orders had been re-cut and that I'd be leaving Gitmo two and a half weeks later than planned. And so it came to pass: we got to do our show. The cast of *110 in the Shade* and I played to full houses and standing ovations every night. It even rained after the final performance. However, it being the Marine Corps and all, there was a stiff price to pay: I would be getting no leave prior to shipping out. That wasn't a problem. I didn't relish the idea of spending two weeks with my parents sitting shiva for me while I was alive and in the room with them.

III

THE NAMESAKE

To everyone's surprise, I survived my enlistment and went on to live a long and interesting life. But I've never forgotten Claude. Every opening night, nervously standing in the wings ready to go on, I say to myself, "This one's for Claude!" And saying it never fails to calm me down and jack me up.

Around 2008, I decided to try and find Claude's family through the internet. After some digging around on the web, I found the photographic studio of someone in Baton Rouge I thought likely to be a relative. I screwed up my courage and wrote to him. The following is our exchange of emails:

Dear Mr. Blackburn,
My name is Max Fogel, and from 1966 to 1968, I was friends with a fellow hospital corpsman named Claude Gregoire. In 1968 he was killed in action in Vietnam, and I have honored his memory throughout my life. Now, as an older man, I've been trying to connect with his family, and in doing so, I've come across your website. Is it possible that you are his nephew? If so, and if this isn't too much of an intrusion into your family's privacy, please reply to this email. And, if you are not, please pardon me for bothering you.
Sincerely,
Max Fogel

Dear Mr. Fogel,
I am his nephew. His sister, Diane, is my mother, and as you can probably guess, I'm named after him. I have always been curious about my uncle, apart from what stories my family tells. There is a side to every person that only their close friends know, that sometimes eludes their family. That's the part of my uncle I've always been curious about. My grandfather passed away almost two years ago and Uncle Claude is interred next to him in Metairie. My grandmother is still alive and still doing relatively well. She speaks about him a good deal. I appreciate you getting in touch with me. Feel free to contact me again.
Sincerely,
Claude Blackburn

Dear Mr. Blackburn,
I knew I was on the right track when I saw your portrait on your website. As I'm sure you've been told, you look a lot like your uncle. From my own experience, I know talking about such things on the phone can be awkward to say the least. Compound that with the fact that you and I have never met, I think that communicating by email will be more comfortable for both of us.

I suppose the reason why I wanted to contact Claude's family was to tie up some loose ends in my own life. When I read his obit in the *Navy Times* many years ago, I felt terrible. He was a great guy and we were best friends. For the last forty-two years, the most I could do was remember Claude whenever I did something I was lucky enough to have experienced. And I've had a really good life, all things considered: a happy marriage to a terrific woman, a career in the arts, good friends, plenty of good times and, until recently, excellent health. It's been an embarrassment of riches. In remembering Claude all this time, I like to think that I've brought him along with me, at least in spirit. I only wish we could have stayed friends through the years and grown old together. And I'm so very glad he has a namesake. If it isn't too hurtful to your grandmother at this late date, please offer my deepest condolences to her and to your mother. Your uncle was an extraordinary person, and it wouldn't surprise me if there were other people who knew him back then who were as touched by his passing as I was. Also, I'd like to ask a favor of you: if you have a photo of him that you could scan and send me, I'd be very grateful. I used to have one, but I left it at the "Wall" in DC about twenty-five years ago. Thanks again for answering my message. Best of everything to you and your family.

Sincerely,

Max Fogel

Dear Mr. Fogel,

I'm touched that your friendship with my uncle still means this much to you so many years later. I've always heard what a great guy he was, but this was always from his relatives—I've never met anyone else who knew him. I have a box of letters that he wrote my mother from California and later Vietnam, but it has been several years since I've read them. They have always been my closest link to who he really was.

Thanks again for your kind words regarding my uncle.

Sincerely—

Claude Blackburn

And that was that. For a while, at least.

A couple of years later, I was hired to perform in a touring play and, as fate would have it, I was scheduled to perform in Baton Rouge. I emailed Claude Blackburn and told him I'd be in town for three days and asked if he would he like to get together to talk about his uncle over lunch. He replied that he would be delighted. We met in a little restaurant in the university section of town and talked about Claude for three hours. I told him everything I could remember about Claude. I told him how, as college boys, we craved conversation about the things that still interested us—foreign films, classical music, jazz, real Italian food, history, all the things we loved—without being mocked and belittled by the guys who talked about nothing but cars, sports and pussy. Young Claude and I might have gone on like that for much longer, but I had a show that night, and he had to get back to his wife, who was eight and a half months pregnant. Before we parted, he thanked me profusely for giving him insight into his uncle that wasn't filtered through his family's grief. We shook hands and he handed me an envelope. In it was a print of Claude in Vietnam, looking very much like the Claude I'd seen in his first visit to my dreams. It sits on my mantle and I look at it every day.

That night, hours after the show, I lay awake in bed, hurting like mad from my arthritis. I finally drifted into a painful sleep. Claude came calling again. He whispered in my ear, "I wish you'd stop complaining about being old. Stop complaining about how much you hurt. Stop complaining about your fucking arthritis, your A-fibs, your angiogram, your A1Cs, EKGs, PVCs, PACs, X-rays, PET scans, CAT scans, MRIs, your goddamn colonoscopy, your PSA, your finger-poked prostate, your echo and stress cardiograms, your aching back, your glacial bowels, your limp dick. Shut up already! You've lived to be old; I never even got to have a real girlfriend! And what about us meeting up for the 1971 Mardi Gras? Oh yeah, that's on me. I got killed. You got the EKG, and I got the KIA."

I was hurt. "Why are you so angry with me, Claude?"

"What makes you think I'm angry with you? You've kept me alive for almost fifty years. I'm just reminding you what you should have realized a long time ago—much of the time, life hurts. My father died two years after I did; my getting killed broke his heart. My mother and sister still can't talk about me without crying. It's only you who remembers me as someone other than just another name on the Wall. By the way, that was a nice thing you did today for my nephew, telling him about the good times we had together. Now I won't just be 'Poor Uncle Claude' to him. But there's just one thing you've got to learn sooner or later: I'm only a ghost in your dreams. And everybody and everything in all your dreams is really about you. Don't feel so damn guilty; I'd have switched places with you in a New York minute. If you really need to be forgiven for your good luck, forgive yourself."

After a while I said, "Claude. What's it like where you are?"

"What's your hurry? You'll find out soon enough."

"But what's it like?"

He smiled. "It's not as bad as you think... But it's no Mardi Gras." ∎

UNTITLED 41
Paddy McCabe

UNTITLED 83
Paddy McCabe

UNTITLED 111
Paddy McCabe

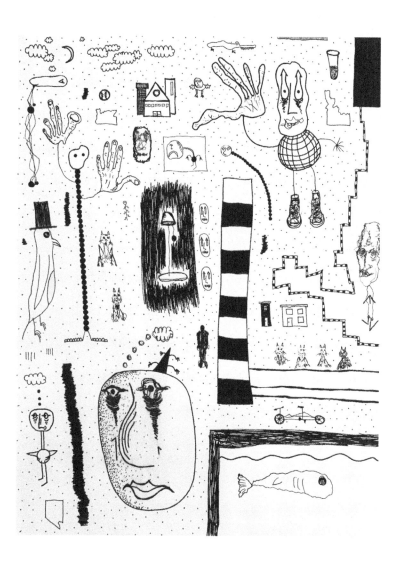

FIRST STEPS
Maud Welch

It takes three ants to open
    the peony, breaking

the well-rounded
    edge, as the afternoon

lake stretches and yawns
    with a gentle wake,

a young squirrel
    balances on a branch,

her button eyes
    surveying the far-off

narrows—where you
    have been out foraging.

Amber light brushes
    our kitchen wall,

wild thyme pauses
    at our sill. I wait

until a motor mutters and you
    undock with ten flat

rocks from the base
    of Pine Mountain.

Today you lay one by one
    into the earth—tuck

point sand and needles
    into thread thin crevices,

and as I join you barefoot
      on the surface of a single step,

I know our shared
      weight is a ceremony.

When the rains begin,
      cascading rounded edges,

how the black rocks will grin
      as they swallow.

STANDING
Tim Raymond

The day I crush the record for *Twilight Princess*'s lowest-percentage speedrun is the day I smash a human person to smithereens with my car. The police are telling me it's not my fault. The black box footage shows he jumped purposefully from behind a parked truck into oncoming traffic.

They tell me to get checked out at a hospital, but instead of that I go home. Home to Nancy, who was my wife once but who is now just a friend and dear roommate.

"Did you take a taxi?" she asks me.

"Yeah."

Nancy is on the lookout for her first serious girlfriend, which I fully support.

"Holy shit, you're bleeding," she says.

So she takes me to the hospital, where after all the doctors say I'm fine. Although, in the coming days I should watch for signs of neck or spinal injury.

I cannot relax, but not because of this dead person, this suicide, whose name is Jens. Was Jens. I had one goal, the record, and the record is crushed. I was driving that afternoon because I couldn't stand being in a house with no stakes. Usually, when I seek calm, I boot up *Zelda* and practice runs.

"Maybe," I tell Nancy, "I sensed he was there and sped on anyway. Generally what follows achievement is destruction."

"Don't be ridiculous. You can't even kill insects."

No, I cannot. In *Twilight Princess*, there is a wolf in the hero, Link. In me there is a wispy and wandering cloud.

On some level, I knew this would happen. The trick to the *TP* low-percentage speedrun is a glitch in item animation, such that if you don't click out of the pop-up triggered by every newfound rupee, then Link will slowly traverse the game's landscape even though he's not supposed to. What this means is you can bypass without keys a few locked gates and doors, which means you can complete the game with fewer items, which means a lower percentage overall, which is the point. Watching your character gaze at gemstones for hours upon hours is the point.

And yet I had let so much rest on this apparent stillness

that, when it stopped, I forgot how to traverse my landscape. My gemstones have been stripped, my rupees spent.

My therapist, Max, who understands my relationship to emotions, is not surprised that I'd rather discuss the game than the accident. My recent idea is that I will regard this new deficit in my life as an opportunity, like how he helped me do with my divorce. This time around, I will pursue an activity without a perfect precipice I can free-fall from.

"I'm thinking handstands," I tell him, if for no other reason than I like the word's associations. In the TPSR standings, I am number one, of thousands, and will shape my body accordingly.

In the meantime, I will wean myself off of *Zelda* with *Eastward*, a *Zelda*-like game that's heavy on the JRPG elements, namely a ton of dialogue and story, which make it a heinous choice for speedrunners.

"I," goes Max, over the Zoom, "love both of these ideas."

"It's one idea with two parts, actually."

"All the same."

"Nancy liked it too," I tell him.

So I give it a shot. *Eastward's* prologue has so many dialogue boxes to work through that I almost abandon all hope. My first attempts at wall-assisted handstands leave me bruised on the floor. My glasses broken. My wrist tweaked.

I manage. My car's still in the shop, to be fixed on the dime of Jens's relative, so I walk to the convenience store by Poison Spider's miniature fire station. For me, I buy Gatorade. Nancy calls cherry sours her guilty pleasure, so I load up on those as well.

The trip takes an hour total, and when I arrive home, there's a car on the street and a woman in our living room. She's older than us by ten years maybe. She and Nancy are chatting.

"Look," Nancy says, "it's Mira."

"Jens's aunt," Mira says.

"You don't have to say anything," I assure her.

"I've not even started yet."

"And you don't have to."

But she wants to, I can see, and I am no bully. She says to just let her speak her piece, that I can't be blaming myself for what happened to her nephew.

"I don't."

She can't sleep, apparently. She had to say these things out loud to me.

"How'd you get our address?" I ask her. The real question. I don't imagine the police would reveal it. The *Tribune* didn't. I'm not on social media, and while Nancy is, she's careful about privacy.

"I showed the student intern my tits," she states, then immediately walks it back. "Sorry, I don't know why I said that. But I did do it. It was lunchtime, and no one was around."

In this way, Nancy and I are introduced to Mira, the aunt. Sister of Jens's mother, who was much older than her. Mira was a surprise baby, which explains Jens being thirty-five to her forty-six. She has in her possession countless dialogue boxes, and try as I might, I cannot sort through them fast enough.

A week later, Nancy is still talking about her. She refuses to admit she likes her, perhaps out of respect for me. But this is not a respect I need, which she knows.

"Such a bizarre situation," she is suggesting.

"Why? Because her family member's death is in my orbit? He wanted to die."

"You process in your way, and I'll let my take be my own, thanks."

"We can't all implode because of it," I insist. "Find good people where you can. It was you who said that."

Her expression reads otherwise, but we both know which words were whose. Nancy's a bad liar. So bad she won't even attempt it.

When I chat with him about it later, Max agrees with her, which is fine by me because at the same time I'm sure he's on my side. As therapist, he is in the business of near-universal sides.

It's just interesting, I'm telling him, because life is supposed to be this huge open-world adventure, where you go wherever you want. Yet this development with Jens and Mira seems very linear, as though I've conquered one challenge and the Cosmic Game is presenting the logical next. I simply don't know my role in it.

"Yeah, I mean," Max says, "you won't know until you've explored a bit, huh?"

"Uh huh."

"This is the person managing all of Jens's affairs and settlements, yes? Be gentle, then."

I am cloud, I could remind him, but instead I nod. Maybe my role is to squeeze money out of her. How you can sue for emotional distress. Or maybe I'm supposed to see her tits. Or help Nancy get a peek at them.

What I've learned about handstands is that I'm bad at the pose, and that they hurt my ass muscles for some reason, yet I do think better when the blood is rushing to my head. And what I have thought today is, I should buy new glasses already.

I've been fucking up at work. The mistakes aren't major, but I'm not rotating produce that needs rotating. I can't see bruises on the apples, and I had my boss order more avocados when there were two extra boxes in the cooler.

I go downtown to the Vision Center, just because I don't know any other place. I select the best approximation of the glasses I had before, white translucent plastic, then stand there while the person fits in the lenses.

Upon leaving, I swear I see Mira exiting the Chinese restaurant across the street.

"No!" I yell to her, for whatever reason.

She does see me and jogs over, to confirm that I'm all right. My fixed car is right there.

"The intern," I ask her, "is a boy or a girl?"

"A *woman*," she says.

"Right, a woman. And you work where?"

"The *college*," she tells me.

"Right, the college."

"Which I have to go back to now. Sorry, are you sure you're okay? You yelled no at me."

"Sometimes I do that."

I too return to my place of work then, for Nancy's employed there as well. I am in Safeway produce, and she's an assistant in their pharmacy. We met originally at Casper College, where she got her pharm tech certificate and where I dropped out of a computer science program.

"She works at the college," I tell her now, at the pharmacy's counter.

"In the writing center, yeah," she says. "She told us that."

"Oh."

"And has some financial stake in the convenience store in the union? Where Jens worked."

"Really?"

"Were you not listening to her?"

"I was listening."

To this, she shrugs, then with intention caps a bottle. "Why don't you just text me, dude?"

"My phone's at home."

The proper place for it, obviously. I do my runs low percentage.

When that afternoon I visit the writing center, Director Mira is waiting for me with a card full of information. Her phone number and email address. A PO box. Even her Insta handle, oddly enough. In this way, the lines of communication open. Nancy is embarrassed, she says, but I know she means shyness and not shame. That weekend, Mira comes over for dinner, which transforms into pizza in the living room and me docking my Switch to play *Eastward* in front of them, until I'm overstimulated and mad about it.

I don't like an audience. I have to sprint my characters away from the dark miasma, but the screen's so black I can't discern snakes from a bush.

Mira is talking. About everything. She is exhausting me, and I hope she doesn't stop. The last person Nancy had over got high on the couch and called me a weirdo, in the way that I should agree. Then she puked in our bathroom. I don't know what it is, whether it's the dating apps or the small town, or our age. There are lovely people in the world, so why does my friend struggle so to locate one?

Mira is divorced. Mira is bisexual. Mira's ex-husband did not like Jens's presence in their lives. Mira could get in trouble for bribing the intern at the registrar for information. Mira could go down for exposing those boobies on campus.

Mira is attracted to Nancy, moreover, and even I can see it. How her look lingers on her. How she's careful not to get too close, lest the energy between their hands overwhelm her. But Nancy seems nervous or something, and I think she ate too much pizza and feels bloated.

She ballooned when we were married, in fact, which was how I first realized she was unsuited to life as we'd constructed it. Her relief was immense when at last I brought it up. Over the pancakes we eat on Sundays.

"What did you do with Jens's ashes?" I ask Mira. "Did he have a request for them?"

"I'm such a garbage person," she says. "He did, but I ignored it."

"So what'd you do with them?"

One thing I like about Mira is that she exercises her eyebrows whenever she speaks, as though these muscles in particular are how she churns the words out.

"I tossed them in the North Platte River, on the part that's not pretty."

"What did he want instead?"

"Not that."

"Are you not sad about his death?" I ask her, at which Nancy's eyes go wide. But Mira is fine with my question. She prefers that people be straight with her, she explains, as opposed to dancing around whatever they assume she's feeling.

Same, of course.

"Jens," she is saying, "was, or could be, how can I put it, a dick. A dickhead." And then, after pausing, her eyebrows pulsing: "He refused to get a therapist. That's not true. He got one, because I forced him, but the therapist wasn't very good and Jens didn't listen to them anyway. He had some pretty nasty tendencies."

I am a big fan of hearing about tendencies, regardless of what they are.

"I'm not surprised," she admits, "that his final act was what it was. It's horrific to me, but you seem so even-keeled about it. I swear to God."

"My therapist is good," I offer up, which is strange because Max is not why I'm even-keeled. Finding him was not what righted my ship. I evened my own keel long ago, and therapy was but one aspect of maintaining the evenness.

"Well, thank you both for inviting me over," Mira tells us. "Yes, I am sad about it." Then she cries a little.

My own tendency, among many, is to rattle inside myself until I find something to occupy my energy. It's why instead of sleeping I trek outside to the closest point of entry to the river, which is not so far away from the house. It does not, despite the ashes, appear to have adopted any human, Jens-like qualities.

On my way home, I see Mira's car parked down the street, though earlier I watched her leave. I don't go and check, but it seems the cab of the car is empty.

Then come morning it's gone, and Nancy is acting shifty, as though she's not been brewing coffee every day for the whole of her adult life.

"Did you sleep with her?" I ask.

"Who?"

Her nostrils are flared, and her lips are stretched over her teeth, like will happen after she farts.

"Mira," I say. "You liar."

"Fine, yes," she confesses. "I'm sorry, okay? I'm embarrassed. I'm a fucking awful lay, man."

She isn't, if such a thing existed.

"Really, I wasn't trying to hide anything."

No, definitely not. I'm frowning only because I wonder if this constitutes an achievement on my part.

I don't believe Mira would care how she's done or lain with, but who am I to say? Or know to any extent? I resolve to bridge these gaps between us. Step one is another dinner, this time with takeout sushi, again at the house. Step two is to not dance around anything and be up front, whatever Nancy's opinion about it.

"Did you want to stay at our house again?" I ask.

"You don't have to answer that," Nancy says.

"Yes," says Mira.

"And lie with her again?" I say.

"Yes."

Nancy's face finds her palms, suddenly.

"Because you enjoyed it."

"Yes."

"Can you tell me," I ask her, "more about Jens's tendencies? I don't get it, did he hate the river or something? Or was the river's ugly section the nearest place when you were deciding what to do?"

"Um," she starts, an eel in her cheek. "Yeah, it's hard to say. The river's always a good metaphor for life and death, I suppose. It just flows on and on, right?"

"Why is flowing a better metaphor than stillness?" I say.

"I don't know, maybe it isn't. I'm saying I don't know. But I would add that, this one time, when he was a kid, he almost drowned in a river."

"So if he was a kid, you were one too?"

"Well, a teenager by then."

"Why was he more connected to you than to his mom?"

"Cancer."

"I'm so sorry," says Nancy.

"Technically, she beat the cancer," Mira states, "but the transplant that beat it led to this rare lung disease. Anyway, trace it back to whatever you want. His dad isn't dead but may as well be."

I don't know what this means, exactly, yet lack the opportunity to ask.

"This one time," proceed her boxes, "Jens showed up at my house barefoot and claimed some thief broke in and stole his shoes. But then when I got in his car to drive him home, his shoes were there in the back seat. He'd get really angry and scream at me, then blame me for triggering him. He chopped my hair off once, because he was losing his, and justified it by saying family supports family."

I go blank then, to this, for my hair has thinned as well.

"What, should I say more?" Nancy wonders.

"No, I want to think now," I tell her, and I excuse myself to my room, where I handstand. I still need the wall, but at this point I can hold it for twenty-one seconds. After twelve, my sinuses sting.

I am contemplating my parents, who aren't dead, and for this I am glad. They have long been divorced. Our relationship was poor until the day I changed everything. We were sitting at a very tense and silent dinner, steaks, and somehow I knew my life would forever be tense and silent if I didn't inject something warm into this dead and bloodless air.

I did love them, I ultimately expressed, even if they thought I was some loser. Which they did. But then, after that, our dynamic shifted.

Who would have had to say what simple line for Jens not to fling himself in front of a car? My car. My slow and safe car that's blue. Not that I'd want it reversed necessarily, were such a procedure possible. Perhaps, I figure, him returning to the nemesis river is precisely what needed to happen.

The next day, as Mira whistles in our kitchen, I see my world record's been broken by a margin of less than one second. Some upstart gamer dodged slightly better than me in his showdown with Ganondorf.

So, the destruction that follows achievement. I wish to know how far it goes. Will I be homeless or moved when Nancy and Mira inevitably decide to live together? On their wedding day, might I break my wrist while handstanding on unfamiliar terrain? Or will nothing change ever, and we'll have coffee and whistles every other morning for as long as there's a future?

"You okay?" Nancy comes in and asks me, her hair a joyful nest.

"I'm going to need a sick day," I tell her, then ring up the store.

Later, Max says he's proud of me. I too am proud. I've set my sights once again on the record, yet in a way disconnected from Twitch and other platforms. There is no record of my runs, no streams of them, and I have zero audience. I am up to thirty seconds against the wall, with which I have built a dynamic of flirtation as opposed to reliance. We are peers, the wall and me. We have progressed beyond the teacher and student, the lender and client, the aggressor and aggressed upon. In *Eastward*, I am stumbling through New Dam City to track down the lost children.

Potentially I'd blame these children, if I didn't know much better. Sometimes what's driving us is a mechanism so convoluted and complex that no technician in the world could effectively parse it. Intuition, energy, fear, hope. Not that everything must be parsed, as Max has shown me.

The college is bustling, despite it being summer. I've come at lunchtime, because lunchtime is when Mira visits the Chinese restaurant. Cashew chicken, day in and day out. I've tasted it too, and it is rich.

At the convenience store in the union, there are two employees, both of whom present as students. I'd rather not presume, but their hair is so greasy as to be ropy. They're discussing *Minecraft*. The Dungeons port, if I'm hearing correctly.

"Is your boss Mira?" I ask them.

"No, our boss is that guy," one says. "Why?"

"Did you work with Jens?" I ask.

"Who?" the one says.

"Oh man," exclaims the other. "Jens. Yeah. Jens."

Here is what I learn. Jens was fired essentially for dereliction of duty. He did not stock the shelves or manage the shipments. He could not be trusted to engage thoughtfully, much less kindly, with the customers. One time, a bunch of Snapple bottles were lying broken on the floor, and he simply could not account for it.

"He was pretty nasty, then?" I say.

"Nasty?" says the one who knew him. "What's that mean?"

"I mean his tendencies were malicious?"

"*Jens?*" he says. "No, dude, I felt sorry for him. He seemed more scared than nasty. Like a puppy in a shelter or something. Like on the side of the road. Like, I don't know what the right word would be for him."

"Disabled," the other one says.

"You didn't even know him, Kyle."

"I have a puppy cousin, man. I'm telling you."

"We all have cousins."

"I don't," I say.

The knowledgeable one eyes me. "Hey, are you going to buy something, or what? Maybe you should go, actually. The manager's not here today."

So I go. At the registrar, I observe the clerks. None of them strikes me as student-like. One is a woman, but clearly not an intern. She has an authority about her. She also has glorious age.

I do ask if they hire interns, in my best collegiate imitation. They say no, thank you for inquiring, but there's kind of lot to all of this.

Yes, I mouth while driving home. Quite a lot.

When I see Mira next, she's holding hands with my friend, who is smiling. Who seems brighter these days. Who more than usual is not letting the monotony of pills grate on her.

Is it she who almost drowned? She who hid her shoes in the car? She who cut the hair and screamed and blamed and sucked the life from every room she entered? Mira's eyes look tired.

Of course I do not dance, thus on we run.

"You lied to us, and I want to know the reason."

"Who you talking to, chief?" says Nancy.

"The girlfriend," I say.

Mira's face is tight, her eyebrows stunned.

"So?" I ask her. "Why was Jens scared?"

Her reaction is somewhere between the dog who can't conceal his guilt and the villain who's pleased to have been outed. We all exist within this space, Max might preach, to which I would argue we're not all in each other's houses.

"I'll just go," Mira is saying.

"I don't want you to go. I want you to stay here and say why you lied to us."

"Lied about what?" asks Nancy.

"I don't totally know," Mira says.

"You've had plenty of time to think about it. Do you not have a therapist?"

Mira grins at me, which is a humor I can't crack. There's nothing that I can think of that's at all worse with therapy.

"I still don't know what the lie is," Nancy says.

"For one, she didn't show any intern her tits," I start. "For two, Jens was not the narcissist she pretended he was."

"I didn't use that word."

"For three, he didn't almost drown."

"That part's true, actually."

"So is *she* the narcissist?" Nancy asks me.

"I don't know," I say, because I don't. A narcissist wouldn't be contrite. Or a narcissist likely would pose as contrite. Or a narcissist would leave. Or I don't know what one would do or not do.

"All right, then the hair story," Nancy goes. "Who cut the hair, you or him? Be real."

We are examining her meager locks when she whispers her reply.

So she starts crying. Nancy is alarmed, but this is not what I want.

"Why'd you say that stuff about him?" I ask. "Is it grief? Mira, you said he was nasty."

"He didn't talk to me basically his entire life," she says. "Is that not? We helped him get this apartment, but he'd still come over and sit in our living room and say nothing. I said my ex hated him, which is not completely true. He hated me going on and on about him, how confused I was and stressed by him. I blamed him, I suppose. I thought I'd get cancer from him somehow. He'd sit there for hours! I don't know, my mind can go weird places if I let it. I'll just go."

"Stop saying that," I tell her. "It's annoying."

"Did you lie to me too?" Nancy says. "About our stuff?"

"White lies," Mira admits. "Normal lies. Dating lies. Did you?"

"Yeah," Nancy says.

"Did you know he'd kill himself?" I ask.

"No."

"Did it help to dump all your rotten parts on him?"

"Yes."

There's another question in me too, but as I'm piecing it together Nancy jumps in.

"Fine, so what now?"

Yes. For now, Mira stops talking about leaving and leaves. While handstanding, I lose focus and crank my neck in an awful direction. It feels like, finally, we have come full circle. The injury from the accident I never sustained. Nancy is laughing out loud to herself a lot and spouting clichés about how dispiriting dating in middle age is. "A whopper, this one," she says. "Boy."

We're in a holding pattern. A week passes without contact. Then Nancy receives a text in which Mira apologizes for having lied again. Her ex left her a bit before Jens was enmeshed in her life. He demanded she seek counseling for, as he used to put it, her dramatics.

"Which was fair," she writes. "I lied to him for months about seeing a therapist. I didn't go even a single time. I am now, though. I found one online." And she includes a screenshot of her BetterHelp account to prove it.

"That is weird as shit," Nancy says to me.

"But nice," I say. "If his death leads somewhere."

What now, what now. Two weeks, three weeks, a month, until our own house goes quiet. *Eastward* is done and sad. I'm no record holder, but my neck's feeling better. I did lose some of my progress.

"Such is progress," Max states.

Such is progress. The day I do my first unassisted handstand, a month later for barely more than a second, Nancy and I make pancakes for three people instead of two. We don't even realize it until after the table is set. See there those three heaping plates, before empty seats. Is the third for his ghost or hers?

"Huh," Nancy says.

Meaning, which thing have I destroyed now? Yet again, our life as we knew it? The holding pattern? Our day of rest is sliced fatally through.

"What do you think?" she's saying, her eyebrows glitching softly. "Want to, or?"

"Okay," I tell her, as though my answer were waiting on me, my assent locked and loaded, then set about keeping the pancakes warm. ∎

THE IMPOSSIBLE THING IS
rose auslander

the girl on our block who went for a walk in the woods. & the man who used to come by & play the drums & once when he was playing, church bells rang. & the old women in flowered house dresses who loved to listen for ambulances & say whadaya gonna do & I wasn't sure it was a question, I mean what they did was walk slowly up to church & back downhill, and after a while, they didn't do that. You know, the girl, she walked on soft paths of dead leaves & pine needles & listened for the sound of wings. & back home our bluestone sidewalks silently cracked & sank & the tree of heaven rooted, rose up & refused to leave, though God knows we tried. I mean it all started to go slow motion, brownstones crumbling, the old women taking longer to sit & forgetting to stand back up, the drummer gone touring in Europe & the church bells forgetting to ring & the girl, the girl still walking in the woods.

THE PEACE SIGN
Richard Huffman

T he VA shrink went through the usual list. "Any thoughts of harming yourself or anyone else? Still having nightmares? During the day… any flashbacks?"

Gary assured her suicide wasn't on the table. "Maybe if I believed in some religious claptrap. I guess that makes life more livable for folks, believing in fantasies."

The nameplate on her desk read Doctor Elizabeth Scott. "Maybe some people get a social benefit from it," she said. "Being around other people. Doing some community work. Volunteering for something. You're still healthy. Your mind is sharp."

"If you say so." He could see she didn't like him very much. She tried to maintain the professional curtain, but he knew eyes. Could always read a person by their eyes. "You religious?" he asked, almost an accusation.

Her hair was a shiny auburn color and hung low on her forehead, almost covering her right eye. She played with it for a second before flicking it away from her eyebrow. Gary could see he had made her uncomfortable. She was just a kid, by his standards. Maybe thirty. Didn't wear a wedding ring. Probably took a job with the VA as a last resort. Knowing the VA, he assumed the pay would be a hell of a lot less than a civilian job. But maybe it wasn't. What did he know? Nothing.

"Let's think about upping your meds a little," she said, ignoring Gary's question about her religion.

He tried to make amends. "Sure. Look… I appreciate you listening to me. It must be hard doing this all the time. Vets bellyaching about their crap. I remember an episode of *The Twilight Zone*… I think it was. This young guy eats other people's sins. Not saying that's what you do, but the idea of having to…"

"I wouldn't be doing this if I didn't like what I do," she said, straightening her back, sitting erect in the chair. Her iPhone beeped. She glanced at it. "Sorry, but time…"

"Yeah. I know. Thanks for listening to me. I can't figure it. A body would think, as time passed you by, that memories you'd rather put away would fade. So why does it get worse? Didn't bother me when I was younger. Too busy then, I guess." Jesus, he thought, now you get into it when you know the session is over. You need to tell her about Timmy. Fess up.

"Is the eighth of next month, same time, okay?"

"Uh-huh."

She tappity-tapped her keyboard. "Your new meds are in transit," she said.

* * *

Outside, Gary took the cigarette pack out of his jacket pocket and pulled one out and cupped his hand around a match and lit up.

"You got a spare?"

The guy had a ring of gray hair around an otherwise bald head. He wore a faded fatigue jacket. A few medals pinned near the collar. Bristly white beard.

Gary handed him the pack.

"Mind if I take an extra for later?"

Gary shrugged. "Take as many as you want."

"Thanks. This'll do. One now. One later. Gotta smoke 'em before I go into the apartment. They don't allow smoking. That's the price a guy has to pay, living in guv-ment-subsidized housing. I tell you, man, don't get old without money... or someone to help out. You got family?"

"Back East. I don't see 'em much. Holidays. I guess they'd help if I needed something... but they have their own lives, kids, stuff."

"Uh-huh. You got your own place?"

"It isn't much. Just a small house near downtown. Good enough for me."

The man held out his hand to shake. "I'm James," he said. "Thanks for the smokes. Must be nice having your own place."

"Gary," he said, shaking the hand. Dry, thin, bony. Dark spots on darker skin.

"You see that guy in there?" James said, nodding at a man sitting inside, on the other side of the glass front.

Gary looked. The man was staring, seemingly at nothing. Lost in space.

"That guy was a full bird colonel," James said. "Probably about our age. Old farts. All that power he had. If he was in Nam... you in Nam? If he was, he probably sent guys out to get their asses blown off. I wonder if he thinks about that? If he's just staring off like that trying to get a grip on things."

"Maybe. I wouldn't know."

James took a long drag on the cigarette. He pursed his lips and let out a spiraling smoke ring. "You take the van out here? You'd think there'd be more than two a day. All that money that goes to the VA. Billions. You'd think they could afford another van. Guess I shouldn't bitch, though. My apartment ain't bad. I get around on my bike mostly. But going anywhere out of the way is a pain in the ass."

"When's the van picking you up?"

James looked at his wristwatch. "Another half hour or so. Sometimes it's late."

Gary nodded over his shoulder toward the parking lot. "I'm going to Santa Cruz, if you want a lift."

"Sure. Beats the hell out of standing here getting blown around by the wind." He smiled and patted Gary on the arm. "Ready when you are. I just have to get my day pack. Left it over there in the bushes so it wouldn't get ripped off."

Gary watched James hustle across the driveway, disappear into the bushes and emerge with a day pack slung over a shoulder. Why would he think leaving his pack in the bushes was safer than keeping it with him during his med appointment? Weird, but then... who wasn't?

* * *

The hour ride back turned into half a day. First it was the artichokes.

"Hey," James said, "could we stop off in Castroville at the Giant Artichoke? I mean, no big deal if we don't... if you're in a hurry to get home or somethin'. I haven't had deep-fried 'choke hearts in years. Love those things."

"I don't need to be home at any particular time. But you go ahead with the artichokes. I'm not a big fan of fried food."

"Oh, one of those health nuts."

Gary took the turn off the highway into Castroville. "No, not a health nut."

There wasn't much to the town. Couple of gas stations, small shopping center, trolley-car diner, and the Giant Artichoke, where all things artichoke could be bought. Signs proclaimed Castroville as the Artichoke Capital of the World. Gary pulled into the gravel parking lot and parked near a large plastic artichoke. Bright orange. A couple of people were standing in front of it. A young boy was taking their picture.

* * *

Artichokes and Marilyn Monroe, the first artichoke queen. There were posters of her on the walls. A blurry newspaper print showed a very young Norma Jean Baker wedged between a trio of nondescript men with a crumpled sash proclaiming her the artichoke queen. A brief biographical article hung alongside describing her early life with an insane mother and a series of twelve foster homes. Gary shook his head. He could relate. Only it was his father who'd gone to the loony bin.

He looked back over his shoulder at the counter where James was ordering. "Hey, you want anything?" James asked

"No, I'm okay."

"C'mon, man... you sure... it's on me. Gotta repay you at least somethin' for the ride." The clerk was looking at Gary, waiting. He seemed impatient, bored. He tapped the eraser end of a pencil on the countertop. His hairnet sloped to one side, half covering an ear.

Gary glanced at the menu board over the counter. "Milkshake. Chocolate," he said. James gave him a thumbs-up and completed the order. For no reason Gary felt one of those times coming on as he walked to a table on the semicovered patio. Daggers of light between roof slats made the floor seem like it was moving. Things were off-kilter. He was in an undulating trough that shouldn't be there. He balanced uneasily and sat in a chair, relieved.

James had his day pack with him and shrugged it off his shoulders and laid it on the floor and kept one foot on it when he sat. "The guy said about ten minutes. I ordered a large basket so we can share. Ranch dressing dip okay by you? Man, that's the only way to go. All that other stuff, dips, I mean... bunch of hooey."

"Order number seventeen!" came a voice over a wall speaker

James looked at his receipt stub. "Bullshit. No way they can fry fresh 'chokes that fast. That guy's gonna try pawnin' off some old greasy shit." He stood quickly and took a few steps, then came back and grabbed his pack and slung it over his shoulder and strode up to the counter.

The argument could be heard throughout the restaurant. James was telling the guy that he wanted fresh fried... not something sitting under a heat lamp for hours. Gary wondered if he should intervene... but getting up from his chair seemed like it would take an effort of tremendous strength. He was afraid to get uprooted. Unmoored.

A young Mexican girl in a multicolored skirt brought him the milkshake. Her skirt was embroidered with animals that sparkled and seemed alive when she moved. She was very courteous, called Gary sir. "Here's your milkshake, sir." It made Gary smile. Pulled him back. He asked how old she was.

"Ten?" Gary said, feigning concern when she answered. "Mighty young to be waitressing." She looked confused for a minute.

"I'm just jokin'. You're about the best waitress I ever had."

She said thank you and turned and walked away. Still some decency left in the world, Gary thought, watching her go, the embroidery reflecting and shimmering before she disappeared into the mysterious workings of the Giant Artichoke's kitchen.

James was still at the counter. Gary could see that he was leaning over, watching his artichokes sizzle in a vat of oil. Gary sipped the milkshake. It was cold and creamy and made him wonder why he didn't have one more often. He hadn't had one in so long... he couldn't remember the last time... maybe ten, twenty years ago. He picked up a menu off the table and read it through. Things were getting out of hand, price wise. Thank god Linda had made sure the mortgage got paid every month. Renting a place now would be impossible.

He felt James brush against him, cursing under his breath before he plopped down the basket of fried 'chokes and set his pack on the floor and scraped the chair legs across the floor, metal screeching against concrete, and sat on the chair, scooting it closer to the table.

"How's your shake?" he asked as he concentrated on dipping an artichoke into the ranch dressing. "Now that's what I'm talking about," he said when he bit into the brown nugget. "Anybody thinks they can put one over on ole Jimmy-boy, better think again."

"Why didn't he listen?" Gary asked.

James squinted. "What?"

Gary stared at him, trying to keep himself on track. "When I told him."

James looked confused.

Gary shook his head. "I... never mind."

"You okay, man?"

"Sure. I didn't mean... it's nothing." He tried to laugh. It came out different than he'd intended.

* * *

On the way out the door, Gary nodded at the picture of Marilyn Monroe. "We would have gotten along," he said.

"Yeah. You and every other guy on the planet." James glanced at the picture and opened the door and went into the sunlight and shaded his eyes.

"I get it," Gary said, following James.

"Get what?"

"What she was going through. How she was twisted up inside. Trying to be someone she had no idea how to be, and finally got so confused it just wasn't worth it anymore."

"Sure." James stood beside the car waiting for Gary to click open the doors. "Thanks for stopping, man." He burped. "My gut will probably make me pay later but it's worth it. They were better than I remember. Going to need some exercise to work it off... Hey!... Let's stop at Moss Landing and rent some kayaks. Haven't done that in years. We can grab a six-pack and kayak into the slough, relax, watch the otters, have a few brewskis. Can you handle it? I mean with your leg. I noticed the limp."

Gary waited before answering. He thought about going home. Watch some TV, veg out. Pet the dog. Sure, if you wanted to dig him up. But there wouldn't be any TV, would there? Stupid. Breaking the remote. Maybe take another walk downtown. Look into store windows. Go through the bookstore. Buy a book, go to a restaurant, back table, read, go home, take sleeping pills. Would three do it? Finally get some real sleep without the nightmares. Maybe something wrong with the old noodle. Wires crossed. Synapses closing down? Wake up at two, then three, then four. Christ, how many pills did a guy need? Get up. Walk around the neighborhood. Go back downtown. Bums in every alcove, every doorway. Sleeping before getting rousted so they could steal enough to buy more drugs.

Maybe the cops would stop him, ask a few questions. At least it would be something. Was this how it would go until the last day? Waiting. Watching the clock. Was the midnight hour near? Maybe five minutes to go and figure it all out then.

"Okay," Gary said. "Let's go kayaking."

They stopped at a grocery store before getting back on the highway. Gary waited in the car while James went in for the beer.

"Want some nuts?" James asked as he slid back into the seat. He held out an opened cellophane package of peanuts and set the six-pack on the floor at his feet.

"No." Gary started the car, shifted into drive and left the parking lot.

James watched him. "You're a bit of an odd duck, aren't you?"

"How's that?"

"I mean nothing bad about that. I fit into that category too. But you seem… I dunno… alone? I can see you leaving sometimes. Inside your head, I mean. Something eating at you, isn't there?"

Gary sighed. "None of your concern."

"Okay. I wasn't… Never mind."

* * *

Gary's kayak was dark red and had been scratched up a bit. James had insisted on a new-looking yellow one when they tried to give him one like Gary's.

They stuffed the beer in one of Gary's day packs and stowed it in the kayak's small sealed compartment. James put his day pack in his canoe's compartment. The sign in the rental office read, "No smoking or alcoholic beverages allowed." "Bullshit!" James had whispered under his breath. He balked at wearing a life jacket but they wouldn't let him go without it.

They were lucky. The tide was close to evening out. They'd be going into the slough with it helping them along. An hour later, when they could paddle back in, it would have reversed. The winds were light. A few clouds were far off, in the west, which gave the promise of a nice sunset.

They paddled into the ocean inlet and rounded the corner, went under the highway bridge, and entered the slough. It took a few minutes to get away from the noise of cars and trucks. Gary thought he saw something out of the corner of his eye and looked down into the water. He wondered if it was just him looking back at himself… his shadow following along. Or it could just be a large, murky fish. Lazy, hiding under the kayak for the shade.

"Otters," James said. Gary looked to where James pointed. A pair of otters snuggled together on a little muddy beach. "Hey, hand me a beer, would ya?"

Gary removed the top of the storage space and pulled his day pack out and wrangled the plastic holder off the six-pack. James bumped his kayak against Gary's as Gary handed him two beers.

"Ah," James said. "Still cold." He snapped the can open and tilted beer into his mouth. "Nice." He pushed his paddle against Gary's kayak and looked back over his shoulder and drank the rest of the beer.

"Thirsty?" Gary said.

"Yep. You?"

"Not so much. I can take some time."

James squinted at Gary. He opened the second beer and drank in gulps and lowered the can. "You drinkin' or not?"

"No hurry. I only need one. You can have the rest. I'll be driving back. Don't need another DUI."

"Another?"

"Just when I was a kid. Spent the night in jail. Fined, drunk driving school. Don't need to ever redo that."

They paddled at the far left of the slough, away from the electric power plant and its two five-hundred-foot chimneys. Gary thought it odd that an electric power plant overlooked the wetlands, probably spewing out who knows what. Not anything good.

"Hey," James said, "let's check it out."

Gary looked to where James was paddling. A narrow waterway came off the slough and disappeared into head-high tule weeds. It was barely wide enough for a kayak. He quickly lost sight of James when he entered the passageway, which immediately made a turn, then another turn, going farther into the weeds. He could hear James paddling. "Where did you go?" he said. "Not sure I like this." He couldn't be more than fifty feet into the weeds but he was already lost. He couldn't see anything but the weeds and the sky.

"Over here. Just keep paddling."

Gary began to sweat. How was he going to turn around? Weeds scraped against the bottom of the kayak. He thought about jumping in, lifting the kayak, and turning it. He pushed his paddle down into the murky water. Mud. He kept pushing. Just mud that stuck like glue to his paddle. He would never get out if he went over the side. Stuck forever. He thought he wouldn't mind if Linda were with him. He should have died when she did. He'd thought about it back then… dying… but had been too afraid to do it. He heard something rustling through the weeds. What could live back here? He peered through the dry stalks. A movement then and maybe a shadow? He should have kept a better watch. Stationed himself on higher ground. But there was no higher ground. Something was under his boat. It had been out there in deeper water. How could it follow in here? Water six inches deep. What kind of thing could manage that? Nothing. It couldn't be something alive. Only the dead. The dead could go anywhere. Maybe he was. Now in this labyrinth that had been waiting for him all these years. A maze for mice, for rats, for him.

James's yellow kayak suddenly appeared, coming backward. He was using his paddle to push against the mud. "There you are," he said. "This is a mess, ain't it? Kinda cool, though, being back here all alone where nobody can see us."

Gary didn't say anything.

James managed to get his kayak at a forty-five-degree angle to Gary's, the nose of the kayak in the weeds. The dry rustle against the sides. The weeds bending from the intrusion. He took his pack out of the storage compartment, unzipped it and pulled out a sealed baggie. "Want some coke?"

No, Gary thought, *I don't want any fucking coke. I just want to get outta here.* He shook his head.

James shrugged. "Whatever." He opened a small paper packet and took a short straw from a pocket and snorted. "You sure?" he said, sniffling and rubbing under his nose.

"No!"

"Okay, partner. No problem." He snorted more coke into each nostril, rewrapped everything and put his pack back into the bin. "Ah, man, this is the life."

James started talking, nonsense cocaine philosophy, yakety yak yakety. Gary half paddled and half pushed his kayak backward. The water deepened. In five minutes they were back out on the slough. James was still rapping.

A group of rented kayaks had circled around one that was longer, sleeker. Somebody yelled across the water. "You're not allowed in there! Can't you read? There are signs everywhere!" The other kayakers turned and stared their disgust at Gary and James.

"Hey...go fuck yourself!" James yelled back.

* * *

After they returned the kayaks the girl told them that they were eighty-sixed from ever renting a kayak again. "I heard what you did," she said in righteous indignation.

James took a step forward. "You think I give a shit?" he said.

The girl's eyes showed her fear. She backed up.

* * *

On the car ride back James kept verbally abusing the kayak people. Finally Gary told him he didn't want to hear any more. James went silent for a moment. Gary shifted his eyes to meet James's hard stare.

James nodded. "Uh-huh. You think I'm an asshole for the way I do. It's the only way, man. You think it was only over there where 'kill or be killed' was a thing. Just as bad here. Course you don't see things the same way I do. How could you? Consider me bein' your prophet.

Something's got a hold on you. I can see it. You're going to explode someday or end up like that colonel back at the clinic."

* * *

Even though it was close to five o'clock, the traffic wasn't bad going into Santa Cruz. On the other side of the freeway, it was the usual end of the workday jam. "Fucking mess," James said, shaking his head at the mass of cars. "Can you let me off at the Emeline exit. I have some shit I have to take care of at the wacko center, if it's still open."

Gary got off at Emeline Avenue, refused to take the five dollars James tried to give him and watched him shoulder his pack and walk off. He took a left, then a right on Button Street and pulled into the driveway of his small yellow house with trimmed shrubbery and a manicured lawn. He opened the door and stood outside for a few moments and felt the cool breeze that foretold fog was on its way in. He finger tested the newly painted door trim. Still a little tacky. It was supposed to be fast-drying enamel. Maybe they thought fast meant two days.

Inside it felt like it had been deserted. No dog to come whining up to him. No TV that he usually left on to dissuade thieves, of which there were plenty in his neighborhood. He opened the cabinet door and took out the Chivas Regal and poured three fingers' worth into a tumbler and plopped in a piece of ice, twirled the drink around a few seconds, fished out the ice and almost threw it on the floor, remembering in time that Sport wasn't there to gobble it up. He tossed the cube into the sink. It slithered across the porcelain and down into the garbage disposal. He sat in the recliner and sipped the drink. His reflection stared back at him from the blank TV screen. Gary squinted. It seemed like he could see the remnants of the last image before he had turned it off. He couldn't remember what it was. As he looked deeper into the TV, he swore there was something there, beyond the screen, a show playing. At first it was just gray shadows, like the ones back in the slough in the water. The dread of it hit him then. He knew what this was going to be. His heart was a drum beating against his chest.

He could see their faces clear as day. Three Southern California beach boys. They were in the bunks across from him. Neighbors. They acted like it was nothing. Like they were just waiting for the next wave. Like being in Vietnam wasn't really a part of their world. He tried to talk to them. Said, "Hi, how goes it?" They stared at him like he was from Mars or some social outcast trying to bust into their inner circle. Only the one, who looked like he was about twelve years old, gave a brief smile before he realized that befriending a stranger would break the inner circle. Timmy, they called him.

Four days before going into the field, the mortars started. He ran into the bunker. It smelled of rot, stale cigarettes. Some new guys were there, in the dark. Everyone scared to death as the mortars walked in, ever closer. He'd have felt better if he'd had his rifle. Not for another four days. He swallowed the bile that was pure gut fear when he heard the small arms fire. Bap-bap-bap into the sides of the sandbagged bunker. The return fire of the M50s from the guard towers. Grenades maybe, or land mines going off. Even inside the bunker, the staccato light of flares parachuting down. Faces lit unnaturally bright for a few seconds then fading back to dark shadows. It was over in a half hour. The longest thirty minutes of Gary's life.

Flares were still descending as he walked back to the barracks. All quiet. An unreal world exposed. Fifty yards out, rolls of concertina wire he hadn't noticed before now looked alive, undulating coils brought to life. The silhouettes of men in the guard towers. The muzzles of their M50s hot, aimed at whatever lay hiding on the other side of the wire. It was suicide… gooks trying to cross that much open ground. Too far out to see their bodies. Ah… but there was one. His silhouette tangled in the wire. A marionette loose of its strings. Gary waited for it to get up, like it would in a movie after the scene was over and the director said, "Cut!"

A white parachute on the ground not far off. Its magnesium flare still glowing. Odd.

Back inside the surfers had built a child's fort of their mattresses on the floor and were half-in, half-out, giggling. They looked at Gary, grinning. One flapped his arms clucking, imitating a chicken. Gary wouldn't have denied it. They were above it all. Having each other for protection. No need for bunkers.

Gary laid back on his bed. His bunkmate had gone into town earlier. Missed the whole thing. Gary felt numb.

"Hey, there's a parachute out there!"

Gary opened his eyes. The one, Timmy, was standing in the doorway looking out like an excited child, "Hey, guys, that'd be a great souvenir for my sister."

They encouraged him. "Go get it. We'll stand guard."

Stand guard, Gary thought. *Against what?* He should tell the kid to forget about it. Get some sleep.

"What if it's not out?"

"Jesus, Timmy, you big wimp." one said, egging him on. "Here take a canteen of water just in case. Douse it."

Gary sat up. Pushed himself onto his feet. The two of them turned and looked at him. "Yeah... wadda you want?"

"He shouldn't..."

"Fuck you, man. You think you're going to get it instead of us?"

"No, but..."

"Go back to sleep, dude. We got this."

Timmy was looking back at him, a grin on his face. A little boy's mocking sneer to keep up with his pals.

"Sure," Gary said. "Go ahead. Pour water on it if it isn't completely out. That should do it." He might as well have told him to pour gasoline on a fire.

* * *

Staring at the TV screen, Gary thought back on it. *I didn't really think the magnesium flare would still be hot, did I? No way would it still be. The kid would have his trophy. A white parachute. How many flares hit the ground still burning. One in a million? And what kind of fool would throw water on it? Just some dumb kid.*

* * *

The next day, the two surfers packed up and were gone. They didn't say a word. They looked wore down. A lousy way to start their field duty. Already scarred. It would only get worse. Their trio broken up. Invulnerability gone.

* * *

A bird hitting his glass window pulled Gary out of it. He looked around the living room. Went to the kitchen. Drank a beer. Into the bathroom. Took a couple of buproprion tabs. Walked outside. The fog just settling. He found the bird on the ground. A dove. It was still alive. Gary took his shirt off and carefully picked up the dove, concealing its eyes so it wouldn't be afraid. He cuddled it against his chest. Felt its warmth on his skin, through his shirt.

He took it inside, thinking about what he should do. Whatever it was, he wasn't going to let it die. Not this time. ∎

ROMAINE IS NOT A BLUEBERRY
Thomas Wawzenek

When I was a kid, I always wanted to go blueberry picking. There were many times when I, along with my younger brother and sister, would ask my father to take us, but he always refused, saying that he didn't want to drive ninety minutes from Chicago to some farm in Michigan just to pick blueberries that we could just as easily buy in a store.

But there was one summer when we did pick romaine lettuce. I know you may think it strange, and wonder why we didn't pick iceberg or green leaf lettuce instead.

We were on a road trip driving through California, Salinas Valley to be more exact, when my father noticed a number of romaine lettuce farms along the way. That summer my father wanted to take the family on a road trip to the West Coast. He felt he needed a break from his job and that it would be good for our family to share some time together. Back then, my father worked for the Florsheim Shoe Company, whose headquarters were in Chicago, and he was part of the marketing team. One of his ideas, which was soon copied by many shoe stores throughout the country, was that anyone who bought a pair of shoes at Florsheim received a complimentary shoehorn. My father was a big believer in shoehorns. In our house there were five shoehorns hanging from the kitchen wall, which were designated for each family member. We didn't have those cheap plastic or tin shoehorns, but ones that were made out of animal bone with a wooden handle that was intricately carved. To this day, I don't know where my father purchased them. My father made sure my brother, sister and I used our shoehorns whenever we put our shoes on before going to school or church.

"Using a shoehorn saves the back of your shoes, and the back of your shoes is everything, think of it like the spine in your body," he would always say.

At the dinner table, he would tell us about college students who would buy a pair of shoes at Florsheim and refuse to take the free shoehorn. "I just don't understand it, what's wrong with young people nowadays?" my father would say. And when I turned fourteen, I became like those young people who refused to accept the free shoehorn. I felt rebellious and would get under my father's skin by not using a shoehorn. I would often tell him that shoehorns were for squares. My father couldn't understand the generational divide about using a shoehorn. The shoehorn to my dad was just as indispensable as carrying a pocket comb or a handkerchief.

As we continued to drive through Salinas Valley, my father said in an enthusiastic voice, "Hey gang, what do you think of the idea of picking some romaine lettuce!" I think my father wanted to make it up to us for all the times he had refused to take us blueberry picking.

My sister, Mia, who was six, and my brother, Billy, who was eight, both let out a cheer. I don't think they were necessarily excited about the prospect of picking lettuce, they just wanted to get out of the car because the air-conditioning had stopped working. In my teenage angst I moaned, "Are you serious? Lettuce picking?" Even though a couple of years earlier, I had bugged my father about taking us blueberry picking, I now felt too cool to want to pick any fruit or vegetable from some farm.

Billy, who was the quintessential middle child, already learning how to play the peacemaker, said, "Maybe this will be fun."

And with that response, I gave him a quick poke to the ribs with my elbow to shut him up so as not to encourage my father.

My surly attitude didn't deter my father's enthusiasm. He really seemed in awe of all the lettuce farms and said, "It will be fun. Just think, we will be picking fresh lettuce that we can eat with our dinner!"

My mother, sitting in the front, gave my father a dubious look and told him that she didn't think any of these farms allowed people to pick lettuce, and besides, she added, we were staying in a motel and eating at restaurants, so when were we going to eat fresh lettuce? But my father quickly dismissed her concerns.

"I know for a fact that all farms welcome the public to pick some of their crops because it's good for customer relations. And we can all snack on the lettuce in our hotel room at night while watching TV," he responded.

As a little sidebar here, I have to add that whenever someone in my family questioned my father, he would always respond, "I know for a fact," but he never stated where he got this fact from and none of us challenged him about it.

We approached another lettuce farm and my father turned down the entrance road, ignoring a large NO TRESPASSING sign.

"This looks like as good of a place as any," he said.

"Dale, what are you doing? We're trespassing," said my mother.

"Do you want us to get arrested?"

My father ignored her concerns and drove another couple hundred feet until we were stopped by this elderly man in overalls who stood in the middle of the road with his hand raised for us to stop. We all figured he had to be the owner of this farm.

The farmer walked over to the driver's side of the car and gave us a wary look. The farmer might have thought for a moment that he was in some time warp and witnessing a Depression-era family from Oklahoma looking for work. "You do know this is private property. Are you folks lost?"

My dad gave him a smile and said, "No, sir, we're not lost. I don't mean to trespass on your property, no, sir, no harm intended, I'm a law-abiding man taking my good family on a road trip. I'm just driving through so that we can pick some romaine lettuce from your fields."

The old farmer scratched the white bristles on his unshaven cheeks and shook his head. "No, no, no. I have a rule where I don't allow people to pick lettuce on my farm. I don't see what good it will do having people running about like rabbits on my property."

My father wasn't going to be deterred because this old farmer had some kind of rule. He tried to convince the farmer that we only wanted to pick a few heads of lettuce and then go on our way. He even told the farmer that this would be a great learning experience for city kids. "All I'm asking is to let us pick a few heads of lettuce."

The farmer studied us as his eyes moved to each of our faces. My father, being a man born and raised in Chicago, knew how to persuade a person. He pulled out his wallet and pushed a twenty and a five-dollar bill toward the farmer. "All I'm asking is for a few minutes. What do you say?" And for good measure, my father opened the glove compartment and pulled out a shoehorn and handed it to the farmer as well. For some mysterious reason, my father always kept extra shoehorns in the glove compartment.

I think it was the twenty-five bucks from my father's wallet that convinced the farmer to let us pick some lettuce, though I'm sure my father thought it was the shoehorn that did the trick. The farmer then directed where my father should park the car. As we all came out of the car, the farmer stood with his hands on his hips and looked us over as if we were potential laborers.

The farmer motioned for us to stand in front of him. He cleared his throat and said, "Before you start, let me give you a little background about romaine lettuce. Did you kids know romaine lettuce is the most nutritious lettuce you can eat? It is also the type of lettuce that is often used in Caesar salad."

I was overcome with despair and thought, *What are we doing here? How do I get out of this?* It went through my mind to just collapse and pretend that I'd fainted as a way of getting out of this situation. But in the end, I decided it was best to just to sit on the ground as a way of showing my displeasure.

My mother became upset with me and said, "Michael, what's wrong with you? Stand back up!"

Mia then began to cry, saying she was thirsty and didn't want to pick any stupid lettuce. And my father added to the confusion by asking, "What do you got here? Three hundred acres? Four hundred?"

"What? Acres?" The farmer was visibly upset that his little speech about romaine lettuce had been interrupted. He closed his eyes for a second as it trying to remember where he left off, but when he opened his eyes again, he gave us a blank look. The farmer decided to forego the history lesson about romaine lettuce and said in a weary voice, but still trying to sound commanding, "Now listen, I want all of you to stay on the edge of the field, I don't want you kids horsin' around and rompin' through my fields."

"You hear that, kids?" my father piped in. "Don't go acting like a bunch of dunderheads."

"And each one of you is only allowed to pick two heads of lettuce. Just two heads apiece," added the farmer.

"Sounds good to me, this will be fun, let's go, gang!" said my father as he clapped his hands together.

I got back on my feet, realizing it was inevitable that we were going to be picking lettuce, if I liked it or not. I said to my family, "This is so, like, totally uncool. You guys better not, like, tell any of my friends about this when we get back home."

We went to the edge of this large field, where we saw the rows of romaine lettuce extend to the horizon. The farmer pointed to a small area at the edge of the field where we were allowed to pull heads of lettuce. The farmer gave us a burlap bag for our harvest. Billy and Mia were surprised to see that lettuce grew on the ground and not in trees. They had been looking forward to climbing up a tree and pulling lettuce from the branches. Mia had a difficult time trying to pull a head of lettuce from the ground and started to cry again. I felt bad for her, she looked miserable, so I helped her pull a couple of heads from the ground. I also helped Billy, who was struggling as well. My mother gave me a smile as she tousled my hair. She gave me her usual qualifying compliment by saying, "You can be very helpful… when you want to be."

After we were done, my father shook the farmer's hand. "Thanks so much. You don't know how exciting this was for all of us. I can't wait to tell my friends back in Chicago that I actually picked lettuce on a farm!"

For the first time, the farmer gave us a small smile. I think he was smiling because he was thrilled to get twenty-five bucks for ten heads of lettuce—way over the market rate he would normally get from a distributer.

I wanted to salvage the afternoon that was wasted on lettuce picking. I thought maybe the farmer had horses on the farm and we could go horseback riding, so I asked him, "Do you, like, got any horses on this farm?"

"No, I don't have any horses now. There hasn't been a horse on this farm since I was boy. I still remember that horse, he was a good horse and I named him…"

But before the farmer could go any further with his little story, which I was certain would prolong our stay, I blurted out, "This farm is, like, so lame."

My father tried to cover up that remark by thanking the farmer again in an enthusiastic manner, but the farmer looked distracted because he was wondering why his farm was so lame.

He wanted to respond to my comment as he opened his mouth a few times, but before he could get any words out, my father quickly herded us back into the car.

As we drove away, I turned around and watched the farmer stand in the middle of the road, staring at the shoehorn. My mother turned around and said to me, "What's wrong with you? How many times have I told you not to call something lame."

It was at that point when Mia announced she had to go the bathroom while Billy said he was dying of thirst. But none of this dampened my father's spirit. He whistled softly to himself, content that we as a family had just shared a meaningful experience together and had ten heads of romaine lettuce in the trunk of the car. ∎

NO PARTICULAR SHORE
Patrick Dundon

I used to think that to give voice to my feelings
was a kind of power, but now I walk behind you

in the desert and watch your white shirt fill
with wind. You jot down a lyric, and I see

smoke from some anonymous fire. I think
I hear a car door slam and my mother yell

and smell the exhaust as she drives away, then
I look up and it is your face, your smile, the word

trust carried on your breath, hot with wine.
When we play music in your living room

between two mirrors, you at your harp,
me with my flute, and we fall into our private

hallway of curtains and lamps, I want to know
what strange flickerings brought me here

to my own body, propped somewhere
between relief and neglect, fresh from dream.

I once thought I could scrub the underside
of my loneliness with therapy, could pull

from my life a willful catharsis, and the ample
hands of light would lift me into my senses,

but no, I still wander in this garden where
I watch the leaves of an oak tree open, a small

resurrection, and I am submerged in your breath
like seaweed swaying in a hypnotized slow-dance

toward no particular shore.

NOTES ON CONTRIBUTORS

GREG AMES is the author of *Buffalo Lockjaw*, a novel, and *Funeral Platter*, a collection of short stories. His work has appeared in *Best American Nonrequired Reading*, *Southern Review*, *The Sun*, and *McSweeney's*, among others. He teaches in the English department at Colgate University.

rose auslander is the author of the book *Wild Water Child*, the chapbooks *Folding Water*, *Hints*, and *The Dolphin in the Gowanus*, and poems in the *Berkeley Poetry Review*, *New American Writing*, *New Ohio Review*, *Baltimore Review*, *RHINO*, *Rumble Fish*, *Tinderbox*, and *Tupelo Quarterly*.

DREW CALVERT lives in Claremont, California. His stories have appeared in *The Kenyon Review*, *The Threepenny Review*, *Gulf Coast*, *The Missouri Review*, and elsewhere. His awards include an Arts Fellowship from the Iowa Writers' Workshop and a Fulbright grant for creative writing. He is at work on a book of short stories and a novel.

HARRISON COPP is currently a first year undergraduate at Yale University. While he has always been drawn to the power of storytelling – whether that be through books, short stories, or film – he has limited experience writing stories. "Fata Morgana" is his first piece of published writing. For literary inspiration, he looks to the short stories of Haruki Murakami and Hemingway, the poems of Ocean Vuong, and the films of Wong Kar-Wai.

MARK CRIMMINS's first book was published by Adelaide's Everytime Press in 2020. That book, *Sydneyside Reflections*, was the first to be published in his multivolume sequence of second-person travel memoirs. Mark's stories were nominated for Pushcart Fiction Prizes in 2015, 2019, and 2022. His fiction has also been nominated for a Million Writers Award and a Best of the Net Award. In 2022, his single-sentence story "A Tiny Island" won the Editor's Choice Award for best fiction in Kansas' annual magazine *Inscape*. Mark's stories and flash fictions have been published in over sixty literary journals, including *Columbia Journal, Confrontation, Queen's Quarterly, Apalachee Review, Eclectica, Kyoto Journal, Kestrel, Atticus Review, Fiction Southeast, Tampa Review, Del Sol Review, Cagibi,* and *Chicago Quarterly Review.* After receiving his doctorate in Twentieth Century Literature (with a thesis on Bellow) from the University of Toronto, Mark was an Assistant Professor and Lecturer in Modern and Contemporary Transatlantic Fiction at the University of Toronto from 1999 to 2016. He is currently an Associate Professor of English Studies at the Chinese University of Hong Kong, Shenzhen. He is seeking a publisher for his first collection of stories, *Characters Madmen Alone Can Read,* and his first novel, *The Meditations of Max Botnik.*

DANTE DI STEFANO is the author of four poetry collections including *Ill Angels* (2019) and the book-length poem *Midwhistle* (2023).

MICHAEL DOWNS's books include a novel, *The Strange and True Tale of Horace Wells, Surgeon Dentist, The Greatest Show: Stories,* and *House of Good Hope,* which won the River Teeth Literary Nonfiction Book Prize. He has won a fellowship from the National Endowment for the Arts and a Fulbright award to Kraków, Poland.

PATRICK DUNDON is the author of the chapbook *The Conspirators of Pleasure* (Sixth Finch Books, 2020). His work has appeared or is forthcoming in *The Iowa Review, Gulf Coast, Washington Square Review, Copper Nickel, The Adroit Journal, DIAGRAM,* and elsewhere. He's a graduate of the MFA program at Syracuse University and currently lives in Portland, Oregon where he teaches creative writing at the Independent Publishing Resource Center.

JOSH EMMONS grew up in Northern California, and after stints in the American Midwest, South and East Coast, now lives in Pasadena, city of roses. He's published two novels, *The Loss of Leon Meed* and *Prescription for a Superior Existence,* and a short story collection, *A Moral Tale and Other Moral Tales.* Currently at work on a new novel, *The New Romantics,* he's also writing a television pilot that revives the Sam Spade character from *The Maltese Falcon.* His story in this issue of *Chicago Quarterly Review,* "Bull's-eye," grew out of a hard day he once spent at an archery range, seeing "the world's most pierced man, Fakir," at a tattoo parlor in Santa Cruz at an impressionable age, the later experience of divorce, lockdown-era home fitness, and ambivalence about kombucha. He has a daughter, Maggie, whose dog, Louis, is important to her.

PHILIP ESKENAZI is a writer of fiction. He holds a PhD from Erasmus University Rotterdam, where he teaches philosophy of science. In addition, he teaches executives about decision making, drawing on his vast personal experience of bad decisions. Philip's first story was recently published by *The Missouri Review*. He lives in Delft, the Netherlands, and is working on his first novel.

KIRK GLASER's poetry has been nominated twice for the Pushcart Prize and has appeared in *The American Journal of Poetry*, *Nimrod*, *The Threepenny Review*, *Catamaran*, *The Cortland Review*, and elsewhere. Awards for his work include an American Academy of Poets prize, C. H. Jones National Poetry Prize, and University of California Poet Laureate Award. He teaches writing and literature at Santa Clara University, where he serves as Director of the Creative Writing Program and Faculty Advisor to the *Santa Clara Review*. He is co-editor of the anthology, *New California Writing 2013*, Heyday Books.

JUSTIN GROPPUSO-COOK is a writer-in-residence at InsideOut Literary Arts Project and poetry reader for *West Trade Review*. His poems have recently appeared or are forthcoming in *Best New Poets*, *Ghost City Press*, *Bear Review*, *Harbor Review*, *Luna Luna Magazine*, and *EcoTheo Review* among others. He received the 2021 Haunted Waters Press Award for Poetry and was a finalist for *Black Warrior Review*'s 2022 Poetry Contest. His chapbook, *Illuminated Pupils*, was a semifinalist for the Tomaž Šalamun Prize. More information can be found on his website www.sunnimani.com.

COLTON HUELLE is a friendly neighborhood fiction guy hailing from scenic Manchester, New Hampshire. He is a student in the MFA program at the University of New Hampshire, where he also teaches composition and creative writing. His work has appeared or is forthcoming in *The Los Angeles Review*, *SOFTBLOW*, and *The Prism Review*.

RICHARD HUFFMAN has had a lifelong passion for creative writing. First short story ever published being in a grade school newsletter. More recently, stories in *The Reed*, *Good Times*, *Catamaran*, *phren-Z*, *CQR*. He has several novels in the wings, lacking perfection. Gritty historical westerns. Race relations in and after the Vietnam war, and a 'mystery thriller.' Fortunate to live in Santa Cruz, California, a hotbed of talented writers and poets.

RICHARD JACOBS lives in Pennsylvania. His short fiction has appeared in the *Sewanee Review*, the *Penmen Review*, *October Hill Magazine*, and the *Lindenwood Review*. He is at work on a novel.

STEPHEN EARLEY JORDAN II was born in Iaeger, West Virginia and raised in Huntington, West Virginia. Jordan attended Alderson-Broaddus College, where he earned a BA in Writing and a BA in Literature. After his first book in 2006, *Beyond Bougie*, Jordan toured colleges and universities where he coordinated writing workshops on creative nonfiction and was a guest speaker for issues of race, class, and gender. He is the author of various books of poetry, essays, and creative nonfiction. His most recent publication is *Gods Mourn Too*, essays on writing and questions for thought. Jordan currently lives in San Juan, Puerto Rico. StephenEarleyJordan.com

MARKUS KIRSCHNER is a writer and teacher. He has taught writing at Columbia University, Adelphi University and currently teaches at The Reader in Berlin, Germany.

AMY MARQUES grew up between languages and places and learned, from an early age, the multiplicity of narratives. She penned children's books, barely read medical papers, and numerous letters before turning to short fiction and visual poetry. She is a Pushcart Prize, Best Small Fictions, and Best of the Net nominee and has work published or forthcoming most recently in *Streetcake Magazine*, *MoonPark Review*, *Bending Genres*, *Gone Lawn*, *Jellyfish Review*, and *Reservoir Road Literary Review*. You can find more at https://amybookwhisperer.wordpress.com.

JESSIE REN MARSHALL is a fiction writer and playwright. Some of the places you can find her work are *Gulf Coast*, *ZYZZYVA*, *Joyland*, *The Gettysburg Review*, *The Common*, *The New York Times*, and at jessierenmarshall.com. "Mrs. Fisher" will appear in her story collection *WOMEN! IN! PERIL!* (Bloomsbury, 2024). She lives off-grid with her dogs on Hawai'i Island and is working on her debut novel, *ALOHALAND*.

PADDY MCCABE studied English and Creative Writing at Oberlin College, where he serialized comic strips in the school newspapers. He grew up in Chicago, but now lives in Columbus, Ohio, where he is a PhD student in English at Ohio State University. His main areas of study are comics, film, and environmental humanities. Several of the artists he most admires are cartoonists (Lynda Barry, Chris Ware, Nick Drasno, Emil Ferris, to name a few), and his art is generally inspired by reading comics. In addition to the kind of visual art seen here, he also makes comics (both strips and longer form narratives) and writes fiction. He lives with his cat, Princess. Princess wakes him up too early and sometimes destroys his things. She also likes to interrupt his work by sitting on his paper as he draws. He loves her all the same.

EIREENE NEALAND's stories, poems and translations have appeared in *ZYZZYVA*, *Drunken Boat*, *Chicago Quarterly Review*, *Poetry International*, *Catamaran*, and *The St. Petersburg Review*, among other places. Her books include *The Nest*, a collaboration with architect Megan Luneburg (Nova Kultura 2017) and *The Darkroom*, a translation with Alta Ifland (Contra Mundum 2021) of Marguerite Duras' experimental film *Le Camion*. She currently lives on a boat in California.

Ricardo Eliécer Neftalí Reyes Basoalto (1904 – 1973), better known by his *nom de plume* and later legal name, **PABLO NERUDA**, was a Chilean poet-diplomat and politician who won the 1971 Nobel Prize in Literature. Neruda became known as a poet when he was just thirteen years old, and wrote in a variety of styles, including surrealist poems, historical epics, overtly political manifestos, a prose autobiography, and passionate love poems such as the ones in his collection *Twenty Love Poems and a Song of Despair* (1924). Inimitably, from Neruda and the egalitarian stride of his poems, an international Whitman emerges, the poet for everyman. In Neruda's odes, especially, the legacy he has bequeathed to us is in the astonishment of the awareness of living simply but deeply. The three books of odes he composed, for regular newspaper publication in *El Nacional*, in Caracas, in the 1950s, were possibly some of the happiest periods of Neruda's creative life.

KRISTY NIELSEN has published fiction and poetry in numerous literary journals. In addition, she co-wrote a screenplay based on two of her short stories. The resulting feature film, *A Measure of the Sin*, is available as video on demand.

JACK NORMAN is a short story writer from North Queensland, Australia. He is currently based in Brisbane, Queensland where life is expected to change upon the arrival of a new baby girl. Jack has appeared before in *Chicago Quarterly Review*. He is mostly interested in stories concerning rural Australia and the often-parodied characters who still live there.

MARCUS ONG KAH HO / 王家豪 was born and raised in Singapore. His stories have appeared or are forthcoming in *Washington Square Review*, *The Adroit Journal*, *X-R-A-Y*, *Hayden's Ferry Review*, and *Salt Hill Journal*, among other publications. He is at work on a novel and a short story collection. Read more at www.marcusongkh.com.

ANDREW PORTER is the author of the short story collections *The Theory of Light and Matter* (Vintage) and *The Disappeared* (forthcoming from Knopf in April 2023), and the novel *In Between Days* (Knopf). His short stories have appeared in *The Pushcart Prize Anthology*, *Ploughshares*, *One Story*, *The Southern Review*, *The Missouri Review*, *The Threepenny Review*, and on NPR's *Selected Shorts*. Currently, he teaches fiction writing and directs the Creative Writing Program at Trinity University in San Antonio.

Past finalist for the PEN Nelson Algren Fiction Award, **MELISSA PRITCHARD**'s fiction has appeared in *The Paris Review*, *A Public Space*, *Ploughshares*, *Ecotone*, *Conjunctions*, *storySouth*, *LitMag*, *The Georgia Review* and other magazines, anthologies and journals. She has received an NEA, three Pushcart Prizes, two O. Henry Prizes, the Flannery O'Connor Award and Carl Sandburg Literary Awards, the Janet Heidinger Kafka Prize and a Marguerite and Lamar Smith Fellowship from the Carson McCullers Center. Two of her books have been named *New York Times* Editors Choice and another received a Barnes and Noble Discover Great Writers Award. Others have been named "Best Books of the Year" by the *San Francisco Chronicle* and the *Chicago Tribune*. One of her story collections was an *NPR*'s "Summer Reading" selection. She has published four novels, four story collections, a volume of essays and a biography.

A fifth novel, *Flight of the Wild Swan*, will be published by Bellevue Literary Press, NYC, in early 2024.

OREL PROTOPOPESCU has written prize-winning works for children and adults. *A Thousand Peaks, Poems from China* (with Siyu Liu, Pacific View Press, 2002), is a New York Public Library Best Book for the Teen Age. *Metaphors & Similes You Can Eat And Twelve More Poetry Writing Lessons* (Scholastic, 2003), a book for teachers, has been used in classrooms around the world. *Two Sticks* (FSG, 2007) was on Bank Street College of Education's "Best Children's Books of the Year, 2008" list. *Thelonious Mouse* (FSG, 2011) was the Crystal Kite winner, 2012, of SCBWI's Metro NY region. *A Word's a Bird*, Orel's bilingual poetry app for iPad, was chosen by *School Library Journal* as one of the ten best children's apps of 2013. Her poetry has been published in a number of journals and she won the Oberon poetry prize in 2010 and 2020. Her first biography, *Dancing Past the Light: The Life of Tanaquil Le Clercq* (University Press of Florida, 2021), received a starred review in *Library Journal*.

JESSICA NIRVANA RAM is an Indo-Guyanese poet and essayist. She is the 2022-23 Stadler Fellow in Literary Arts Administration. Jessica completed her MFA at the University of North Carolina Wilmington and received her BA from Susquehanna University. Her work–about inheritance, expectations, and radical self love–appears in *Glass: A Journal of Poetry, Hayden's Ferry Review, HAD,* and *Honey Literary,* among others. Jessica is currently a poetry reader at *Okay Donkey Mag.* Find her @jessnirvanapoet on Twitter.

DARREN OBERTO was born 1978 in Ann Arbor, Michigan. He received a bachelor of fine art degree from Kendall College of Art and Design in 2001. Following his formal education, Darren relocated to the Rogers Park neighborhood of Chicago. He then entered into a rewarding apprenticeship with his mentor, Christopher Molloy, who fostered a creative niche at the Alley Gallery in Evanston, Illinois where Darren is now co-owner and resident artist. His work is multidisciplinary but radiates from a nucleus of traditional painting. He is interested and concerned with all media and conceptual horizons that are defined by art, science, and the human experience. He considers himself a "maker" and has an obsession with creating that permeates every aspect of his life.

TIM RAYMOND is an autistic person from Wyoming. His fiction has appeared recently or will appear in *Conjunctions*, *Nimrod*, and the *Best Small Fictions* anthology, among others. He lives in Seoul, South Korea, with his partner and cat.

WILLIAM V. ROEBUCK completed his diplomatic career in late 2020, after twenty-eight years of service in postings across the Middle East, including Baghdad, Tripoli, Damascus, and Jerusalem. He served as U.S. ambassador to Bahrain from 2015-17. For his 2018-20 service in northeastern Syria as Deputy Special Envoy for the Global Coalition Against ISIS, Roebuck received the State Department's Distinguished Honor Award for Gallantry. He was a runner up for *The Missouri Review*'s Jeffrey E. Smith Editors' Prize for Nonfiction in 2021 and a finalist for the same award in 2020. His work has appeared in the *Chicago Quarterly Review*, *The Missouri Review*, *The Briar Cliff Review*, *The Foreign Service Journal*, and elsewhere. Roebuck was born and raised in eastern North Carolina and currently resides in Arlington, Virginia, where he serves as Executive Vice President of the Arab Gulf States Institute in Washington.

MALCOLM ROTHMAN was a regular on the Chicago theatrical scene since 1978, performing on stage, TV, film, voiceover and narration, audiobooks and for twenty-two years portraying Harry Caray at corporate and private events until his retirement. Stage credits include performances with the Guthrie Theater, National Jewish Theater, Court Theater, Candlelight/Forum Theaters, Marriott's Lincolnshire Theater, New American Theater, Steppenwolf Theater Company and many others throughout the Midwest and nationally. His memoir, "Family Photos," appeared in the *Chicago Quarterly Review* and was chosen as a Notable Essay by *Best American Essays 2020*. In addition, his story "Good Dog" appeared in Issue #35 of the *CQR*. Malcolm was a Navy Hospital Corpsman and served in Vietnam from 1969 to 1970.

VARUN U. SHETTY is a writer and critical care physician. He grew up in Mumbai and lives in Cleveland, Ohio. His work has appeared or is forthcoming in *Frontier*, *Five South Online*, *Cleaver*, *Hobart*, *Healing Muse*, *Complete Sentence*, *Reckoning*, and others. He won the 2022 F. Sean Hodge Prize for Poetry in Medicine. You can read more about him at www.varunushetty.com.

PAUL SKENAZY grew up in Chicago, moved to California for graduate school, but often returns to his childhood home in his imagination. He taught literature and writing at the University of California, Santa Cruz. He wrote book reviews for the *Chicago Tribune, Washington Post* and other newspapers and magazines, as well as critical books on James M. Cain and other noir writers. He is the author of two novels: *Temper, CA,* winner of the Miami University Press Novella Contest (Miami Univ Press, 2019), and *Still Life* (Paper Angel Press, 2021). He lives in Santa Cruz with his wife, the poet Farnaz Fatemi.

WALLY SWIST's books include *Huang Po and the Dimensions of Love* (Southern Illinois University Press, 2012), selected by Yusef Komunyakaa for the 2011 Crab Orchard Open Poetry Competition, *A Bird Who Seems to Know Me: Poems Regarding Birds and Nature,* winner of the 2018 Ex Ophidia Poetry Prize, *Evanescence: Selected Poems and Taking Residence* (2021), with Shanti Arts. His recent poetry and translations have appeared in *Asymptote, Chicago Quarterly Review, Ezra: An Online Journal of Translation, The Montreal Review, Pensive: A Global Journal of Spirituality and the Arts, Poetry London, The Seventh Quarry Poetry Magazine (Wales),* and *Transom. A Writer's Statements on Beauty: New & Selected Essays & Reviews* was published in 2022 by Shanti Arts. His translation of *L'Allegria/Cheerfulness: Poems 1914-1919* by Giuseppi Ungaretti is forthcoming from Shanti Arts in 2023.

ERNIE WANG's short fiction has been published in *McSweeney's, Mississippi Review, Prairie Schooner, The Southern Review, Story,* and elsewhere. His essays have been published in *Gulf Coast, The Southern Review,* and *Threepenny Review* and one was recognized as a Notable Essay in *Best American Essays 2022.* He is a PhD candidate at the University of Houston.

THOMAS WAWZENEK is a Chicago writer and his plays have been staged in Chicago, Milwaukee and New York as well as at various theatre festivals. Wawzenek has also collaborated with actors and musicians in performing and recording "Stories in Motion," a spoken word project that integrates his short stories with musical and theatrical elements. He has been a staff writer for numerous publications and websites, has ghostwritten books, and currently works as a freelance writer. He regularly contributes art reviews to *Third Coast Review,* an online magazine, specializing in Chicago-area

CHICAGO QUARTERLY REVIEW

arts and culture coverage. Wawzenek received his creative writing degree from Columbia College Chicago. To learn more about his work, visit his website at wordbeat.net.

MAUD WELCH holds a BA from Bates College and is currently an MFA candidate at the Naslund-Mann Graduate School of Writing. She resides in her hometown of Louisville, Kentucky. Her work has been published in *Rust + Moth, New Ohio Review, New Delta Review,* and *Appalachian Review.* She is a recent recipient of the Matt Clark Award in Poetry.

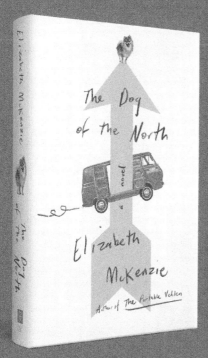

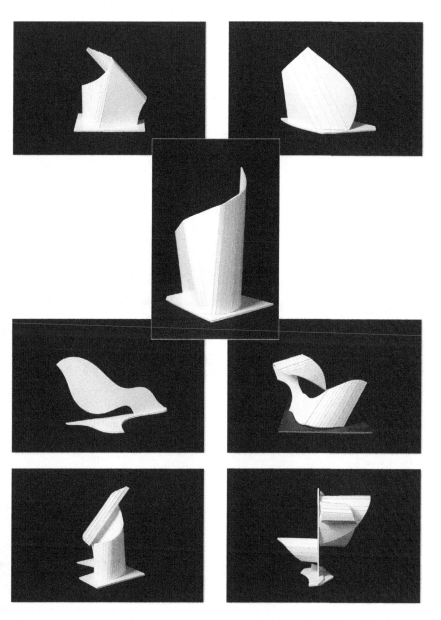

"Art Post Cards from Italy" for mailing or framing. $10.00 Per Package.

Concept Sculptural Prototypes made of Foamboard
(Architects, Landscape Architects and Developers)

Contact: Alicia Loy Griffin 323. 293.1858 (studio) alicialoy@icloud.com alicialoy.griffin.com

The
Nelson Algren
Committee

On the Make
Since 1989

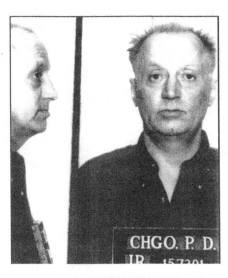

CHGO. P. D.

CHICAGO QUARTERLY REVIEW
Issue: 36
Fall 2022

"After Imaginative Storm, writer's block is a myth."
- *Abdullah Erakat, journalist and screenwriter*

Party Like it's 1893–or 1931

Journey back to the past of night life in *Chicago by Day and Night,* a quite unofficial guide to Chicago's more salacious attractions around the World's Columbian Exposition of 1893. This pocket book for the man-about-town is annotated and explicated by Paul Durica and Bill Savage.

Northwestern University Press

Then skip ahead to 1931, where Chicago journalist George Ade attempted to explain American urban and rural drinking culture (to a generation who had never raised a glass legally due to Prohibition) in *The Old-Time Saloon,* annotated and introduced by Bill Savage.

The University of Chicago Press

BLACK ENSEMBLE THEATER
2023 SEASON OF EXCELLENCE

REASONS: A TRIBUTE TO EARTH, WIND & FIRE
WRITTEN AND DIRECTED BY DARYL D. BROOKS

MARCH 5 – APRIL 16
PREVIEWS: FEBRUARY 25 & 26 ~ MARCH 3 & 4

Reasons takes us on a journey of how Earth, Wind & Fire was formed from humble beginnings, to become the sonic revolutionaries that changed the course of music. They took a vision that no one said would work, and turned it into a musical powerhouse that still lives on today.

the Real Housewives of MOTOWN
Written and Directed by Michelle Reneé Bester

May 20 – July 9, 2023 | Previews: May 20, 21, 26 & 27, 2023

We've seen how life was for the musical superstars of the Motown era but it's time the wives be given a voice. Join us for this exciting musical journey as we discover what life was like for the women married to the stars!

CHAKA KHAN CHAKA KHAN
Written by Reginald Williams
Directed by Daryl D. Brooks & Michele Reneé Bester

AUGUST 19 – OCTOBER 1, 2023
PREVIEWS: AUGUST 19, 20, 25 & 26, 2023

A rousing musical tribute and journey through the incredible five-decade career of the undisputed "Queen of Funk" – Yvette Marie Stevens – better known as "Chaka Khan," beginning with her becoming the lead singer of the phenomenal funk/rock group "Rufus" and continuing through her solo career.

JACKIE TAYLOR'S THE OTHER CINDERELLA
Nov 19 - Dec 31 | Previews: Nov 11 & 12, 17 & 18

Now in its 47th year, "The Other Cinderella" is indeed a Black Ensemble Theater classic. Cinderella was raised in the projects. The Brothers are from the hood, the Fairygodmamma hails from Jamaica and everybody in this Kingdom has soul! The music is divine and the dancing is contagious in this uplifting feel good classic tale that has entertained audiences of all ages for more than 4 decades. And as the King says "This is a Kingdom where everyone is welcome!"

CALL 773.769.4451 FOR TICKET INFORMATION/RESERVATIONS OR PURCHASE TICKETS ONLINE AT BLACKENSEMBLE.ORG

SCAN ME

Black Ensemble Theater | 4450 N. Clark Street | Chicago, IL 60640

SCAN ME

Dialect of Distant Harbors
poems

"These words drenched themselves in color
nipples like seeds through thin white fabric
they rampaged through streets, breath sour with bhang."

"I take my father's gnarled hand,
each skein sprouting a story.
His fingers zigzag through newsprint
past caravans of walking migrants
the chimera of home."

"Sometimes the third eye is a camera,
sometimes a fist to the heart."

Mukherjee's *Dialect of Distant Harbors* is a hybridic journey of storytelling, translations, reportage, lyrical
unfoldings, and acts of witness. Though steeped in elegies for the dead, it is also praise-filled and
empowering as she guides us through a detailed terrain of muslin petticoats, Weird Al, Calcutta heat,
and "black / diamonds under bare feet," as well as the rich odors of smeared chutney, woodsmoke, and ink.

—Simone Muench, author of *Orange Crush* and *Wolf Centos*

Published Proudly by
CAVANKERRYPRESS

Dipika Mukherjee

Order at cavankerrypress.org or press.uchicago.edu
ISBN: 978-1-933880-93-8

The Stuart Brent Children's Book Club

TODAY A READER,

Tomorrow a Leader

www.stuartbrent.com

Share your passion.

CavanKerryPress
Welcomes
Our 2023 Titles!

Boy
by **Tracy Youngblom**

Boy explores how death and loss color memory and influence the ways family members relate to each other and to their shared history.

Pub Date 2/7 | 978-1-933880-99-0

The History Hotel
by **Baron Wormser**

The History Hotel presents an emotional kaleidoscope of historical and existential realities, the poem-essences of moments, eras, lives and memories.

Pub Date 3/7 | 978-1-933880-98-3

When Did We Stop Being Cute?
by **Martin Wiley**

When Did We Stop Being Cute? speaks of growing up, encountering racism, loss, tragedy and coming of age, set to the soundtrack of the '80s.

Pub Date 4/4 | 978-1-933880-97-6

Deep Are These Distances Between Us
by **Susan Atefat-Peckham**

Deep Are These Distances Between Us dictates a literature of nurture; of love, spirituality, care, transcendence, and the power of story to connect us.

Pub Date 5/2 | 978-1-933880-96-9

Italian Blood
by **Denise Tolan**

Italian Blood traces the bloodline of a family from first cuts to open wounds to healing, revealing how legacies of violence can only be broken by speaking the truth.

Pub Date 10/3 | 978-1-933880-95-2

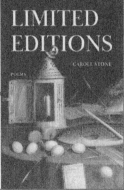

Limited Editions
by **Carole Stone**

Limited Editions details the process of caretaking for an ailing spouse, coming to terms with letting him go, mourning, and, miraculously, rediscovering the joy of living.

Pub Date 11/7 | 978-1-960327-00-0

CRDT
CERQUA RIVERA DANCE THEATRE

"These are historic times that call for bravery and leadership. Being quiet is not an option for this company."
– Cofounder and Artistic Director Wilfredo Rivera

Cerqua Rivera Dance Theatre uses dance and music to nourish the mind and the soul. The company unites artists and audiences to explore themes that shape our community.
more on Facebook, Instagram, and www.cerquarivera.org

Now on Sale:

It's the night before the beginning of the Aztec empire's new millennium, and the Chosen One--so named because he is to be sacrificed in orderto make the sunrise the next morning--has run off with the Emperor's daughter. If he is not found, the sun will not rise and the world will end. By the writers of the legendary Chicago musical Summer Stock Murder.

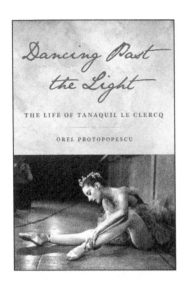

66

*[A] rich, compelling biography.
... This thoughtful and elegant
narrative is full of wonderful
stories about the world of ballet.
A fitting tribute to the life and
legacy of a beloved dancer
that will enthrall balletomanes
everywhere."*

—Library Journal, Starred Review

*"Protopopescu has told the story
of Le Clercq with grace, weaving
in the background of some of
the most influential people in
her life, all of whom are worthy
to have their own stories told.
Protopopescu allows the reader
to peer through a keyhole into
Le Clercq's world, a place that
few of us were privileged to be."*

—Jacques d'Amboise, New York City Ballet
principal dancer and author of *I Was a
Dancer*

Dancing Past the Light

The Life of Tanaquil Le Clercq

OREL PROTOPOPESCU

Hardcover $35.00

Dancing Past the Light cinematically illuminates the glamorous and moving
life story of Tanaquil "Tanny" Le Clercq (1929–2000), one of the most
celebrated ballerinas of the twentieth century, describing her brilliant stage
career, her struggle with polio, and her important work as a dance teacher,
coach, photographer, and writer.

Enhanced with a wealth of previously unpublished photos, and with
insights from interviews with her friends, students, and colleagues, *Dancing
Past the Light* depicts the joys and the dark moments of Le Clercq's dramatic
life, celebrating her mighty legacy.

UNIVERSITY PRESS
OF FLORIDA

@floridapress
upress.ufl.edu · 800.226.3822

"Patricia Engel
is a wonder."
—LAUREN GROFF

THE
FARAWAY
WORLD

STORIES

PATRICIA ENGEL

NEW YORK TIMES BESTSELLING AUTHOR OF
INFINITE COUNTRY

Jamie O'Reilly
A Voice for the Soul of the City

Listen to Songs
Read her Blogs

jamieoreilly.com

MUNRO CAMPAGNA
ARTIST REPRESENTATIVES

410 S. Michigan Ave. Suite 439
Chicago, IL 60605
+1 312 335 8925

steve@munrocampagna.com
www.munrocampagna.com

Illustrator
Clint Hansen

Portrait of
Amanda Gorman

The KENYON Review

SUMMER ONLINE WRITING WORKSHOPS

Designed for writers who can't take time off for a residential workshop, our online program offers a unique opportunity to learn from three different faculty members in one genre-specific, generative workshop, which will meet every day, **June 18–24, 2023.**

Applications open: March 15 – April 16

Faculty includes...

POETRY
Tina Cane
Anthony Cody
Shira Erlichman

FICTION
Marie-Helene Bertino
Helen Phillips

CREATIVE NONFICTION
Paul Lisicky
Dinty W. Moore

TRANSLATION
Kaiama L. Glover
Daniel Saldaña París
Kelsi Vanada

To learn more and apply, visit
https://kenyonreview.org/kenyon-review-writers-workshops/

Chicago's Maxwell Street Klezmer Band
Celebrates Four Decades
of Sharing the "Joy of Klez"

Sunday, June 4th, 2023, 2:00 PM
Old Town School of Folk Music, Chicago
www.oldtownschool.org

For more 40th Anniversary Events,
visit www.klezmerband.com

To support our mission of reviving klezmer music, become a supporter of the Klezmer Music Foundation. Your donation enables:

- The Junior Klezmer Orchestra
- Community bands across Chicagoland
- The Salaam-Shalom Music Project
- Concerts for Senior Citizen Residences
- School Concerts

"A shared life of simchas (celebrations)...You've been part of our lives, just as we've been privileged to be part of yours."
- Grandmother of the Bar Mitzvah Boy, 2023

"The Maxwell Street Klezmer Band conjures joy from thin air while at the same time freeing the deep waters of the soul."
- Rich Warren host/producer Emeritus WFMT Radio, Chicago

KlezmerBand.com

Donate at KlezmerMusicFoundation.org

BASED ON THE JUDY BLUME BOOK LOVED BY MILLIONS

ACADEMY AWARD® NOMINEE
RACHEL McADAMS   ABBY RYDER FORTSON   ACADEMY AWARD® WINNER
KATHY BATES

Are You There God? It's Me, Margaret.

FROM THE DIRECTOR OF   THE EDGE OF SEVENTEEN

IT'S FINALLY THAT TIME
04.28.23
ONLY IN THEATERS

WRITTEN FOR THE SCREEN AND DIRECTED BY
KELLY FREMON CRAIG
PRODUCED BY JAMES L. BROOKS

 LIONSGATE

SUNDAY SALON CHICAGO
IS AN IN-PERSON LIT READING SERIES
THAT TAKES PLACE EVERY OTHER MONTH
starting in January, with occasional Zoom events during
the in-between months to include non-local authors

NAMED ONE OF CHICAGO'S BEST LITERARY ORGANIZATIONS
BY NEWCITY

THE SALON SERIES HAS BROUGHT WORD POWER TO
NEW YORK CITY, NAIROBI, MIAMI & CHICAGO
MAKING OUR BEST LOCAL AND NATIONAL WRITERS AVAILABLE
TO A LARGER COMMUNITY FOR OVER 16 YEARS

WE MEET AT THE REVELER*
3403 N Damen Ave. & Roscoe St., in Roscoe Village, Chicago
FROM 7PM TO 9PM ON THE LAST SUNDAY OF EVERY OTHER MONTH
(w/Roscoe Books present to sell authors' titles at ea. event)
Our alternative venue is at Roscoe Books, when announced
2142 W. Roscoe St., Chicago, 60618, just 3 blocks west

EAT, DRINK YOUR FAVORITE DRINKS, MAKE NEW FRIENDS
AND ENJOY EXCELLENT READINGS WITH US!

OUR EVENTS ARE ALWAYS FREE

Find us at https://sundaysalon-chicago.com
https://www.facebook.com/Sunday.Salon.Chicago/
www.roscoebooks.com

*masking is required/encouraged due to Coronavirus,
and The Reveler is operating at normal capacity. Our Zoom events
require registration, so please check our website or Facebook page.

THANK YOU, CQR, FOR SUPPORTING US!

Chicago Danztheatre Ensemble presents a night of "humanity and hope" in collaboration with CIRCA Pintig

Daryo's All-American Diner
by Conrad A. Panganiban
May 5-20

The Wasteland
by T.S. Eliot

WRITERS ALOUD

A monthly first read by and for writers who don't necessarily think of themselves as writers

First Sunday of the month, via Zoom

**Want the Zoom link? Want to read your writing?
Contact Karen.o.fort@gmail.com**